LOVE STORIES

LOVE STORIES

Language, Private Love,
and Public Romance
in Georgia

PAUL MANNING

Teaching Culture: UTP Ethnographies for the Classroom

UNIVERSITY OF TORONTO PRESS

Copyright © University of Toronto Press 2015
Higher Education Division
www.utppublishing.com

Library and Archives Canada Cataloguing in Publication

Manning, Paul, 1964–, author

Love stories : language, private love, and public romance in Georgia / Paul Manning.
(Teaching culture: UTP ethnographies for the classroom)

Includes bibliographical references and index.

Issued in print and electronic formats.

ISBN 978-1-4426-0897-9 (bound). —ISBN 978-1-4426-0896-2 (pbk.). —ISBN 978-1-4426-0898-6 (pdf).
—ISBN 978-1-4426-0899-3 (epub)

   1. Khevsurs—Sexual behavior. 2. Khevsurs—Social life and customs. 3. Ethnology—Georgia
(Republic)—Xevsureti. I. Title.

DK673.5.K48M35 2015   305.899'969   C2014-907126-4
                                                  C2014-907127-2

We welcome comments and suggestions regarding any aspect of our publications—please feel free to
contact us at news@utphighereducation.com or visit our Internet site at www.utppublishing.com.

North America   UK, Ireland, and continental Europe
5201 Dufferin Street   NBN International
North York, Ontario, Canada, M3H 5T8   Estover Road, Plymouth, PL6 7PY, UK
                                       ORDERS PHONE: 44 (0) 1752 202301
2250 Military Road   ORDERS FAX: 44 (0) 1752 202333
Tonawanda, New York, USA, 14150   ORDERS E-MAIL: enquiries@nbninternational.com

ORDERS PHONE: 1-800-565-9523
ORDERS FAX: 1-800-221-9985
ORDERS E-MAIL: utpbooks@utpress.utoronto.ca

The University of Toronto Press acknowledges the financial support for its publishing activities of the
Government of Canada through the Canada Book Fund.

Printed in the United States of America.

Dedicated to my mother, Betty Manning, and to the memory of my late father, Harvey Manning.

CONTENTS

———◆———

ILLUSTRATIONS

———◆———

FIGURES

TABLE

ACKNOWLEDGMENTS

———

Fɪʀsᴛ ɪ ᴡᴏᴜʟᴅ ʟɪᴋᴇ ᴛᴏ ᴛʜᴀɴᴋ ᴍʏ ᴇᴅɪᴛᴏʀ, Anne Brackenbury, for all her help, advice, and inspiration to finally write this book. The research on which it depends could not have happened without Paata Bukhrashvili, Khvtiso Mamisimedishvili, David Toklikishvili, and Kevin Tuite. For help with formulating the basic ideas, as well as with reading and commenting on specific sections, or more general encouragement, I am indebted to Deborah Cameron, Kate Dougherty, Bruce Grant, Nicholas Harkness, Alaina Lemon, Constantine Nakassis, Lauren Ninoshvili, Shunsuke Nozawa, Debra Occhi, Elana Resnick, Zaza Shatirishvili, Rupert Stasch, and Nino Tseradze. Special thanks are due to my copyeditor, Martin Boyne, for greatly improving not only the form, but also in many places the content, of this book. I thank Anne Meneley, Florian Muehlfried, Perry Sherouse, and Kevin Tuite, as well as the two reviewers, Laura Miller and Don Kulick, for their detailed and insightful comments on the whole text. Anne Meneley deserves special thanks for many discussions on the materials and approach over the years.

Some of the material here has been discussed in a different form in Manning (2007, 2012a, 2014a).

INTRODUCTION: SETTING THE STAGE FOR ROMANCE

T HIS BOOK is a historical ethnography of sexual relations in the mountainous region of Khevsureti in the country of Georgia in the early twentieth century. These sexual relations seemed paradoxical to outsiders, Georgians and others, since they were sexual relations without any actual sex, and they represented a sphere of romance so sharply opposed to marriage that it has often been called "anti-marriage" (Charachidze 1968; Tuite 2000). Such paradoxical sexual relations, the opposite of sex and the opposite of marriage, would have disappeared without a trace had it not been for the existence of two indigenous ethnographers, Natela Baliauri and her husband, Aleksi Ochiauri, upon whose work this book is largely based. Ironically, these ethnographers became ethnographers because they were exiled from their communities for breaking the very rules of sexuality and marriage that their ethnographies later made part of the ethnographic record of Georgia. They continued describing their erstwhile homes from their exile in the lower valleys of neighboring Pshavi, watching helplessly as their communities disappeared forever when the Khevsur world was uprooted and destroyed by a single order from Josef Stalin in 1952, leading to the entire population of Khevsureti being forcibly resettled in the plains. Natela Baliauri spent the rest of her life mourning this lost world in letters to her friends: "Khevsureti doesn't exist anywhere anymore . . . the labor of the women was lost . . . the tempering of the men, the horse races and the burnishing of swords and shields. I love my Khevsureti, but how could I rescue it?" (cited in K'alandadze 1995: 7).

In a sense, however, Baliauri *did* rescue Khevsureti in her ethnography, which moldered in archives until it was published at the end of the socialist period in 1991. Her ethnographic work is a "love story" in two senses. On the one hand, it expresses her heartbroken love and pining for the lost world of Khevsureti; on the other, it provides a unique insider perspective on the "love stories" of the Khevsurs themselves. In a parallel manner, this book tracks the transformation of the living "love stories" of the Khevsurs into still images of a lost world, framed within a larger narrative of a parallel "love story," that of the Georgian romanticization of these mountain peoples: here images of Khevsur romance began a second life as they circulated in Georgian media, becoming the themes of romantic novels, films, and even contemporary advertisements and Internet forum debates. This book is composed of two kinds of "love stories" covering both the first and second lives of Khevsur romance: its private life as a living practice among the Khevsurs, and its public life as an always second-hand source of exotic fascination and fantasy in the Georgian nation. My own fascination with this topic is informed by this more general Georgian interest in the Khevsurs, one produced by having seen ubiquitous images of the Khevsurs and Khevsur romance circulating in Georgian media culture. From reading Georgian novels and ethnographies set in Khevsureti, to standing at metro stops or sitting in socialist-period cafés adorned with frescoes of Khevsurs, to watching Georgian films set in the region, or drinking Georgian "Khevsur" beers with labels and names celebrating Khevsur heroes, I have become fascinated by the fantasy of Khevsureti and Khevsur romance, which have also seemed to be some sort of secret key to understanding Georgian modernity. I am also intrigued because it all has the air of a detective story, a set of mysteries to be solved: how did the private sexual lives of a few thousand people living nearly a century ago become a matter of public concern and the locus of private fantasy for the Georgian nation as a whole? How did anyone even come to find out about the sexual lives of this obscure people in the first place? And what were those sexual lives really like anyway? Here, amid all the hearsay evidence, Natela Baliauri is the key witness in all the links of this chain. So, most of all, this book is the result of my encounter with Natela Baliauri's singular ethnography, as well as my desire to retell her own love story and the other love stories she told.

A BRIEF INTRODUCTION TO KHEVSUR LOVE

In traditional Khevsureti, casual sexual liaisons between boys and girls initially took the form of a relationship known as *sts'orproba*, a term that means literally something like "a relationship between friends of the same age" but that more specifically means an elective, casual, specifically sexual relationship between opposite-gender age-mates who are otherwise ineligible to get married. A Georgian ethnographer writing in this period describes the general outlines of this erotic relationship:[1]

> *Sts'orproba* begins this way: a girl goes with a bottle of vodka to lie down with a boy, even if they don't know each other close up and only like each other from afar. First—kissing, lying in each other's arms, hugging and caressing with great shyness and restraint happens, but later, when they little by little

get to know one another, this hugging and kissing becomes freer. (Tedoradze 1930: 131)

A very similar kind of erotic liaison takes place in the neighboring valleys of Pshavi, what is called there *ts'ats'loba* ("relationship between *ts'ats'alis*," a term whose literal meaning is obscure; Tuite 2000), which another Georgian ethnographer, Sergi Mak'alatia, describes as follows:

> *Ts'ats'loba* among strangers (non-relatives, *utskhota shoris*) is first of all based on liking each other and on love. If a boy likes a girl, or a girl a boy, they declare "sworn brotherhood-sworn sisterhood" (*nadzmob-nadoboba*) to each other. After their coming together lying together is arranged between them. Newly brought together *ts'ats'alis*, in the first period, lie down in some hidden, concealed place outside the house, in the stable or the cow shed, or in the forest under a cloak without taking off their clothes. The boy always goes to the girl at the appointed place, the girl pretends to sleep and the boy has to wake her up, with his caresses and with sweet talk, whose content revolves around *ts'ats'loba*. After a several years the "sworn brother" (*nadzmobi*) begins praising his "sworn sister" (*nadobi*) and touching her with his hands, which ends in kissing and embracing. (Mak'alatia 1934: 9)[2]

Khevsur and Pshavian romantic practices are seemingly similar, but from an indigenous perspective they are polar opposites. Among the Khevsurs, the girl comes to the boy where he sleeps inside and wakes him, while in the Pshavian practice, the boy comes to the sleeping girl, often outside. While local ideologies of ethnic difference make minor opposed details like these very significant, outsiders—other Georgians, as we will see in the later chapters—take these to be essentially the same practices, often using the two terms interchangeably.

WELL, *DID* THEY, OR *DIDN'T* THEY?

I have described this as a *sexual* relationship, yet the above descriptions leave unresolved the question of whether the couples had actual *sex*: Did they? Or didn't they? Of course, even in our own society, it is not exactly clear what specific physical acts are meant by *sex* (Cameron and Kulick 2003: 2–3). Therefore, a cultural account of sexuality of our own society or any other must be careful not to universalize our own commonsense notions, or give terms like *sex* an illusory concreteness. This is a *linguistic* as well as a *cultural* ethnography, so we must attend to the linguistic expressions and terminology of the culture we are studying. In the space of difference between their world and our own, both in form and content, we can hopefully learn something about both.

The Khevsur term *sts'orperi* (literally "equal-color") meant something like "peer" or "friend of the same age." But it usually meant "sexual partner in a relationship of *sts'orproba*" or, more simply, "casual lover." Thus this is a sexual relationship that held between equals or peers: opposite-sexed peers as a subset of all peers. This relationship was initially defined as being elective (so choice, desire, and freedom were involved), so the peers had to be similar (*shesaperi*) in desirability, a similarity to which, perhaps, the element *peri* ("color, kind") in the term *sts'orperi* also drew attention.

In addition, the relationship usually occurred at a certain degree of social distance: the relationship occupied a "Goldilocks zone," a zone where desire is permitted between those others classified as siblings between whom sexual desire should not exist, and those more distant kin and strangers who were defined as potential marriage partners in this exogamous society (where marriage partners are defined as being neither kin nor coresidential within the same village). In marriage, sexual desire or personal choice was also normatively irrelevant, because people often married strangers by parental arrangement, or marriage happened "by abduction." Marriage by abduction could represent either what we would call elopement, if the girl was a willing partner, or something more akin to rape if she was not; in either case it happened against the wishes of the parents. *Sts'orproba*, for this reason, as mentioned above, is sometimes defined as a zone of sexual practice in opposition to marriage: "anti-marriage" (Charachidze 1968; Tuite 2000). We might instead treat it as one defined by desire, which is absent in the relations between those classed as siblings, and not particularly relevant to those whom one is supposed to marry. Social distance and sexual desire, avoidance and intimacy, went together. *Sts'orproba* defined a "middle zone" of others between whom the expression of elective, sociable sexual desire was appropriate and possible.

Sts'orproba, then, as an expression of sexuality, was rigorously opposed to marriage at all points, and specifically cannot be interpreted as a form of premarital courtship: *sts'orperis* could not marry, and *sts'orproba* expresses sexual desire, whereas marriage does not. At the same time, *sts'orproba* was sexual, but paradoxically it did not involve what North Americans (or other Georgians, for that matter) would call sex. *Sts'orproba* was strongly opposed to sexual activity that might lead to childbirth (*garq'vna*, "fornication"): for Khevsurs, the physical expression of this desire had to remain *uteslo* ("without seed"; Tuite 2000). But much more importantly, for the most part the sexual expression of *sts'orproba* amounted mostly to affectionate caresses, kissing, and talking. *Sts'orproba* was a relationship that gave expression to sexual desire, but the expression of this desire was kept in check by rigorous social norms. However, these norms were very different both from somewhat variable North American notions of what heterosexual "sex" is (which can include both vaginal intercourse as well as a wide range of other activities; see Cameron and Kulick 2003: 3) and also from those of other Georgians.

Unlike other Georgians, Khevsurs did not link sexual desire to marriage, nor did they link sexual desire to sex. Moreover, other Georgians tend to define *sex* as vaginal intercourse, something that would lead to the rupture of the hymen of a virgin, and therefore preservation of virginity is an important boundary for other Georgians: a woman who has lost her virginity is almost by definition neither desirable nor marriageable for Georgian men. For Khevsurs, virginity was a non-issue; the relevant absolute boundary was, instead, childbirth. Khevsur sexual expressions have, both for North Americans and for Georgians, a paradoxical quality: *sts'orproba* is romance that can never lead to marriage, and Khevsurs seem to have had no specific concept of sexual activity that corresponds either to what North Americans, or other Georgians, would call "sex." Khevsurs didn't even distinguish between erotic desire and "romantic" love, talking only of "desire" (*survili*).

As a result of this "ambiguity," Georgians even today spend a good deal of time trying to understand these paradoxes and decipher this desire: was it sex, or purely platonic, chivalric love?

This ethnography initially seeks to understand this seeming paradox of a form of sexuality that has been called both "anti-marriage" and "sex without sex," in terms of the culture and society in which it was found. But the paradoxical quality of this relationship, initially limited to a small group of people living in the mountains, as described in Georgian ethnographies, novels, and films, has also fired the erotic imagination of the whole Georgian nation, to the extent that teenagers in Georgia today still debate on Internet forums tantalizing questions about whether Khevsurs did or did not have sex. Forms of sexuality and desire go from being local practices *here* and *now* to fuelling fantasies about people *there* and *then*. Strangely, Georgians' fascination with Khevsur sexual life coexists with their fascination with Western (i.e., European or American) sexual life. Both of these erotic worlds represent fantastic, unattainable "elsewheres" that have a kind of "virtual potential" to construct and express sexual fantasies without any real-world interactions or consequences (Galbraith 2009). But unlike completely fantastic worlds created only in the imagination, these are *real* elsewheres that permit things that are not permitted in one's own real life (e.g., making out with random others, having sex outside of wedlock, having virginity not be a barrier to marriage). They also challenge societally accepted norms that take on a seemingly naturalized character, showing that other ways of doing things are always possible somewhere else. But at the same time these two elsewheres are fundamentally different: the "close distance" of the elsewhere of Khevsur sexuality allows Georgians to have an impossible erotic fantasy in a Georgian setting, but it also affords the possibility of criticizing what is not allowed sexually in

Georgia from the perspective of an authentic Georgian tradition, from *inside* the nation, rather than from the exterior perspective of "the West."

Yet the two "real elsewheres"—the sexual worlds of the Khevsurs and the sexual worlds of "the West"—can also seem strangely alike as uncanny mirror images of normative Georgian sexual life. In a recent article provocatively entitled "Georgian Traditional Sex," the author, Aleko Tskhitishvili (n.d.), posed in semi-serious form the facetious question, "Was there ever sex in Georgia, or not?" In some sense the answer is obvious, since the existence of every Georgian points to at least one act of heterosexual vaginal intercourse. However, the author uses the word *seksi* (an English borrowing), and by it he apparently means something different from this prosaic kind of sexual reproduction. Scouring sources from Georgian literature and from the same ethnographies I use in this book, he searches for traces of another kind of sex, a kind of sexual sociability, a purely elective, Western-style "play" form of sex, pursued entirely for its own sake and unencumbered by any connection to biological reproduction or marital obligation. He eventually finds in the Georgian mountains a form of traditional "ancestral sex" that has this paradoxical quality, since it is absolutely opposed to marriage and it doesn't seem to involve any actual sex. Trying to find a name for this sex, which is not actual "sex" (*seksi*), he borrows another (somewhat archaic) English slang word *pet't'ingi* ("petting"). So he ends up using these terms, derived from the "elsewhere" of Western sexual traditions, to explain terms such as *sts'orperi* and *ts'ats'ali*, from the "elsewhere" of "Georgian traditional sex," where the separation of love from marriage ended up making traditional Khevsur marital relations seem like a form of fornication:

> *Ts'ats'loba* or *sts'orproba*, it seems, was a pure Georgian traditional [form of] petting.... There were frequent cases in which a man and a woman loved their *ts'ats'ali* [or] *sts'orperi* their entire lives, but marriage was forbidden to them; therefore, factually, they engaged in fornication with their legal spouse ... only to fulfill marital obligations. (Tskhitishvili n.d.)

Here the fantastic sexual worlds of the Khevsur and the equally fantastic sexual worlds of the "Imaginary West" become translational equivalents. The question "Was there ever sex in Georgia, or not?" is answered with a paradox: "There was, and there was not, sex in Georgia"! In Georgian, this paradox is also a pun, because "There was, and there was not ..." is the standard opening for Georgian (and other Eurasian) fairy tales, so his answer also translates as "Once upon a time, there was sex in Georgia." The search for real traditional sex ends up assigning sex to the fairy-tale world of fantasy.

But for my readers, mostly North Americans, the sexual worlds of the Khevsurs are no more and no less alien than those of the Georgians. There is a long line of anthropological ethnographies that show the seemingly endless diversity of human sexualities

and therefore explicitly challenge deeply held or widespread naturalizing and univer-
salizing assumptions about sexuality: classics such as Bronislaw Malinowski's deliberately provocative and somewhat luridly titled book *The Sexual Lives of Savages in
North-Western Melanesia* (1929) and Margaret Mead's *Coming of Age in Samoa* (1928),
followed by a range of contemporary ethnographies of sexuality such as Don Kulick's
Travesti: Sex, Gender, and Culture among Brazilian Transgendered Prostitutes (1998) or
Patrick Galbraith's work on the Japanese virtual sexuality of *moe*, the euphoric response
to fantasy characters among *otaku* and *fujoshi* subcultures (2009). Following their lead,
this ethnography also draws a portrait of a form of sexuality that challenges a set of
deeply held and highly naturalized beliefs about a supposedly natural and universal
association between romantic love, sexual desire, and marriage (cf. Ahearn 2003). Here
we have a cultural system in which these things were kept apart, their relations carefully
managed. Unlike classical anthropological approaches, which tend to reduce romantic
love to its kinship outcomes, that is biological reproduction and social alliances, here
romantic love is constituted as an entirely autonomous domain pursued solely for its
own intrinsic pleasure. Therefore, it also seeks to challenge the sociological axiom that
there is something specifically "modern" (and Western!) about an autonomous domain
of romantic or sociable "love" pursued for its own sake (as articulated by, e.g., Giddens
1992). If classical sociology treated unfettered "love" as a harbinger or diagnostic of the
modern, classical anthropology tended to ignore it as an inconsequential sideshow to
kinship (reproduction and marriage). Certainly, in many societies and cultures, autonomous love is mostly of the tragic, unrequited variety, the stuff of fantasies and poetry
about star-crossed lovers, usually with the moral that it is an emotion that one cannot
act on without tragic outcomes. My ethnography is written against the backdrop of
these varied sources, and it could well be read in tandem with them, especially Abu-
Lughod's (1986) excellent study of Bedouin love poetry, to which I am deeply indebted.

GEORGIAN STEREOTYPES ABOUT KHEVSURS
AND "THE ROMANCE OF THE MOUNTAINS"

By the late socialist period, Khevsureti was well-established as a stereotypical exotic,
romantic "lost world." In the 1965 film *Ballad of the Khevsurs* (discussed in chapter 7),
a film that is probably responsible for popularizing more of these stereotypes about
Khevsureti than any other source, the Khevsur hero (Imeda) tells a visiting doctor
from Tbilisi, the capital city of Georgia:

> IMEDA: Eh, this place is forgotten by God and Man alike, everyone looks at it with
> the eyes of a tourist, looking for only romance and exoticism, they cannot see
> how hard the life of the Khevsur is.

DOCTOR: Khevsureti and Romance were for me, until this very day, one and the same too.

As Imeda suggests, Khevsureti is stereotypically associated, from the nineteenth century onwards, with exotic images of sturdy, manly mountain dwellers romantically outfitted in colorful costumes, daggers, swords, and a smattering of chain-mail armor. The Khevsurs are a bold, free people who settle scores with blood, who have never been slaves or had slaves, whose women are just as free and bold as the men, and whose difficult lives of great material poverty lead to correspondingly great moral virtues. The narrator of the aforementioned film sums up this romantic mythology of the virtues of the Khevsurs as formed by their harsh material conditions:

> One who was born in these inaccessible mountains and valleys, who is not frightened by lack of roads and bad weather, dizzying ascents and descents, who from youth became used to galloping on horseback on these barren paths as thin as threads, believes that nowhere can be found a better place than his homeland. Heavy and hard is the life of the mountain man, but, well, where is the life of humankind easy? Where people live, from there you hear groaning. With such thoughts a people comforts themselves; a people who have never had a master, who have neither been anyone's serf nor had serfs themselves. Here live the Khevsurs, hospitable, valiant, taciturn, strong-legged Khevsurs. Poor, but not beggarly. The proud, free Khevsurs.

These pervasive stereotypes, which date back to the nineteenth century, link the Georgian-speaking mountain peoples, and especially the Khevsurs (whose dialect, however archaic-sounding and diabolically difficult to understand, is still Georgian), with a picturesque lost Georgian fantasy world full of danger, exoticism, and romance. Alongside this "romance of the mountains" are found stereotypical images of "mountaineer romance," a set of often salacious speculations and rumors that in Khevsureti, as well as neighboring Pshavi, sexual matters take a very different course than in the rest of Georgia: *there*, things are permitted that would be a scandal anywhere else in Georgia; or, conversely, *there* is a world of chaste chivalric romance, such as is found celebrated in medieval Georgian epic poems. Regardless, what they had is *different* from what we have, Georgians might say. This sexual mountaineer romance, like the masculine romance of the mountains, is for modern Georgians an exotic elsewhere pregnant with possibility, one that permits Georgians to engage in romantic or sexual fantasy in the imagination while the fantasies still remain, technically, in Georgia.

The best way to illustrate such pervasive stereotypes is probably through the world of branding and advertising, a line of work that is largely about making (frequently

random) associations between mundane products and fantastic, stereotypical human figures who embody the "personality" of the brand. Since advertisers have so little time and space in a given ad to conjure up a positive set of associations for their brand, brand creators often fish in the common pool of powerful cultural stereotypes of various kinds for these brand personalities, which can include mythologized figures of the producer or inventor (e.g., Betty Crocker, Steve Jobs), aspirational selves embodied in images of the ideal consumer (typified by ads that boil down to a celebrity holding a bottle, or the "brand synergy" of bands like U2 and brands like Apple), to exotic images of social others, human, or animal (as seen in the remarkable number of North American brands that still have images of American Indians on them, for example). One can therefore look at this material not only to learn something about how brands and advertising work as media, but also as a source of information about the symbolic field of stereotypes from which the images are drawn.

Images of "mountain romance" used in Georgian beer advertising illustrate this nicely. In the postsocialist period beginning in 1991, which was characterized by civil wars, corruption, and general economic malaise, the Georgian economy produced one seemingly authentic economic miracle. Georgia suddenly became a country that produced quality beer for domestic consumption and boasted many indigenous brands of beer, at a time when virtually all other products in Georgia were either of low quality or imported from abroad. But Georgia is not a country normally known for its beer; it is known instead for its wine. Georgian beer marketers were therefore confronted with a basic question of branding: how to persuade Georgians that "Georgian beer" was not a contradiction in terms? How to situate a product like beer within the imaginary framework of the nation as an *authentically* Georgian product in the same way that wine was considered to be? For a period, the solution seemed to present itself in what Ann Uplisashvili and I have called elsewhere "ethnographic branding" (Manning and Uplisashvili 2007).

Georgian marketers needed to associate this new product, beer, with the idea of an authentic, traditional Georgia. To do so, Georgian beer marketers raided the repertoire of ethnographic representations and ethnographic figures of what I have called "the romance of the mountains," looking for traditional Georgian beer-makers and beer-drinkers out of which to build brand icons. Here the people of the Georgian mountains, for whom beer is an important ritual drink, provided these brand-makers with traditional ethnographic figures after whom to name their beers, and suitably masculine Georgian highlanders in traditional dress to put on the labels of their new beer brands (see Figures 0.1 and 0.2). So many manufacturers did this that, for a short time, the beer aisle of a store looked a little like a Georgian ethnographic museum.

But some of the mountain people, notably the Khevsurs and Pshavians, had other advantages for brand image. Not only did they make and drink beer (which allowed

FIGURE 0.1: Label for Aluda: A Khevsur beer. (Castel-Sakartvelo)

Georgian brand-makers to create fabulous mythological ancestors for their largely standard European lagers), but romanticized images of Khevsur and Pshavian men also represented what brand-makers like to call "aspirational" figures: stereotypical Khevsurs and Pshavians are macho, gallant, romantic figures, the kind of person any male Georgian beer drinker might like to be, thus inspiring consumers to buy the brand that is associated with their aspirational selves. Aspirational branding, like most branding, involves creating nebulous associations of products with imagined persons, rather than talking up the actual properties of the product itself.

These same mountain locales are also notorious for being the abode of romance in the more strictly sexual sense. If Georgian brand-makers made use of masculine images of mountain people in their iconography of brand, that is, in the images and logos that adorn the bottles, in their advertisements for these brands they sometimes also made coy reference to the libertine sexual traditions of the mountains. As we will see repeatedly, the reception of mountain sexuality by the Georgian public takes two opposed and seemingly paradoxical forms: on the one hand, there is a view of Pshavian and Khevsur tradition that is characterized by tasteful and chaste restraint; on the other hand, there is a view that is reduced to anatomical couplings of the most vulgar sort. To illustrate these most recent echoes of the lost world of Khevsur romance, I will discuss two commercials for different Georgian beer brands.

FIGURE 0.2: The wheat beer Pshavi (Kazbegi 1881 JSC)

The first is a commercial for Kazbegi's wheat beer Pshavi (Kazbegi JSC), which displays the traditional contexts of production and consumption of beer in an idyllic scene of life in the mountains of Pshavi, with a traditional Pshavian poem voice-over:[3]

roca k'i gazapkhuldeba,	When spring comes,
gamoighvidzebs kveq'ana,	The world awakens,
silaghe, simkhiarule,	Freedom, happiness,
daseirnoben q'velgana.	Wander about everywhere.
shasvi pshavuri—et'q'vian,	Drink Pshavian, they say,
khorblis ludia sviani,	It is a wheat beer with hops,
gvitkhari rame ghvtis madlsa,	Tell us something, by the grace of God,
erti kartuli gziani.	Having a Georgian way.
ludi pshavi—kartuli mtis ist'oria.	Pshavi Beer—the history of the Georgian mountains.

This 2005 commercial opens with springtime flirtation between a Pshavian boy and girl (Figures 0.3a and 0.3b) otherwise engaged in traditional occupations (the man carrying a sheep, the woman carrying water), moving on to an older man (symbolizing respect for elders and tradition, perhaps), and then to a man engaged in brewing beer

FIGURE 0.3A AND 0.3B: Exchanging glances (Pshavi commercial, Kazbegi 1881 JSC, 2005)

using traditional methods. From here the ad moves seamlessly from traditional scenes of beer production to those of beer consumption, finally juxtaposing the traditional Pshavian beer poured from a traditional serving pitcher with the modern bottled beer brand "Pshavi."

Importantly, the ad narrative takes the form of a traditional Pshavian poem. Like the Khevsurs, the Pshavians are also noted for being poets, and their poetic cycles are the focus of Georgian folklore (something I discuss in more detail in chapter 4). Kazbegi commercials are always clever, always tasteful, and Kazbegi is certainly the corporation that began the process of ethnographic branding in Georgia. This particular commercial is perhaps the most complete grounding of a beer in idyllic scenes of traditional beer production and consumption, appropriate for the Kazbegi product which is most directly linked to this project of ethnographic branding. And yet, at the same time, it also makes a veiled, but tasteful, reference to the "free love" of the mountains by opening with a flirtatious exchange of glances between two Pshavian youths.

The second beer commercial I wish to examine is a notorious, even shocking, commercial for the now-defunct beer company Lomisi (a beer named after an important mountain shrine). Lomisi's ads were best known for their spokesman (who appears in this commercial as well), a somewhat creepy older man who announces their somewhat unimaginative slogan, "*k'ai ludia—lomisi*" (It's good beer—Lomisi), with a gravelly voice. Like all beer producers in this period of the heyday of ethnographic beer advertising (circa 2000–2005), following the lead in general of the branding strategy of the Kazbegi company, they occasionally produced commercials containing ethnographic elements. One of these, the commercial from 2003 under discussion here, caused quite an uproar; in it, a man is portrayed flirting with a barmaid, ostensibly discussing the properties of the beer, but in thinly veiled sexual double entendres.

On the surface, without the text, the ad is brutally simple: the frankly quite ugly customer and the improbably well-endowed barmaid move quickly from double entendres to having actual sex in the back room of the bar.

FIGURE 0.4A AND 0.4B: Exchanging glances (Lomisi commercial, 2003)

However, once the text is taken into consideration, the commercial takes on additional significance. The text, like that of the first commercial, consists of a traditional mountain poem. The man approaches the bar and ogles the woman's breasts while ostensibly talking about the beer (Figures 0.4a and 0.4b):

MAN:	*ise lamazad kapdebà,*	So beautifully does it foam,
	veghar movts'q'vite tvalio.	I could no longer tear my eyes away.
WOMAN:	*magas keba ar unda,*	It doesn't need praise,
	lomisi unda dalio!	You must drink Lomisi!
MEN'S CHORUS:	*lomisi unda dalio!*	You must drink Lomisi!

In case we missed the fact that he is *really* talking about her breasts, in the next line he directly addresses them, and indeed reaches out to touch them:

MAN:	*ts'q'urvili mak'lavs, mitkhari,*	A thirst is killing me, tell me,
	dzudzus kvesh tu gak khalio.	Whether you have a mole under your breasts. [the girl slaps his hand, smiling]
WOMAN:	*ts'q'urvilma rom ar dagkhrchos,*	So that your thirst doesn't strangle you,
	lomisi unda dalio!	You must drink Lomisi!
MEN'S CHORUS:	*lomisi unda dalio!*	You must drink Lomisi!

Finally, he leads her through a door in the back of the bar, and we see a beer glass foaming over with pointed significance to what we are not seeing. The woman returns, clearly in a state of post-coital bliss, and says something inaudible but along the lines of "thanks to Lomisi, I got all cooled off." The man returns, clearly zipping up his fly, and raises a glass of Lomisi, finishing her poetic line by shouting something even more inaudible. The camera pans to the spokesman, who concludes with the slogan:

OFFICIAL SPOKESMAN: *k'ai ludia, lomisi* It's good beer, Lomisi.

The most obvious aspect of this commercial, then, is that it connects Lomisi beer with a kind of plebeian form of masculine sociability and sexual imagination involving fantastic worlds where ugly men can have casual sex with pretty barmaids in the back of the bar.

But with such a straightforward reading, one aspect of this commercial might escape notice: the lecherous man and the busty barmaid are engaging in a traditional extemporaneous *poetic duel*, one in which joking, flirtation, and double entendre play an important role. This connects the verbal exchange in this commercial with a specific folkloric genre called *k'apia*, which is associated with Georgian mountain groups, particularly the Khevsurs and Pshavians. More specifically, the director of this commercial intended a clear allusion to a famous scene of *k'apia* that is the centerpiece of the film *Ballad of the Khevsurs* (see chapter 7). *K'apia* is defined, however, not only by its use in joking exchanges, but by the fact that it involves paired extemporaneous poetic dialogue. This commercial, like the Kazbegi commercial for Pshavi, links beer consumption to mountain traditions of folk poetry (chapter 4) and to stereotypical representations of these mountain traditions in socialist films (chapter 7).

There is, then, a strong parallelism between the two commercials: a traditional mountain drink, beer, is linked to Georgian ethnographic traditions, and the vehicle chosen to do this is poetry. The main difference between the Lomisi commercial and the scene from the Khevsur *Ballad* is that in the former, the sublime traditional elements of flirtation, poetry, and dueling are coupled with a grotesque contemporary element. Georgian mountain traditions of love are here reduced to being primarily about having casual, extramarital sex. The commercial brings together two very different visions of Georgian tradition, Georgian romance, and Georgian masculinity: one sublime, one grotesque.

LANGUAGE AND DESIRE: GENRES AND PRACTICES

This book is first and foremost an ethnography, but no ethnographic question can be framed without some sort of theoretical questions and some sort of theoretical framework chosen from among many alternative approaches. Understanding this framework will help the reader understand why I have organized the ethnography as I have. First, this book is, among other things, a linguistic anthropological ethnography of sexuality, one that attends to the key role played by language alongside other more conventionally erotic expressions of sexual desire. Second, this book, potentially controversially, follows Cameron and Kulick's approach to language and sexuality (2003) in treating sexuality as centrally about the cultural articulation of erotic desire rather than primarily as a matter of expressing identity. As Cameron and Kulick (2003: 106–7) point out, "sexuality is centrally about the erotic," that is, about desire (including, obviously, the varied things that we would call "sex"). They make this point to stress that, with respect to both linguistic and nonlinguistic practices of sexuality, sexuality is not simply a matter of expressing identity (a subject that preoccupies the literature on language and sexuality, as Cameron and Kulick show), though it is also that. It is first and foremost about erotic *desire*, so a study of language and sexuality, such as the one I am undertaking here, "acknowledges that sexuality is relational and transitive: desire is always for someone or something," and "the relationships between the two [the subject and object of desire] are materialized through language" (Cameron and Kulick 2003: 107).

But desire is not simply a natural given, always the same across cultures. It is shaped by culture, and also by language and linguistic interaction:

> Although we may experience our sexual desires as uniquely personal and intensely private, their form is shaped by social and verbal interaction—including . . . the silences, the explicit and tacit prohibitions that are part of that interaction. It is in the social world that we learn what is desirable, which desires are appropriate for which kinds of people, and which desires are forbidden. (Cameron and Kulick 2003: 131)

As an ethnography of language and sexuality in the unfamiliar culture of the Khevsurs, this book will necessarily attend to the way in which the cultural constitution of "desire" among the Khevsurs is perhaps both similar to and different from the forms and expressions of sexual desire in Western cultures. Further, as an ethnography of language and desire, it will also place special emphasis on the way in which both the physical and linguistic manifestations of desire are structured by relatively stable, conventional, recognizable, and repeatable forms of behavior or utterance recognized within cultural systems, what are traditionally labeled "*genres.*" Love does not merely exist; it can only exist in, and by virtue of, specific cultural forms of expression, that is, genres. These genres are both linguistic and nonlinguistic. This work will center on the relationship of genre as a conventional cultural category in relation to the individual erotic desire that these genres allow to be expressed: "The study of language and sexuality should in principle encompass the linguistic genres (e.g. flirting, personal ads, pornography and erotica, sex talk) in which people perform and represent their erotic desires, the way they construct themselves as desiring subjects and address the real or imagined objects of their desire" (Cameron and Kulick 2003: 107). I will expand the concept of genre to include both nonlinguistic genres of *physical* sexual expression, such as kissing, alongside linguistic genres expressing desire, such as pillow talk. This ethnography, then, will be organized in terms of genre, maintaining as much as possible a symmetry between linguistic genres and other nonlinguistic genres of erotic behavior, so that a change in linguistic genre expressing a change in degree of intimacy is usually paired with a parallel change in nonlinguistic genres. The erotic career of a couple can then be presented as a series of paired linguistic and nonlinguistic erotic genres. Just as the erotic career of North American teens moves through recognizable stages with recognizable genres (Meeting, Flirting, Creating, Maintaining, and Ending a Relationship; see Pascoe 2010), with both linguistic and nonlinguistic aspects, so too is it with Khevsur romance. Nonlinguistic erotic genres are not merely expressed or described in linguistic genres; they are created by them.

The fact that sexuality involves shared genres of sexual practice, both linguistic and nonlinguistic, draws attention to the way in which *sts'orproba* also represents a kind of community of practice: an "aggregate of people who, through engagement in a common enterprise, come to develop and share ways of doing things, ways of talking, beliefs, values—in short, practices" (Eckert 1996: 1). Such a perspective allows us to maintain a parallelism between linguistic and nonlinguistic genres, but it also highlights the fact that as children in a given community become adults, they move with their age cohort into a normative community of heterosexual practice, in which, among other things, the valuation of their gender is transformed by "a transition from a normatively asexual social order to a normatively heterosexual one, transforming relations among and between boys and girls" (Eckert 1996: 2). As Eckert states in an earlier work:

> In order for the cohort to emerge as socially heterosexual, boys and girls, many of whom have known each other most of their lives, must begin to see each other differently. The familiar must be rendered mysterious; the ordinary must be rendered desirable. This requires a complex process of mystification and mutual objectification, as girls and boys feel constrained to stop seeing each other as "just people," and start seeing each other as a class of desired objects. (Eckert 1994: 11)

For Khevsurs, this transformation of gender roles and practices happened suddenly and was expressed by linked changes in both linguistic and nonlinguistic practice: at the ages of 14–15, Khevsur boys and girls began to leave aside childish genres; they no longer engaged in childish pastimes and no longer recited childish genres of poetry (Gogoch'uri 1974: 57). By the ages of 16–17, boys and girls begin to engage in *sts'orproba* (Baliauri 1991: 9). Khevsur marriages were usually arranged quite early by their parents, but the marriage itself happened quite late: most Khevsurs would engage in *sts'orproba* for around a decade before they finally consummated their marriage, a process that itself had several stages. As a result, when Khevsurs speak of "husband" and "wife" for an unmarried person, they mean "designated husband or wife" or "betrothed."

The sexualization of gender happens unevenly for different members of any adolescent cohort, so that at any given time, a sexual cohort will contain both relatively new, inexperienced members and relatively old, experienced ones (Eckert 1996). Similarly, the community of practice of *sts'orproba* had central and marginal members: it contained new members (e.g., girls who had not yet engaged in the practice) who needed to be paired with more experienced partners, and it also contained boys and girls who were *sts'orpriani* (those whose desirability was expressed by having had many *sts'orperi* partners) as well as those who were *usts'orpero* ("lacking in *sts'operis*," those who had no such partners because they were undesirable). The latter, those who were undesirable in themselves, often participated in romantic practices centrally, but vicariously, as "mediators" (*elchi*), becoming experts in facilitating desire between others, taking pleasure in, or gaining power over, a process in which they themselves did not directly participate.

Sexuality is primarily about desire, involving a desiring subject and an object of that desire (Cameron and Kulick 2003), but genres or forms of expression of desire, like any other shared cultural practice, can also secondarily be mobilized as a marker of individual or collective identity. While we tend to privilege "sexual identities," that is, identities strongly defined by sexuality ("I am a gay/lesbian/heterosexual etc."), as the central kind of identity that arises from sexuality, the possible relations between sexuality and identity are culturally and historically variable, just as sexuality itself is (Cameron and Kulick 2003: 8). Thus, sexuality can be foundational to individual and collective identities that are not in themselves "sexual identities." Khevsurs explicitly defined their collective identity as a community of shared practice: to be a Khevsur was to follow Khevsur "rules" (*ts'esi*), in *sts'orproba* as in many other things. These rules defined Khevsur collective identity in opposition to other communities of (sexual) practice, such as the strangely similar-and-opposed sexual practices of Pshavian *ts'ats'loba* or, worse, the completely debased sexual anarchy prevailing among the Russians (discussed in chapter 5). Indeed, those who violated the rules of the Khevsurs were said to have "become Russians." Khevsur rules of sexuality involved both expression of sexual desire and restraint, and thus expressed, embodied, and inculcated a certain cultural model of personhood (cf. Caton 1990: 109–25). Not merely is *sts'orproba* a set of cultural genres for the expression of desire, but these genres also express nonsexual Khevsur virtues of personal freedom and autonomy (i.e., absence of sexual coercion, which made possible the free expression of individual desire) and concerns for honor, shame, and self-restraint (cf. Abu-Lughod 1986). *Sts'orproba* involves the self-regulating tempering of individual desire (*survili*) by a concern for one's name (*sakheli*) and capacity to experience shame (*sirtskhvili*); this results from having the ethical virtue of *namusi*, which can mean honor, conscience, or shame (in a particularly sexual sense). All of these things are central both to Khevsur identity and to the rules of *sts'orproba*.

THE KHEVSURS IN HISTORY

This is a historical ethnography. The first half of this book is based largely on the works of indigenous ethnographers writing at a time when the practices described in the book were still alive and well. I rely particularly on the writings of Natela Baliauri and her husband, Aleksi Ochiauri, both of whom were themselves Khevsurs living in exile in neighboring Pshavi, as well as on the work of a "circle" of Georgian folklorists and ethnographers who were friends of this family (beginning with Ak'ak'i Shanidze, Giorgi Tedoradze, and Sergi Mak'alatia) and doing ethnography in a living culture. In the case of Baliauri's and Ochiauri's work, the time of writing is not always clear; the ethnographic "present tense" of quotations is the first half of the twentieth century, at a time when ethnographers were still able to witness Khevsur culture in something like an intact state, before the Khevsurs were forcibly removed from their homes high in the mountains and resettled in the plains of Georgia in 1952, at the end of the Stalin period. Naturally, given the mediated nature of my data, I can only talk about what the original ethnographers said, and if I am silent on a point, it probably means there is nothing written about it.

I propose to give here merely an extremely schematic history of both the country of Georgia and the Khevsurs. Suffice it to say that the Khevsurs were one of many Georgian mountain-dwelling groups, including the neighboring Pshavians and other groups (Figure 0.5), a very small and relatively isolated group occupying small mountain villages, and who, owing to the harsh conditions and poverty of their abode in the high mountains, never numbered more than a few thousand souls. The Khevsurs spoke an archaic-sounding dialect of Georgian that is fairly distant from standard Georgian, befitting a people who were sometimes thought to be a lost group of Crusaders, since they wore exotic costumes decorated with crosses and used swords and chain mail incongruously alongside rifles and muskets well into the twentieth century. Their distance from centers of power and the difficulty of reaching these villages meant that Khevsurs lived lives relatively free from direct outside interference and rule: the principles of autonomy and self-governance of these warlike communities resemble classic ethnographic examples of what E.E. Evans-Pritchard (1940) called "ordered anarchy," that is, states without rulers.

As a result, Khevsur relations with the states in the plains were checkered. In the period of Georgian feudalism, in which most peasants were serfs, tied to the land in feudal bondage, little more than slaves of their feudal lords, Khevsurs were one of the "free" mountain groups that had neither lords nor serfs. When Georgia became part of the Russian empire in 1801, serfdom continued, and was even reinforced, until the Russian emperor ordered the emancipation of the serfs beginning in the 1860s. The emancipation was an event that transformed Georgian intellectual society and marked the beginning of modern Georgian print and urban culture (Manning 2012a). But all this had little impact on the Khevsurs, who were, after all, already free peasants and would not have much contact with Russian bureaucracy in their day-to-day lives for decades yet. Despite attempts by the Russian state to "restore" Orthodox Christianity to these erstwhile Christians, the "pagan" Khevsurs remained highly skeptical of Russian-Georgian church rituals, priests, and churches, viewing them for what they were: an extension of the political power of the Russian colonial state into the local community.

When Georgia was integrated forcefully into the Soviet Union after a few years of independence (1918–21) in the wake of the Russian Revolution and civil war, the Khevsurs remained more or less as they were before, tolerating occasional incursions into their mountain fastnesses but largely remaining autonomous and settling most of their political affairs with other mountain communities as they had done in the past. With the consolidation of Soviet power, especially in the Stalin period (from the 1930s until Stalin's death in 1953), the Soviet State increasingly sought to bring the mountain-dwelling people of the Caucasus under direct state control, often by exiling them from the mountains. While large groups like the neighboring Chechens were punished by the Soviet State and deported en masse to Central Asia over a period of a few days toward the end of World War II (1944), resulting in the death of more than 100,000 civilians, the very small Khevsur population was deported under comparatively easy conditions in 1952 and resettled to the plains of Georgia. The history and ethnography of the Khevsurs as a settled group ends there, and from chapter 6 onward this book deals with a community that exists increasingly only in the form of circulating images.

PLAN OF THE BOOK

The early chapters of this book will in general begin by following the trajectory of a typical romance, paying attention to the different linguistic and nonlinguistic genres at each stage (chapters 1–3). In the first chapter, we follow the trials and travails of girls who act as romantic mediators, and examine Khevsur society as an uneven terrain across which these girls seek to build casual erotic relationships between boys and other girls through the conversational art of persuasion. In the second chapter, we follow the boy and the girl to bed for a casual night spent together, and see how conversation and kissing work together as equivalent expressions of erotic sociability. In the third chapter, we follow individual couples as they seek to make something more durable out of these casual one-night liaisons. Here we spend more time focusing on how boys and girls who have become "sworn brothers" (*dzmobili*)[4] defend their relationships from casual lovers and other rivals, how they mark time spent apart, and how they give each other durable signs of love in the form of gifts. I pay particular attention here to the crucial role of stolen bottles of vodka that girls save for boys: this particularly feminine form of romantic gift serves to mark long periods spent apart when it is saved (vodka will last indefinitely), it marks the relationship as being a particularly intimate one, since vodka is only stolen and saved for one's chosen lover, and if the relationship falls apart, it becomes a sign of loss and betrayal, an object that must be disposed of somehow. In the middle of the book (chapters 4 and 5), I will turn from genres that mediate individual experiences and romantic relationships to ones that relate individual erotic desire to a collective normative order. In chapter 4, I examine genres of love poetry with which lovers make their most intimate secrets public, and

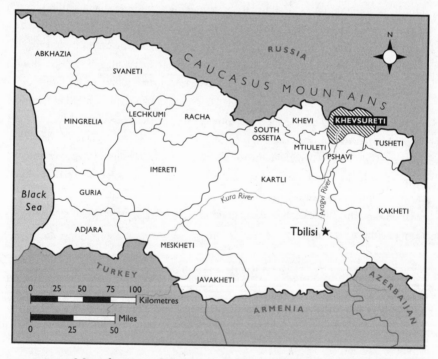

FIGURE 0.5: Map of regions of Georgia with Khevsureti (shaded) in the northeast

explore how and why Khevsur girls write love poems of praise for their lovers in which the author and her love vanish—love poems that seem not to be love poems at all.

Chapter 5 explores Khevsur romance not as a part of an idealized, unchanging culture but as a real historical narrative, where rules are broken and scandals spread. This change to a primarily historical mode of presentation continues in the final chapters, where we turn to the question of how anyone ever found out about the romantic practices of a handful of Georgian mountain people, and how their romantic lives became objects of intense national public scrutiny and vicarious erotic fascination. In the next two chapters (6–7), I will explore how outsiders, specifically other Georgians, became aware of these practices through the new genres of print culture and visual media: newspaper correspondence, ethnography (chapter 6), novels and films (chapter 7). Finally I show how increasingly fragmentary images of this lost world of sexuality continue to circulate in contemporary multimedia genres, including teenage Internet forums.

NOTES

1. As we will see in Chapter 3, Tedoradze is probably wrong about the vodka, which plays a role in transforming this casual relationship into a more durable relationship. Mak'alatia similarly mixes up the casual and committed stages of Pshavian ts'ats'loba in the next quotation.

2. A traveller in the region from 1880 (Mamsashvili 1880: 2) explains this unfamiliar Pshavian custom to other Georgians by comparing it to sworn-sisterhood: "a 'ts'ats'ali' is sort of like a sworn sister (vitom dobili), but who fulfills a romantic role." As we will see, however, for Pshavians and Khevsurs alike, the "sworn brother/sworn sister" stage of the relationship is a more serious stage that both ethnographers have confused here with the initial casual stages.

3. Note that Georgian orthography does not distinguish between upper and lower case. To capture this sense, I have used only lower case in the transliteration of Georgian throughout the book.

4. Among the Khevsurs the same term, meaning something like "boyfriend or girlfriend," is used regardless of gender; compare the parallel Pshavian terms nadzmobi "sworn brother; boyfriend" and nadobi "sworn sister; girlfriend."

1

THE AMBASSADOR

———

THE SEXUAL relationship of *sts'orproba* was a ubiquitous feature of Khevsur life. Virtually every collective social event where opposite-sex young persons were present—weddings and harvests, for instance—was a potential occasion for *sts'orproba*, and whatever the ostensible reason for such a larger social occasion, for many young people in attendance the real point of the event was to engage in *sts'orproba*:

> In Khevsureti not one event would end, if at the end of it *sts'orproba* was not arranged, aside from those times, when someone died and they came to mourn him. In other such minor events the young men and women would gather more for the sake and purpose of *sts'orproba*. . . . (A. Ochiauri 1980: 231)

But since unacquainted boys and girls usually could not initiate this relationship directly, they initially relied on the conversational labors of a third party, the *elchi* ("ambassador, envoy"), usually a girl from the community who did all the negotiations to set up a boy and girl together for a single night. The presence of this mediating figure pointed to the presence of both social distance and sexual desire between a boy and a girl. The *elchi* bridged the social distance between opposite-sex peers and enabled them to express sexual desire. Given that boys and girls might have desires for each other, and yet were unable to act upon them directly, how did desire find expression? Here the *elchi* stepped in to establish a couple, and then she stepped away.

The mediation of the *elchi* was optional at some degrees of social distance, and required at others. The requirement for an *elchi* to mediate defined the relationship as one of a certain social distance, one in which desire was potentially present and permitted. In addition, the *elchi* not only navigated social distance, but also exerted agency over pairings so that they could become expressive of desires. Just as we will see that a large amount of what boys and girls spent the night together doing was simply talking sociably, so too the work that brought them together involved persuasive conversations that mediated social distance and individual desires. This chapter deals with the first stages of romance: the *elchi's* work needed to set up the initial encounter, work that was dominated by the pervasive, and seemingly unremarkable, speech genre of conversation.

Erotic liaisons among the Khevsurs were created by conversation, and whatever else was involved, conversation was part and parcel of the erotic relationship. The importance of conversation in the creation and maintenance of social relationships of various kinds, including romantic ones, was identified early on by the British social anthropologist Bronislaw Malinowski. He used the terms "phatic communion" and the "phatic function" for these functions of language: "a type of speech in which ties of union are created by a mere exchange of words" (Malinowski 1923: 315). For Malinowski, the phatic function was an example of language as a form of social action, serving both to index existing social relations and to create new ones, what he called the "pragmatic" function of language, language as a "mode of behaviour, an indispensable element of concerted human action" (Malinowski 1923: 316). Malinowski emphasizes not only that such phatic speech functions pragmatically as a kind of social action, as a way to establish and maintain social bonds (phatic communion), but also that conversation fulfills this role not because of the content of *what* is said, but by its *very form*: conversation thus takes the form of verbal exchange.

Through the exchange of roles between speaker and listener, the genre of conversation represents a form of reciprocity that expresses not only solidarity, but also equality, between participants; in Malinowski's words, "reciprocity is established by the change of rôles" of speaker and addressee (1923: 314). Malinowski's treatment of conversation as a form of egalitarian reciprocal verbal exchange also connects conversation nicely to other forms of exchange that similarly establish ties of fellowship or love, including "the deep tendency to create social ties through exchange of gifts" (Malinowski 1932: 175). As we will see, conversational exchange among the Khevsurs created and maintained a phatic relationship of equality, one that could also involve reciprocity on several levels: exchanges of words, exchanges of gifts that boys made or bought for girls and the bottles of vodka that girls stole and hid for boys, and, of course, exchanges of spit.

Attention to the phatic dimension draws attention to the channel within which the relationship operates. Social relations, of whatever kind, between two persons require some sort of physical medium, a channel or channels, and they often require a third party to create that channel (Elyachar 2010). Before two people can fall in love, they must talk, and before two people can talk, a channel of communication between them must be opened, and it must be maintained: introductions must be made for people to speak to each other as acquaintances, or telephone networks must be created before a telephone conversation can happen. For there to be conversational dyad, there must be a channel of communication, and initially, a third party, a mediator of some kind, may open this channel of communication: a mutual friend making introductions, perhaps, or in old telephone systems where no telephone conversation could begin without the mediation of an operator.

While certainly two people can do this work themselves, "striking up" a conversation with a stranger at a bus stop or in a bar, in romantic liaisons this work can involve a matchmaker, a kind of social communications engineer, working tirelessly and invisibly to create these channels of communication, what Elyachar (2010) calls a "phatic worker" or even a "phatic pimp." The latter term is useful for this analysis, because particularly in the romantic world of the Khevsurs, girls and boys could not flirt, let alone "make out," until they had been "set up" by the *elchi*, who engaged in a series of "infrastructural" conversations to establish the channel of communication along which the relationship could flow.

THE *ELCHI* AS MEDIATOR

As a "phatic worker," the *elchi* created the conditions of possibility for erotic liaisons. Like other infrastructural workers and the infrastructures they create, the *elchi* tended to disappear into her work: if she was successful, her thankless work would speak for itself; if she was not, she would take the blame. The *elchi* appeared to take a vicarious pleasure in her work, for there was no obvious reward: "She will try anything, make up anything, endure all kinds of humiliation and abuse if only she can make a boy and girl meet each other and lie down together. If anyone asks her, when she is being reviled as she usually is, where she got the strength to do this, she will answer with a laugh: . . . . 'my thanks is—laying sweethearts down together!'" (Baliauri 1991: 150). Not merely a thankless task, the sneaking, skulking subterfuges of the *elchi* could even lead to physical danger. A poem composed by an *elchi* gives some idea:

gadaviare samjera	Thrice I went by
ertis soplelis binao.	The house of a villager.
anabriv kurdi vegone,	Maybe they thought I was a thief,
gamaiq'arnes dzmanio.	Her brothers came out.
mavbrundi, gajavrebulma	I came back, angrily
uk'ughm visrien kvanio.	I threw rocks back at them.
shaudzver garetachia,	I sneaked into their out-building,
t'q'vias makhkonda chkamio.	A bullet made a sound.
samjer mamidzman davsts'q'ien,	Thrice I cursed their fathers' brothers,
aghar vielcheb kalio.	I will never be an *elchi* again.

(Baliauri 1991: 180)

An *elchi* participated in romance, but only vicariously. To perform her thankless work as mediator, the *elchi* also had to be disinterested personally, standing outside the relations she mediated: she was *in* the system of relations of *sts'orproba* but not *of* it, not one of the objects linked by that system. Therefore the *elchi* was often a girl who had never engaged in *sts'orproba* herself; rather, she satisfied herself in taking notice of when others had desire for one another. She might, for example, be physically unattractive and unable to be paired off herself, yet she might have become quite influential in arranging, or destroying, the affairs of others. As a result, *elchis* could become very famous within their villages (Baliauri 1991: 151). The *elchi* was a zealous advocate of desire: she never divulged the secrets of the boys and girls she brought together, but she was quite capable of betraying a promise made to one person in order to achieve the pairings she desired or had promised to another.

The *elchi* was usually a girl, either a relative of or at least someone the same age as those for whom she mediated, for only a girl could traverse—and even transgress—all the boundaries needed to do the work she had to do in creating channels of communication. Unlike a boy, a girl could relatively freely enter the house of the girl for whom she wished to arrange *sts'orproba*, and could even spend the night there. Some families allowed the *elchi* to come in openly and take their daughters away, while others did not. In the latter case, when an *elchi* came to spend the night in another girl's house, the family would set them a place to sleep from which it would be easy to detect attempts to leave, and would position themselves nearby as well, lest the *elchi* help the girl escape from them. But still, through various ruses, the *elchi* managed not only to arrange an escape for the girl so she could meet her lover, but also even to hide the fact of the escape having happened in the first place. She might pretend to talk to the (already absent) girl, or she might start laughing, pretending that the girl herself was laughing, and so on. The girl, for her part, would make sure the doors were unlocked so the *elchi* could sneak in when the lights were put out. The *elchi* would then wake her up and send her on her way, and take her place in the bed until the girl returned from her tryst, at which point she would sneak out again (Baliauri 1991: 150). Sometimes matters were even more complicated:

> Sometimes a boy and a girl are forbidden from lying down together for some reason. Let's say that such a boy and a girl want to lie down together, then the *elchi* goes to the girl's house at that time when everyone has already gone to bed. The girl who is waiting for her does not lock the doors and the *elchi* sneaks into the house. She wakes up the girl and sends her to the appointed place where the boy is waiting for her, while she lies down herself in her [the girl's] bed. If the girl for some reason was unable to get home early and her relatives get up to go to work, the *elchi* lies sleeping with bated breath,

because she is waiting for the girl and she can't get up until she arrives. Eventually [the girl's] brothers and sisters call out: "Get up!" They think that it's their sister lying in bed. The girl [*elchi*] doesn't move. She has her head covered and she lies there sleeping like that. Well, how is she to get up? Someone comes, and removes her head-coverings, and they see the *elchi* lying there. (Baliauri 1991: 152–53)

Boys sometimes also served as *elchis*, but the restrictions imposed by their gender hampered their ability to do this work. Unlike girls, boys could not easily enter a girl's house, and if they did, they had to do so openly; nor, obviously, could they pretend to actually *be* the missing girl (Baliauri 1991: 153). The boy might invent some pretext for openly entering a girl's house, such as having something to tell her family members, or might arrange beforehand to meet up with her outside in a place where there were few people around. In this case he could bring the girl on horseback to meet with the designated boy, and then bring her back home again on horseback. The boy *elchi* assumed a complementary role to a girl *elchi*, in that the boy specifically could not bring a girl to a boy from *someone else's* house to *yet another person's* house (say, from the girl's house to the boy's house) *within the same village*, which is precisely what the girl *elchi* specialized in doing. He might, however, invite the boy to be a guest in his own home and bring the girl there too, or carry a girl to a boy in another village, for example (Baliauri 1991: 153).

AUTONOMY, PERSUASION, AND DESIRE

The *elchi* took on the mediating work, the "phatic labor," needed to create and protect a relationship. Her work encountered different forms of resistance, other than social distance between the unacquainted and possibly a lack of desire. First, Khevsur boys and girls alike had an ideal of personal freedom and proud autonomy (*tavmoq'vareoba*), so they could not be compelled to do much of anything, especially anything sexual, by command or by force (see chapter 5 for some examples). On the contrary, they had to be persuaded, perhaps by reference to kinship and hospitality obligations, or appeals to personal desire. Nowhere is this better displayed than in relations of *sts'orproba*, especially for women: "No one can stop a Khevsur woman from engaging in *sts'orproba*. Only her parents have the right to do so, but they don't. A brother cannot raise his voice to say anything at all, nor can cousins and other relatives. In this respect, a woman is completely free" (Baliauri 1991: 28).

Obviously, objectively speaking, as in most societies, there were a good many substantive sources of inequality and unfreedom in Khevsur society, especially for women. Much of the work of maintaining, hiding, legitimating, and naturalizing Khevsur gender inequality has its roots in a pervasive dualistic model of cosmology in which men are "pure," descended from male divinities, while women are "impure," basically the spawn of the devil. This cosmological account of gender difference had pervasive taken-for-granted effects on a woman's life, regulating where she could go and what she had to do, and had the effect of naturalizing and legitimating many gender inequalities, much as appeals to putative biological differences in aptitude for different tasks between men and women can act to naturalize and legitimate gender inequalities in our own society. But almost none of this factual gender inequality was maintained by the power of command or coercion (domination), but was rather embedded in the tacit presuppositions of a taken-for-granted cosmological order expressed in myths (hegemony). In spite of this dualistic cosmological framework that established basic gender inequalities as being ordained by nonhuman entities (gods and demons), a Khevsur woman could maintain a strong, *non-illusory*, sense of autonomy and freedom with respect to other *human* persons, since autonomy and freedom were defined as absence of coercion by other human persons (see Abu-Lughod 1986: 78–117, 233–259 for comparable Bedouin ideologies of autonomy).

The important point is that from a Khevsur perspective, freedom and personal autonomy of the person, male or female, were ideals that had to be overtly and formally recognized in all social interactions. Consent always had to be elicited, because coercion, as Abu-Lughod puts in with respect to a comparable situation among the Bedouin, "strips acts of their meaning" (1986: 245). For Khevsur women there were specific times of life and areas in which this subjective sense of autonomy and freedom were felt to be particularly characteristic. Women's lives had two major phases: a period of autonomy and freedom among her friends and kin, which was also the period in which she engaged in *sts'orproba*; and a period of unfreedom and exile among hostile strangers, characteristic of married life.

Personal autonomy was a quite general personal ideal among the Khevsurs, and its far-reaching consequences were not limited to erotic matters but in fact underlay all personal and political interactions. Khevsur political society was, compared to the Georgian society of the plains, "free," meaning that there were no explicit social hierarchies and no human political authorities with the power to issue commands in their own right or to ensure compliance with commands by the use of force. As we will see throughout, Khevsurs perceived their freedom and autonomy from the commands of human others to have resulted from their voluntary collective obedience to divinely appointed "rules" (*ts'esi*) that defined them as a "free" people. Political hierarchy (the power of command) was displaced from human actors onto divinities: Khevsurs, who had never known real feudal domination, imagined themselves to be in a feudal relationship of subordination as "serfs," "servants," or "vassals" (*q'mebi*) to otherworldly "lords," divinities incarnated in local shrines (*jvari*, literally "crosses," or what are called *khati* "icons" in neighboring Pshavi; Tuite 1999). Individually, all humans were imagined as being equally subordinated to divinities, but real interactions between humans were highly egalitarian and sensitive to the autonomy of the other. As in the political life of the community, so too in personal decisions about romance: desire was a central expression of this individual autonomy. For Khevsurs, desire presupposed autonomy and consent and was therefore absolutely opposed to obligation or coercion, so the *elchi* had to engage in persuasion in order to produce desire.

As Caton argues generally for similar social organizations, the importance of persuasion is centrally linked to cultural conceptions of personhood that value autonomy:

> Persuasion must be explained in light of cultural notions such as autonomy because an actor would only try to persuade someone whom he could not or should not compel. In other words, actors must believe they are in some sense *free* to accept or reject political policies and that their opinions matter in the decision-making process. (Caton 1987: 96; emphasis in original)

As Caton argues (with particular reference to political dispute processes in such communities), certain forms of speaking (what I am calling speech genres) are particularly suited to this kind of persuasion for both resolving conflicts and arranging romantic liaisons. Conversation or dialogue, in particular, is such a genre: inasmuch as it mediates between a "plethora of voices engaged with each other, dialogue also invokes the notion of autonomy—in fact requires it. A command is not part of a dialogue; a suggestion or question is. If I have no right to refrain or dissent or agree, I cannot engage in a true dialogue" (Caton 1987: 97). In addition, it is not enough to recognize a plurality of voices in order to have a dialogue; these voices must be mediated by a "dialectical process" in which opposing arguments are valued: "they must also listen and hear in their medley a common chord that keeps them in harmony. . . . In dialogue there must be mediation of the opposed points of view. The mediator in tribal conflicts is, in a sense, *a third term* who tries to find the common ground in the dialogue of disputes, and then expand it" (Caton 1987: 97; emphasis added).

Just as a neutral mediator, a third term, is required in tribal conflicts to re-establish a relationship of harmony between two conflicting groups, so too the *elchi* acted as a "third term" mediating between opposed "sides" in matters of romance. She did this through a series of conversations with each party. The conversations the *elchi* had with boys and girls were oriented toward creating desire through persuasion. It is significant, then, that Baliauri's ethnography spends the first part of the discussion of *sts'orproba* showing in detail all of this work, most of which consists of conversation.

THE *ELCHI* AT WORK: A GIRL'S FIRST NIGHT
OF *STS'ORPROBA*

The most straightforward example of the phatic labor of the *elchi* is when a girl was engaging in *sts'orproba*, lying down together with a boy, for the very first time, what is called "lying down and getting up" (*ts'ola-dgoma*, henceforth "lying down"). Here the *elchi* sought to lay down an inexperienced girl with a comparatively experienced and physically attractive boy. The girl was expected to strongly resist the very idea of lying down with a boy, for which resistance her relatives would reproach her, and her cousins and other young women would mock her: "You have no charm!" (Baliauri 1991: 10). Since the consent of the girl was required, the *elchi* first had to "sell" the girl on the very idea of lying down with a boy, while her job with the boy was simply to sell him on the idea of lying down with this particular girl. In both cases the role of the *elchi* was partially conditioned by the avoidance normatively displayed between boys and girls, so her first task was to overcome the expressed lack of desire in order to produce desire, or at least to elicit consent, to the pairing.

Conversation 1: The *Elchi* and the Girl

Since the consent of the boy was not required, first the *elchi* would go to the girl to try to find out what sorts of boy she liked and disliked. The consent of the girl to any proposed pairing was required, yet at the same time the girl was normatively expected to avoid expressing a preference or a distaste for any particular boy. Accordingly, a conversation of the following sort would occur as the *elchi* sought to overcome this resistance and evasion, find an appropriate pairing, and elicit consent. The girl would invent reasons for not doing it, and the *elchi* would counter these with arguments. Baliauri (1991) portrays a typical conversation of this kind. Note that she clearly demarcates that it is an imagined typical conversation, presumably based on many such conversations in which she participated directly through growing up in the community, by occasionally putting in generic fillers like "(name)"; these are in the original text. Note also that this hypothetical conversation takes place between members of the same village, all of whom are treated linguistically as being kin, so the two girls address each other as "sister," "little sister," and so on.

> GIRL: I don't know anything about "lying down"!
> ELCHI: So you need to "lie down" soon. No one learns about "lying down and getting up" from birth, you see don't you, that good or bad, "lying down and getting up" happens to everyone.

GIRL: If everyone "lies down," who have you been lying down with, my (name)?

ELCHI: Stop it, girl, the story of my "lying down and getting up" is none of your business.

GIRL: This is my business, that when the relatives of my [future] husband come, I will lay you down with them [i.e., I will serve as a mediator], but it appears you don't even know the rules properly and here you are teaching me? You are a damnable one, you are.

ELCHI: How stupidly you talk to me, little sister. I tell you, I will "lay you down" with someone and you start cursing me [lit. you call out to devils].

GIRL: You know (name), if you also will lie there where I will lie down, then I will do it, if not, no. Girl, you know, I am a sleepyhead and if I fall asleep who in the world will wake me up before dawn? Otherwise my mother will find out and she will give you a hard time, you know her.

ELCHI: Girl, stop talking. Who do you like, with whom can I lay you down? Tell me, little sister, don't you like this boy (name)? There isn't a more desirable [*dghiani*] boy than him in Khevsureti. *Ba ba ba ba ba bai*,[1] he has more *sts'orperis* than anyone! Don't refuse me. If you don't loathe him, I will lay you down with him tonight, he is very good.

GIRL: Whether he is good or bad, that doesn't worry me, all of them are good in themselves.

ELCHI: If you don't loathe him, I really will take you to him.

GIRL: No, I don't loathe him and I don't really have a liking for him all the same. As far as lying down is concerned, however, I won't lie down with him nor anyone else, stop talking about it or I will go home right now.

A Myth about Desire

At the end, the *elchi* returns to her initial position, that the girl should engage in *sts'orproba* because it is a rule (*ts'esi*) appointed by God. She tells a little myth about its origins:

ELCHI: Why would you go home, little sister? Girls and boys "lying down" together is a rule. Why would you be ashamed to lie with (name)? It's not like he is your husband to be, is he? *Sts'orproba* was created by God. Since the time when humans were created, my father says, boys and girls have desired one another. In those days, they apparently desired each other much more, the ancestral people were perishing from desire, they say. "Lying down" together apparently did not exist. So they could only gaze upon each other. Then God apparently saw Eteri and Abesalomi had died by desire [the plot of a Georgian folktale about star-crossed lovers]. And so he partially removed desire from humans, he transferred desire onto the horns of a deer, onto tobacco, onto the beaded collar of a woman. Sworn-brotherhood and sisterhood [i.e., *sts'orproba*] were not thought up first by you and me, were they? (Baliauri 1991: 11)

The clincher in the *elchi*'s imagined argument with the girl takes her from personal desires to a retelling of a myth about the cosmological genesis of desire. The argument of the myth presents the practices of *sts'orproba* as a "rule," not "something you and I thought up right here," but something instituted by God. As noted above, obeying such a divinely appointed rule is not a threat to personal autonomy in the same way that obeying a command would be.

To understand the myth we need to know just a bit more about the Khevsur cultural concept of "desire." First, the Khevsurs did not speak of "love," "sex," or any number of terms we use in our categories of sexuality, but only of "liking" (*mats'oneba*), "wanting" (*ndoba*), and "desire" (*survili, suruli*). Second, desire was not associated with marriage (marriage partners were subject to strong norms of avoidance or "taboo": spouses could not even address each other by name!). This is why the *elchi* says "it's not like he is your husband to be, is he?" As we will see, *sts'orproba*, which both expresses, and holds in check, desire, is opposed to marriage.

The Khevsurs considered desire to be a potentially dangerous, almost sorcerous, destructive force. Unlike the other terms above, the term *desire* could denote a one-sided longing or pining, which was potentially maddening and destructive to individual and community alike (Gogoch'uri 1974: 106–07). The myth presents heterosexual desire as something that came to be as soon as boys and girls were created, but it was not in itself created by God. In this myth-time, only this single form of desire existed, and since there were no competing forms of desire it was apparently very powerful, even fatal. At the same time, there was no way to express this desire, so those who experienced it had no way to express it physically: "lying down," i.e., the rules of *sts'orproba*, did not exist, so people pined to death, it appears, because all they could do was "gaze upon each other."

God enters into the myth to tame this dangerous, destructive desire in two ways. God instituted *sts'orproba* so that this desire would have an acceptable form of physical expression. Second, he weakened this powerful original desire by taking some of the desire out of sexuality and transforming it into various other forms. Desire was thus transferred from sexual desire to other nonsexual forms of desire, replacing sexual desire with a series of competing nonsexual desires of lesser intensity, the kinds of desires one might have for material objects, like the way a man might desire deer horns (used for drinking) or a woman might desire a beautifully decorated *paragi* (a beaded collar, the most decorative part of a woman's clothing), or anyone might desire tobacco. The Khevsur notion of desire, therefore, cannot be understood on the same terms as our own cultural concept of desire: the Khevsur term did not make some of the distinctions we might make within the sexual sphere (e.g., romantic, platonic, sexual, erotic desires), nor does it recognize different sexualities. Furthermore, while sexual desire for an opposite-sexed human other is presented in the myth as the foundational form of desire, and desire for material objects is a secondary, derivative form, they are all still subsumed under a single category of desire: a relation that requires a human desiring subject and a human or non-human other as its object. Because desire is dangerous and destructive, it is something that must be afforded a proper means or object of expression (either sexual or other), but it must also be kept in check, denied, or restrained.

Conversation 2: The *Elchi* and the Boy

The girl would insist that she was interested in no one specifically, but the *elchi* would pay careful attention to her tone of voice to determine whether she really wanted to lie down with this or that boy, ascertaining from such indirect hints what the girl's real desires were, since the girl would never speak ill of or criticize any boy directly. Once the *elchi* was satisfied that she had the agreement of the girl to lying down with a boy, she would then go to the boy, beginning the conversation in veiled terms, announcing her intent to be a guest in his house that night, and asking what other guests might be present that night. The boy, in turn, would attempt to deduce who his actual guest would be, that is, who the *elchi* was trying to set him up with.

The avoidance the *elchi* had to overcome on the boy's side was a little different but no less daunting. If the girl was expected to display reserve or shyness (*morideba*), and thus not express her desire or lack of desire for this or that boy directly, the boy's primary obligation was self-control or restraint (*tavdach'eriloba*), a virtue in part elicited by, and responding to, the reserve of the girl: a boy was to appear to be indifferent to girls, not pursuing them or even looking in their direction or going into their houses. This is why the first rule of Khevsur *sts'orproba* was that boys must never go to girls; girls must always come to boys.

The Khevsurs saw this rule as distinguishing the romantic practices of *sts'orproba* from the very similar, and yet scandalous, ones called *ts'ats'loba* taking place among the neighboring Pshavians, where no *elchi* was required because the boy went directly to the girl. Even worse, the boy often visited the girl in taboo and impure female sleeping spaces, the *boseli*, literally "stable," because the first floor of the house is both the women's quarters and the stable for cattle, which women tend. *Boseli* is also the Pshavian name for menstrual isolation huts (Khevsur *samrevlo* "impure, mixed place"), spaces that are extremely taboo for males. In Khevsur practice, the girl went to the boy, and they "lay down" together in the *ch'erkho* (the "pure" male upper story of the house) or adjacent *bani* (balcony, flat roof of the lower floor) (Figure 1.1).

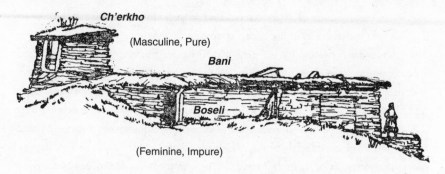

FIGURE I.I: A Khevsur house. In most traditional Khevsur houses the *bani* is smaller and the *ch'erkho* much larger than implied here. Adapted from Mak'alatia (1984 [1935]: 136).

Khevsurs considered Pshavian practices scandalous: for this reason, the use of the Pshavian term for lover, *ts'ats'ali*, among the Khevsurs could be a grave insult (Gogoch'uri 1974: 131). One Khevsur woman poet in exile among the Pshavs commented with evident horror at their scandalous sexual rules (*ts'esi*) (Gogoch'uri 1974: 130):

pshaurad gadavinatle,	I have been rebaptized as a Pshav,
pshaur avighe qelia,	I have taken a Pshavian hand,
sak'virvelia, pshavlebsa	It is strange, what kind of rules
ts'esi akvs rais peria?	Do these Pshavians have?
kalebstan tviton dadian,	The boys go themselves to the girls,
eg ragha chasdenia?	What kind of thing to do is that?

This simple inversion was scandalous for several reasons. Most important for our purposes, for a boy to go to a girl would imply a lack of masculine self-restraint. For a Khevsur boy even appear to be interested in girls and sexual matters was considered unmanly, demeaning, and shameful; for the Khevsurs, unlike the Pshavs, desire was always to be held in check. Self-control was an important way for a Khevsur boy to express his masculinity, which in turn made him attractive to girls. An oft-quoted Khevsur poem defines a good man (*k'ai q'ma*, literally "good servant"; *q'ma* "serf, servant, vassal" means "male member of the shrine-centered community") as one who would prefer to "die in battle" than to "bed down with women"; presumably the more happy-go-lucky Pshavs would not have completely agreed:

k'ai q'ma lashkar mok'vdeba,	The good servant will die in battle,
sts'orebis mjobinobasa,	Settling scores,

tsudai—boslis q'uresa,	The bad one—at the doors of the stable,
kalebtan loginobasa	Bedding down with women.

(Shanidze 1931: 013)

The stereotypical "bad servant" therefore engages in practices that are more or less typical of Pshavian sexual practices.

Khevsur males expressed their masculine virtue of self-control (*tavdach'eriloba*) by appearing to be uninterested sexually in females, instead spending their time in masculine pursuits such as dueling with swords (*k'ech'naoba*) and warfare, for which the Khevsurs were noted. Paradoxically, precisely this self-control and seeming disinterest in women are what made Khevsur males interesting sexually (on all these points see Tuite 2008). Essentially, young men made themselves attractive to women by becoming living embodiments of the warlike virtues of dead heroes (i.e., the good servant). As Baliauri notes, Khevsur boys initially had difficulty being taken seriously by women as sexual beings: "older women treat them as little boys, while girls their age treat them as clowns. For this reason, a boy tries to be amiable, self-controlled, valiant, a good horseman, belligerent, and, at the same time, a good fencer [swordsman]. He should not be idle, nor be a pursuer of women, that is, *kalachuna* ["cowardly man, sissy"], he should dress well . . . good weapons and a good horse are absolutely required for a young man" (Baliauri 1991: 17). As should be obvious, Pshavian practices, which allowed men to go about actively seeking female company, seemed scandalous to the Khevsurs, as lack of reserve, self-restraint, and avoidance made a boy appear to be unmasculine and sexually undesirable. The implication is that Pshavian boys were not really masculine at all.

Hence, from the boy's perspective, a female mediator was required, since he could not act overtly in any way, since even showing desire for a girl amounted to "going to the girl." Therefore, the boy's interest in his conversation with the *elchi* would be to try to figure out which girl she was trying to set him up with, since he would be afraid to meet with a girl he did not like. If he were to find out he would be laid down with a young girl, he would agree, but "out of respect" (*khatrit*) for the girl or the *elchi*, and not because he specifically desired the girl (as we will see, lying down out of respect or a sense of obligation is strongly opposed to lying down out of desire). The *elchi*, in turn, would resist his efforts to find this out:

[The girl *elchi*] goes to the boy and tells him: "I will be your guest tonight. Do you have guests or not, if so, how many. I want them to be few in number." In short, she makes the boy aware for what purpose she has come. At the same time, the boy tries to figure out who the *elchi* is talking about. He is afraid of meeting up with a girl he doesn't like or loathes. If he finds out that he is to be laid down with a very young girl, he will agree, even though he will not enjoy the modesty and shyness of a young girl. (Baliauri 1991: 11–12)

The rest of the conversation between the *elchi*, whom we now know as Tamia, and the boy, would go something like this, according to Baliauri:

BOY: What in the world do you intend, little Tamia?

ELCHI: What do I intend, boy? First just tell me, whether you will be in or not? Or has anyone else [another *elchi*] already talked to you, my little brother (name), about laying another girl down with you, don't hide it from me!

BOY: Oh, I understand, I understand, Tamia, first tell me, who do you have as a guest? Is she a fellow villager or from [another village within] the [wider] community [*temi*]?[2]

ELCHI: Who should I be bringing as guest? Boy, it is none of your affair, who I have. First answer the questions I have asked, and then I will tell you.

BOY: I won't tell you, Tamia, no.

ELCHI: Boy, don't get on my nerves! What is wrong with you, tell me!

BOY: I won't tell you anything until I find out who you are talking about [laying me down with].

ELCHI: Boy, why are you tormenting me?

BOY: I will tell you, my sister Tamia, but if you tell me [you are putting me] with someone bad, I will disgrace you publicly, I will not let you come here again as long as you are alive. Not very long ago [a few days ago] you brought (the name of a girl) to lay with me in bed. I spent that whole night awake. If right now you are talking about someone like that, you should know I will kill you.

ELCHI: Boy, why would you kill me? She herself wants to lie with you. Why in the world would I do something like that?

BOY: Leave here, maybe go tell that girl (the same girl's name) yourself, that supposedly I want to lie down with her too, why not? [sarcastically] She wants to! That way you would be lying to her too!

ELCHI: My brother, don't refuse me and I will tell you.

BOY: Tell me, tell me.

ELCHI: I will bring (name of girl). She is indeed a little girl, but a good girl! It's not a problem, my brother. She will become accustomed (to lying down) and we will have a new girl in the village.

BOY: Oh, Nana (let us say that this is the name of the girl)? When in the world did she begin lying down? If she lies down with me first, as with a decrepit old man, well, what in the world would I tell you [i.e., I can't say no]. Poor Nana, my Tami inflicted me on you!

ELCHI: My brother, don't lie to me, if you don't want her, tell me right now.

BOY: Eh, bring her, for your sake I have spent one night as if lying on thistles, I won't disappoint you.

Conversation 3: The *Elchi* and the Mother

Once the *elchi* had set up a possible pairing, she also had to arrange the logistics of actually bringing the girl to the boy. *Sts'orproba* did not take place openly, but was rather furtive and concealed, and sometimes it could be resisted by the family. Here the *elchi*'s work lay not only in setting up the pairing, but also in concealing it from others who might seek to prevent it. In fact, it began to take on the character of a spy game:

> Once the *elchi* persuades the girl and the boy to lie down together, she asks the boy where his bed is in the house, who sleeps close to him and so on. The boy teaches her everything, after which they agree on some sign, by which the boy will learn of their arrival. So for example they will make some sort of noise, or they will imitate the sound of some animal, they will whistle, toss pebbles and so on. From these signs the boy will learn of their arrival. The Khevsurs call these "signs." This is necessary because it is possible that someone else will be sleeping in that bed. There are cases where the *elchi* apparently brought the girl to the boy and by mistake laid her down with someone else. For example in the village of Akhieli they brought a young girl to sleep with a boy, in the bed, in which the boy was supposed to be sleeping, lay his old uncle and the boy didn't dare to say anything. The *elchi* brought the girl and took the covers off the appointed bed in order to lay the girl, but instead of the "sworn brother" [her appointed lover] she encountered an old man. To avoid such dangers a sign agreed upon in advance is necessary.
>
> After all this the *elchi* goes to the girl's house and tries to bring the girl out of there. She thinks up some excuse and says to the girl's mother:

ELCHI: My Sandua (let's say the girl's mother is called that), let Nana come out to my house tonight, I have some wool that needs to be carded, I want us to stay all night and I don't want to be alone, I'll fall asleep.

MOTHER: Little mother,[3] My Tamia [. . .], Nana would prevent you from sleeping! What a great lover of work I have! In the evening she takes a bite to eat with her to bed and you can't wake her up until dawn, even if we were to turn the whole house upside down.

ELCHI: No matter, my Sandua, we will entertain one another, we won't get sleepy, I would have come to your place, but then I would have to drag the wool to be carded here and back again.

MOTHER: She can come if she wants to, she doesn't do anything for me here at night anyway.

ELCHI [to girl]: Get up, hurry get up, my little sister, let's go. (Baliauri 1991: 13)

The next day, after the couple have spent the night together, the *elchi* would visit the girl and ask her how she liked the boy, how he behaved toward her, whether she would lie down with him again, and so on: "All of this is interesting for the *elchi*. If she finds out that the girl liked the boy, then she will serve as an *elchi* for her again. She goes to see the boy too and asks him, how the girl was, good or not. Or, if he liked her, whether he wants to lie down with her again" (Baliauri 1991: 16). The relationship between them still has not progressed to the "boyfriend-girlfriend" (*dzmobili*, literally "sworn brother") stage (which I will discuss in chapter 3). Rather, the *elchi* would still mediate between the boy and the girl for a second and third time, although in future visits the *elchi* would only lead the girl to the boy's house, and not accompany her all the way to the boy's bed, as happened the first time. If the boy was asleep, the girl would wake him, but for the most part the boy would be waiting awake for her. The story of the *elchi* does not end here; we will see her again, but first we must see what would happen after the *elchi* left the couple together for the night.

NOTES

1   This is an essentially untranslatable admirative expression, roughly equivalent to "good heavens" or "boy oh boy."

2   A *temi* is generally a valley in which there is more than one village, or a collection of related villages, whose residents are also understood to be related to one another.

3   If unrelated boys and girls called each other "brother" and "sister," the kin terms were also used across generations between people living in the same village. However, just as mothers called their children "little mother" (in effect addressing the child as the child would address her), so here Sandua calls Tamia "little mother."

2

SPENDING THE NIGHT TOGETHER

IN THE LAST CHAPTER we saw the way conversation worked as a form of persuasion and mediation that set up the conditions for romance, paying special attention to the "phatic labor" of the *elchi*, who had to navigate social distance and produce desire through her conversational labors of persuasion. In this chapter conversation takes on a slightly different role, not as producing the conditions for romance, but as a pleasurable form of interaction pursued for its own sake, one that attended, and was part and parcel of, the nonverbal forms of erotic interaction also pursued for their own sake: the erotic genre of sexual sociability called "lying down and getting up," which formed the central practice of *sts'orproba*. Again here we find a symmetry between linguistic and nonlinguistic expressions of eroticism. Just as these relations of lying down together for the night were ephemeral, inconsequential forms of expression of intimacy between opposite sex peers, so too did free conversations take place during these trysts, pursued for their own sake and, like the relationships they attended, leaving no lasting traces of themselves. Both talking and kissing, then, have a symmetrical property of expressing what sociologist Georg Simmel (1949) called *sociability*. This explains why casual conversation and casual sexuality occur together on "first dates," and how the two genres—a verbal one and a sexual one—resemble each other as a form of sociable interaction between opposite-sex peers. However, for sexuality to remain a purely free "play form" of sociability, as among the Khevsurs, it must be carefully separated from any and all consequential forms of sexual behavior, specifically marriage and childbirth, as we will see.

The sociologist Georg Simmel famously treated casual conversation between peers as being one of the key examples of a certain kind of interaction that he called "sociability," a "play form" of interaction pursued for its own sake (1949). For Simmel, "sociable" conversation indexes a specific kind of social relationship, one that is purely elective or freely chosen, unconstrained by hierarchy or status difference between those participating in it, without any ulterior motive or social consequence, and undertaken purely for the pleasure it affords. To be a play form, it must be carefully placed within a "magic circle" that protects it from having any personal content or consequence: for if there is any such content or consequence, the relationship or association becomes determined by that content or those consequences (Simmel 1949: 256). Simmel gives two key examples of forms of association that can be transformed into a form of play and pursued purely sociably: flirtation ("coquetry"), which is the play form of eroticism and sexuality, and casual conversation, which is the play form of verbal interaction. Like sociable conversation, genres of sociable sexuality index specific things about the contexts and participants, so that sociable or phatic conversation is felt to be best exemplified by casual conversation between intimates and peers, and in the same way, flirtation can happen only in similar conversational contexts. For Simmel, sociable genres of language and sexuality, conversational sallies and kisses, are also similar in that they are forms of exchange or reciprocity, both of which work to establish and affirm social ties: "Every interaction has to be regarded as an exchange: every conversation, every affection (even if it is rejected), every game, every glance at another person" (Simmel 1978: 79).

LYING DOWN AND GETTING UP: SOCIABLE TALK AND SOCIABLE SEXUALITY

The very term *sts'orproba*, a word that means "a relationship between equals," is already suggestive of the play world of stipulated equality that is, for Simmel, foundational for sociable interaction. The practices of *sts'orproba* were clearly sociable too, including casual sociable conversation and casual sociable eroticism, called *ts'ola-dgoma* (lying down and getting up, that is, spending the night together). As we will see, the lovers alternated between conversation and touching as equal expressions of sexual sociability; and, much like in the last chapter, conversation also served as a mediator to overcome distance, allowing talk to turn to touching.

Once the *elchi* had arranged everything, the only thing that remained was to bring the two parties together for their night together: she would say nothing to the girl on the road, but would simply lead her to the boy's house and, when everyone was asleep, to the boy. If the girl was completely inexperienced in these matters, the boy and the girl might have a joking conversation as follows. The boy would begin by jokingly announcing his suspicion that the girl is not lying down with him out of desire, but out of respect (*khatrit*) or the *elchi*'s pleading (*perobit*) (Baliauri 1991: 13–15):

BOY: Poor girl, what made you lie down with me? Was there no longer anyone else more pathetic than me in our village, so that one, who deserves death (meaning the *elchi*) didn't have to bring you to me? Who knows how much she had to plead with you, in order to make you agree, didn't she? You poor, poor girl. Perhaps she also told you: "He wants to sleep with you" and you are suffering through it for my sake.

GIRL: Out of respect (*khatrit*) for you I am lying down, then, didn't you know?

Joking to a large extent creates intimacy by transgression; that is, many jokes take the form of insults: in an intimate context, an insult that verbally violates a taboo "tests" the intimacy of the partners and can create greater intimacy (if it is taken as a joke) rather than greater social distance (if it is taken as an insult). In traditional social anthropological terms, joking relationships (in Khevsureti, the relationship between siblings and neighbors, up to, say, the relationship between someone and their mother's brother's kin, including potential *sts'orperis*) are the opposite of avoidance relationships (in Khevsureti, typified by one's relationship with one's affines, that is, kin by marriage). Hence, in this context, a boy might jokingly make some highly transgressive, disparaging references to the girl's future affines (remember that Khevsurs are betrothed to their future spouse very early), particularly her future sisters-in-law, as his erstwhile partners in *sts'orproba*. By doing this he would establish himself as a bold conversationalist who is not afraid to take conversational risks, which would make him potentially more interesting and attractive. He begins by disparaging himself as before:

BOY: [Ahh you are indeed unfortunate] to lie down in such a bed, and look at who you have to lie down with, too! What will make a good girl [like you] lie down with me? Don't get angry with me, I'm not talking about you, am I? No, I am talking about when your sisters-in-law come to visit you, but no need to talk about them.

GIRL: [What are you saying], they are very bad girls, if they come to visit me!

BOY: What if I am? It's not like your [future] husband is automatically an idiot just because I said something bad about his sisters. May God allow that you and him grow old together sweetly like sugar as long as I don't see those girls here again. Did they go somewhere else, your sisters-in-law? When I run into them on the road they don't speak to me, as stubborn as if they were seated on mules.

GIRL: Why do you disparage them so? Did they publicly insult you somewhere?

After these joking, but potentially offensive, conversational sallies about her in-laws, he mends fences by drawing attention to his own nervousness about the event they are engaged in: will he offend her similarly by kissing her, or offend her by not kissing her?

> BOY: Girl, let's you and me not remain enemies. It appears in your speech that you are insulted, I have apparently insulted you by talking about those girls. How should I behave toward you, I no longer know. What will offend you or what will make you happy? I am afraid of kissing you, for fear of offending you. I don't kiss you, and you blame me for that, you will begin to complain "You don't consider me a woman." If I kiss you once, I have no idea what you will say to me about that, I will endure it. So I will be careful, if I break my promise there, I don't know.

Joking is a risky behavior, but it reminds us that "one consistent finding of researchers who have studied intimate forms of language is that intimacy is often achieved, at least in part, through the transgression of public taboos" (Cameron and Kulick 2003: 115). As Cameron and Kulick point out, intimacy is something that must be *achieved* in the context of an interaction, and in this case the boy seeks to overcome the resistance of the girl by means of a joking conversational exchange that transgresses a fairly strong taboo—speaking ill of, or insulting, her potential in-laws—and then moves on to discussing the prohibitions and uncertainty of the nature of the physical rules of comportment that lie between them.

And indeed, as they move from their joking conversation to physical touching, their physical comportment with each other is initially very reserved. This initial physical reserve and shyness on the first night would be mediated, in the first instance, by conversation. The boy would begin the night not facing the girl (facing the ceiling), and trying to bring her out, win her over, by sociable conversation alone:

> In general first the boy lies facing up away from the girl and talks to her about different topics. He should be bold [as a conversationalist], or the girl will not like him as a *kalachuna* ("sissy"). If the girl likes the boy, she will become more at ease, and the boy at the same time will not forget his obligations and will turn to the girl and she will lie down on his arm.
>
> Again they begin talking about "girls and boys." Frequently they argue and defend the virtues of their own sex. They laugh. The boy will ask first, who the girl likes or who she "knows." The girl tries to convince him that she doesn't like anyone and doesn't "know" anyone.

> BOY: Girl, then, you. Have you grown up? It seems like you no longer joke. Maybe it's me who's gotten old. And who doesn't grow old who is pestered by Khevsur girls!

GIRL: How do the girls hinder you?

BOY: If they don't hinder me, how do they help me? .[. . . .] Now, I want to question you as to who you "know," or who you like, but my heart trembles with fear, lest you get angry with me.

GIRL: About that question there is no need for your heart to tremble. If I "knew" anyone, you would know that even sooner than I would, but I neither "know" anyone, nor do I like anyone. Nor is there anyone desirable and likeable. Who in the world are you worrying yourself about!

BOY: Then, it seems that you don't like anyone. If you did like someone, what in the world would you do for them?

GIRL: I don't like anyone, aren't I saying that?

BOY: Then I will spend tonight without sleep in vain. I was thinking that if I treated you well, maybe I would get you used to me. Really why in the world would I want to get even older, but wiser, you can do that by getting sick.

GIRL: Then who do you "know"?

BOY: Oh, I know many, your [future] sisters in-law, your mother's sister's daughters. Well, what do I know, I know many others besides, and I know you too, now.

> "Who do you know"—this expression in Khevsureti is a *double entendre*. The first: it means a person you recognize by sight and by character, the second: a boy and a girl getting to know each other at the time of lying together, by lying together. (Baliauri 1991: 14–15)

This sociable conversation would be pursued for its own sake, it would not be limited or restricted in any way, and it would, indeed, be "bolder" than the eventual physical relationship between the boy and the girl. When sociable conversation had overcome the initial distance and reserve, the boy and the girl moved from sociable conversation to more open displays of sociable sexuality:

> In generally their conversation is not restricted. They talk about whatever they want. Afterwards the boy kisses her modestly and embraces her. The girl responds with feeling to his kiss. It is frequently the case that a boy doesn't kiss or embrace a little girl at all, nor does he look at her directly. Those who have met for the first time do not kiss, and the same is said about embracing. (Baliauri 1991: 15)

While the potential objects of conversation were freely chosen and not delimited in any way, the objects of touching and caressing were fairly strongly delimited. The relative freedom of conversation paved the way to more sexual intimacy, and at the same time a large part of sexual intimacy consisted of sociable conversation.

If conversation was an index of intimacy and desire, then the lack of conversation was equally an index of the lack thereof. Generally speaking, it was considered to be important that boys and girls who were set up together be "similar" to each other (*shesaperi* "suitable, appropriate, worthy, fitting") in attractiveness. As far as what was attractive in men, Baliauri does not go into much detail about physical properties, but she intimates here and there that these can be important, but that the most important thing for a girl was that the boy be *dghiani*, "pleasing, well-known," that is, well known and well liked by others (1991: 19–20). Boys were attractive (*dghiani*) insofar as they exhibited the masculine traits of dead heroes (the "good servant") and avoided those of the "bad servant" discussed above; that is, attractiveness stemmed from boys exhibiting an *apparent* disinterest in girls and matters of love. In addition, the boy was to be restrained with women, fearless and feared in battle, with a good sword and horse, having had many *sts'orperis* and also many enemies. As we will see in chapter 4, when girls praised their lovers in poetry, they praised them as being living versions of dead heroes, in terms of the list of generally desirable traits that collected together make them *dghiani*. Attractiveness (being *dghiani*) was not egocentric ("what I like about you"), but sociocentric ("what people in general like about you").

Other than being hard-working and having pleasing personalities that made them well-liked in general by others (*dghiani*) (Baliauri 1991: 20) and showing sexual reserve (*namusi*), women were ideally to be "tall, wide-shouldered, long-necked, with large hands and feet and a small chest," with bonus points for a white neck, which men might praise thus: "She was such a beautiful woman, that her neck and ears gave off light" (81). Women could show a high degree of autonomy in their actions without censure or making themselves unattractive to men: "A woman had the right to be as she herself wished, as long as she had a good tongue [was well-spoken] and was not a 'thief-whore' (*kurd-bozi*)" (81). It is extremely important to underline that having had an active sexual history in *sts'orproba* was absolutely not a cause for censure, but instead an asset: women were considered to be especially attractive and *dghiani* if they had had many *sts'orperis* (28). For Georgians since the nineteenth century, this particular aspect of Khevsur and Pshavian romance has always seemed particularly incomprehensible, since for other Georgians having many lovers (however restrained) is *precisely* what defines a woman as a "whore."[1] However, in the general ethical environment of self-restraint and *namusi*, "having had many lovers" (*sts'orpriani*) was interpreted by Khevsurs as evidence that the woman was *dghiani*, just as was the case for men.

It was not considered good (except perhaps as a cruel prank, as frequently happened with a boy visiting his in-laws) to create couples who were not of similar attractiveness. If, for example, an attractive girl is laid down with an unattractive boy, then

> the girl might pretend to sleep. The boy will notice this too. He can't wake her up by force, can he? Neither showing affection nor causing loss of sleep by force is acceptable. If in the course of *sts'orproba* the girl or the boy fall silent, this is a sign that they do not like the person lying beside them. Sometimes in such circumstances the girl and the boy will get up from the bed. They tell each other: "If you were sleepy, why didn't you sleep alone?" . . . Some fall asleep themselves, saying nothing, but they will remain offended. Feigning sleep and turning one's back . . . means a great humiliation for the person who is lying next to the person who has turned their back. (Baliauri 1991: 140)

Thus, no longer talking was equivalent to more severe forms of disregard for the other person. At the same time, in cases where the relationship was one where reserve was required, then conversation might become the *only* expression of the sexual dimension of the relationship.

INTIMATE CONTACT: PROHIBITION
AND TRANSGRESSION

Just as the *elchi* overcame the distance between the boy and the girl so that they could talk to each other, conversation between these two overcame some of the reserve between them and paved the way for more direct physical expressions of intimacy. Physical intimacy began very strongly bounded, but as the relationship developed, the couple could create intimacy precisely by transgressing these prohibitions and taboos (Cameron and Kulick 2003: 113). Thus distance, prohibition, and avoidance or taboo were essential to creating both the conditions of desire (separating the subject and object far enough so that desire could exist) and also the lines that would have to be crossed to riskily affirm intimacy and realize that desire. At their first meeting, the specific rules for physical comportment were quite exacting:

> The boy behaves very politely to the girl. He kisses her and embraces her a little and he jokes a little. . . . The girl is very shy, she doesn't return the boy's embrace. She lies on her left side so that the button of her beaded collar [which buttons on the left side] is turned down. She arranges her legs so that they are away from the legs of the boy. She keeps her left arm against her side, and she brings her right arm to embrace the boy around the shoulders. The boy lies with the girl resting on his right arm and he holds the girl with his left arm. (Baliauri 1991: 14)

Rules were quite explicit about the positioning of the legs and lower body (distant) and exactly where one could touch one's partner: a girl was expected to be modest and could touch the boy on the neck and even on the chest, but she could not put her hand down his collar, nor could she put her arm below his armpit, and in general her hands could go nowhere near his waist. Excessive kissing was also frowned upon.

The rules for the boy (which express his quality of "self-control") were even stricter. He could not touch the girl on her neck, and his hand could go nowhere near her chest nor under her armpits. Putting the hand anywhere near the collar would be a serious offense, and the hand touching the button of the beaded collar (*paragi*, Figure 2.1) was completely beyond the pale (Baliauri 1991: 15, see chapter 4 for poems about this act). If this button were to be opened, the girl's breast would come into view, but during *sts'orproba* the girl was not afraid of that, because it was night and in any case nothing would be seen; rather, she was afraid that the boy might touch her breast. Needless to say, their lower bodies needed to be kept far apart.

These are the rules of touching that apply at the first meeting between a boy and a girl, on subsequent meetings the boy and the girl become used to one

FIGURE 2.1: Khevsur woman's costume showing the beaded collar (*saq'elo, paragi*), which covers the chest and buttons on the left side. From Tedoradze 1930: 73.

another and trust grows between them. The next day they part ways, the boy kisses and embraces the girl once more, gets up with her and accompanies her a short distance home, they bid each other goodbye and boy returns to bed, and the girl slips unnoticed back into her own bed and sleeps. (Baliauri 1991: 16)

On subsequent visits, the boy and the girl would be less reserved, more daring, with one another: the boy would turn to the girl (and not lie facing the ceiling), embrace her, and kiss her; the girl too would be more daring, and she too would embrace him and kiss him. Hereabouts the relationship might change into something more durable, a true boyfriend-girlfriend relationship (the topic of the next chapter), and the rules the couple would follow could be relaxed in different degrees according to the level of mutual trust and the intimate negotiations of the partners.

Boundary: Sex

Khevsurs believed that maintaining strong boundaries between consequential sexual behavior (in the case of Khevsureti, childbirth and marriage) and *sts'orproba* was the key to maintaining a domain of free, elective, sexual sociability between peers, and indeed, their freedom in general. This domain of freedom was the domain of desire. Forms of sexual expression could be regarded as a sociable "play form" of eroticism, expressing desire, as long as they remained purely elective (free from coercion or obligation) and absolutely inconsequential (i.e., separated from any biological or social consequences). In general, what would be considered a significant transgression, i.e., "going too far," was at least in part negotiated between the partners; however, it is clear that at different degrees of social distance, different expressions of intimate contact would be acceptable or transgressive. At the same time, those transgressions of the ordinary rules that were negotiated by consent between the couple were different from those attempted transgressions that one or the other partner did not consent to. The sanctions for the former primarily resulted when the couple's transgression came to light publicly, for example when it led to childbirth or marital elopement (which happened occasionally and was usually fairly tragic in its consequences); the sanctions for the latter took the form of verbal shamings at the moment and often poems of denunciation (as we will see in the next chapters).

All forms of intimacy were played out in a gray area of relative freedom defined against absolute transgressions. In general, such absolute violations of the rules that could lead to childbirth were called "depravity" (*garq'vna, garq'vniloba*) (Baliauri 1991: 30–31). Tuite summarizes these prohibitions:

> The relationship of *ts'ats'loba* or *sts'orproba* must not be consummated in the form of either marriage or childbirth; it must remain *uteslo* "without seed,"

i.e. without producing offspring. Mountaineer [ethnographers] go to great lengths to emphasize the self-control required of young couples, to assure that their deep-felt affection and passion remains "pure," untainted by the depravity (*garq'vna*) of premarital sex.... All ethnographic accounts agree that the birth of a child to *ts'ats'alis* or *sts'orperis* is a social catastrophe. (Tuite 2000)

Both partners in a Khevsur relationship were expected to be *namusiani* ("having *namusi*"). *Namusi* (an ethical term meaning "honor, shame, respectability," derived from the Arabic term *namus* with more or less the same meaning) denoted a kind of honor that resulted from having self-restraint, modesty, or shame. The opposite type of person, *garq'vnili* ("depraved one, pervert"), was therefore *unamuso* ("having no *namusi*") and was often more or less equivalently compared to a dog (dogs, after all, have sex in public), a Russian (Khevsurs shared with other Georgians a low estimation of Russians, particularly with regard to sexual comportment), or a prostitute (*kurd-bozi* lit. "thief and prostitute," *matushk'a* "prostitute," from Russian "little mother, mama").

In general, for a Khevsur male, maintaining self-control (*tavdach'eriloba*) was a key masculine virtue that he demanded of himself and a woman demanded of him. Self-control derived from several sources: first his own self-esteem (*tavmoq'vareoba*) and his *namusi*. Second, his fear of being publicly shamed by the other men of the shrine and having the divine wrath of the shrine brought down upon him: young men had to swear an oath on the shrine that they have not had sex (*garq'vna*) with women in the context of *sts'orproba* (Baliauri 1991: 30).

Nor, given the general context of sleeping together among others, could a man force a woman to cross these limits easily. There would almost always be a large number of people sleeping nearby in the same space, who would wake up immediately if any unusual noises happened. In addition, Khevsur women had "severe characters" and a high sense of autonomy and respectability (*tavk'virebuli* "proud, having self-respect, respectable"), so "a man never tries to force them to do anything" (Baliauri 1991: 31). Because of the high degree of control women had over sexual matters, ironically, Baliauri somewhat misogynistically tends to present "weak-willed women" as the primary source of depravity (Baliauri 1991: 31):

A girl begins to engage in depravity by opening the chest [undoing the buttons over the chest], when she has laid down with a boy already three or four times; she may think that he will like this. Because she thinks this, she is convinced that the boy won't tell anyone about whatever she will do, and she will undo the button, and give the boy permission to kiss and hold her breasts. If the boy is quick-tempered and lacks self-control, he will follow her lead and in the end the whole thing ends with fornication. (Baliauri 1991: 31)

There were many ways in which a lover might attempt to transgress the limits of what is permitted sexually, and depending on the type of relationship it might be either very little (e.g., a kiss in an avoidance relationship) or a lot (e.g., an attempt to have sex in any relationship other than marriage).

For example, it frequently was the case at large public events where many of the boys and girls had no prior knowledge of each other on which to base their preferences, the *elchis* would choose among themselves who was suitable (*shesaperi*) to whom, pairing boys and girls who were strangers:

> At this time no one asks the the boy or the girl about who they like or don't like. But if they are to stay in the village a lot longer, then they do indeed ask both the girl and the boy too: if they like one another, they lie them down together again; If not then they say to someone else "lie down with this one," "I will lie down with this one" and so on. (Baliauri 1991: 122)

Given the haphazard nature of such pairings between strangers, the resulting lying down was characterized by a great deal of reserve, especially on the girl's part. In such circumstances, very little provocation was needed from the boy to result in relatively extreme sanctions:

> The lying down happens with great reserve (*morideba*), inasmuch as the girl always displays great reserve with a stranger. The boy too should also display great reserve, or in this sort of context a girl won't put up with much from him. If the boy starts going too far, then the girl gets up, whacks him with something, and shames him. For this to happen she needs little cause, because the boy and the girl are not well acquainted and the girl has no reason to defer to him [*mosaridi*]. In the same way the boy too can easily dismiss the girl if the girl lies down without reserve, but he will not say anything, if the people "sleeping around" haven't figured out [what is happening]. Hearing [a quarrel between sleepers] happens very easily because many are sleeping together either on the *bani* (flat roof/balcony) or the *ch'erkho* (top floor). Everyone will hear a girl getting up in an untimely fashion, however. For this reason the girl and the boy are as careful as possible. Kissing strangers is not good. [So] they kiss each other very little. (Baliauri 1991: 122–23)

Regardless of the nature of the transgression, the basic sanction was the same in all cases. If the man thought the woman was going too far, he kicked her out of his bed and verbally shamed her for her forwardness: "Go and sleep with whomever it is that you have been sleeping with that way, but get away from me and after this never come near me again! Are you not ashamed, you are a girl and you engage in that kind of behavior!" If a woman determined that her male partner seemed to want to take things too far, she wouldn't revile him loudly, but tell him politely: "If you are testing me, fine—Enough! If not then I do not know and never learned to lie down in that way." Then she would get up from the bed and leave. She wouldn't say anything, but she wouldn't need to, because everyone would be sleeping in a common area and would figure out what had happened anyway; as a result, the boy's reputation would be ruined and other girls would avoid him (Baliauri 1991: 31–32).

Boundary: Marriage

The obvious way in which *sts'orproba*, as a form of sexual sociability, a "play form" of eroticism, was kept separate from consequential sexuality was through the strong separation between *sts'orproba* and marriage. The ideal potential partners of *sts'orproba* and of marriage were normatively different: the best example of a potential *sts'orproba* partner was someone one knew, from one's own village or kinship group who was not an actual sibling, while the best example of a potential marriage partner was a stranger, from another kinship group and another village (Figure 2.2).

Marriage was a world of unfreedom, especially for women, a literal exile among strangers, because rules of exogamy (which prohibit members of the same kinship group or village from marrying one another) meant that women would not only be married to strangers, but also spend the rest of their lives living among them. Thus the importance of exogamy for the life of a girl cannot be overstated. As previously discussed, a girl's life was composed of two periods of completely different character: a relatively long period of the freedom of unmarried life (Khevsurs married late) living among family and siblings (and those fellow villagers classified as kin and siblings), and the unfreedom of marriage, which forced a girl to live in exile among strangers. Hence, the marriage of a girl was somewhat akin to exile and death, for both her and her family:

> Until a Khevsur girl is married, she is very free, after her marriage her free coming and going, dancing, singing, wearing jewelry, is usually forbidden to her. When she is in her father's house, everyone loves her starting from her early childhood to her old age.... [A] girl in her own village goes into everyone's home freely, day or night. It has no importance whether they are related by blood, a girl can freely go among [fellow villagers] of different clans [*gvari* "surname"], in the same way she can sleep in their home and pass the time there. If a girl's actions are so unconstrained among fellow villagers of

different clans, it is clear, among members of her own clan she is even more free. The boys and girls of a single clan [*gvari*] treat each other as members of a single family. Day and night, they are always visiting each other. . . . At night she wanders far from her village, on fields of hay or fields of grain, she can even spend the night alone in a meadow: she is not afraid of what her kin will say . . . Everyone in the village loves a girl, no one is happy when she gets married. They even cry. (Baliauri 1991: 70–72)

Khevsur marriage is all about its social content, consequences, and obligation. By contrast, Khevsurs saw in the restraints imposed by *sts'orproba* the creation of a world of freedom and autonomy; the prohibitions in effect produced a magic circle where sexual desire could exist within a set of purely elective relationships, separating it from a form of courtship, for example.

Even so, it did occur to boys and girls that they would like to marry their *sts'orperis* or more permanent boyfriends/girlfriends (*dzmobili*) (see chapter 4):

In Khevsureti in the past a *dzmobili* boy did not marry his *dzmobili* girl, and vice versa. Their marrying was a great shame. When they betrothed a girl, it was possible that she would not like her fiancé. Then with crying and with pleading she would address her parents and brothers, "I don't like him and don't marry me to him." The parents' response was like this: "So what, you don't like him, he's not a *sts'orperi*, that you might love. If you want pleasure and love, go marry a *sts'orperi*." (Baliauri 1991: 33)

Of course, the parental advice here could not be serious, but must be read against the knowledge that marrying one's *sts'orperi* or *dzmobili* would be, in fact, an unrealizable fantasy and a major transgression. However, the world of possible *sts'orproba* partners and potential marriage partners did overlap: at many gradations of kinship distance, a potential *sts'orperi* was also at the same time a potential spouse. As Tuite (2000) summarizes a complex situation, eligibility for *sts'orproba* and eligibility for marriage were like mirror images of each other in the way they were both highly sensitive to kinship and social distance: sexual avoidance, and less sociable sexuality, was found precisely with those others that could be sexual partners of a non-sociable sort (marriage), just as sexuality was taboo in those relations from which sexuality was normatively absent (siblings). *Sts'orproba* was ideally found in the "Goldilocks zone" between siblings and potential affines (Figure 2.2).

Given this extensive overlap, there were plenty of people one might lie down with as *sts'orperi* that one might otherwise have married: for example, a boy or girl visiting his or her future spouse as a guest might easily be laid down with one or another of the future spouse's siblings for the night. The important thing was that no one could be

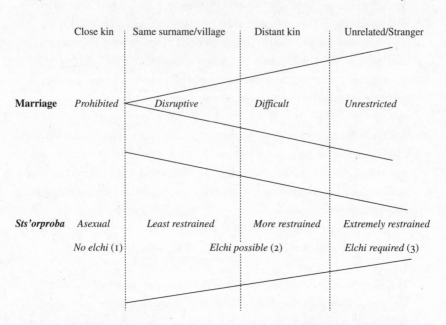

FIGURE 2.2: Overlapping zones of *sts'orproba* and marriage. Adapted from Tuite (2000)

both a *sts'orperi/dzmobili* and *then* a spouse to the same person. Sanctions against the marriage of *sts'orproba* partners largely depended on how far their elective relationship had progressed: the marriage of erstwhile *sts'orperis* produced drama and reconciliation; the marriage of committed boyfriends and girlfriends (*dzmobilis*), like childbirth, was much more likely to lead to suicide or exile.

Just as both the *sts'orperi* and potential spouse relationship had to be carefully separated from siblinghood to avoid incest, at further degrees of distance the potential *sts'orperi* relationship had to be carefully separated from the potential spousal one, because if not, then the relationship of *sts'orproba*, and the freedom and autonomy it produced, would instead come to be seen as a kind of premarital courtship, an inconsequential casual relationship would become consequential, and it would have to be ended: "They talk about it like this: 'If a boy and girl cannot restrain themselves, and look upon one another as possible husband and wife, then it is better that this rule [of lying down together] no longer exist in Khevsureti and be wiped out entirely'" (Baliauri 1991: 98).

SOCIABILITY AND OBLIGATION

As Figure 2.2 suggests, "lying down" was a practice that could happen within a wide range of social relations. So far we have assumed it was the "least restrained" variety, a form of elective sociable sexuality among those who could not marry. However, lying down together at night was not always or even most of the time a purely sociable sexual practice expressive of desire: it could be arranged by several different *genres*, and depending on *how it was arranged linguistically*, the resulting encounter could be either sociable or not, sexual or not, express desire or obligation or merely the need to sleep somewhere.

Boys and girls were laid down together at night for a variety of reasons (the need to sleep, desire, obligation), each reason corresponding roughly to relations of different degrees of social distance, and to each such reason and relation there were different linguistic genres for negotiating the process of lying down. In addition, the *elchi*, if present, played different roles.

(1) *Simple Lying Down.* First, because everyone slept in a common area and guests had to be put somewhere, it was said to happen "by chance" (*shemtkhvevit*), or without a mediator (*uelchod* "without an *elchi*") or without an explicit formal linguistic genre of mediation (*utkmelad* "without words"): "This is simple lying down, no *elchi* is required and no one says to them: 'lie down together!'" (Baliauri 1991: 72). This "simple lying down" was particularly appropriate for closely related or otherwise well-acquainted boys and girls for whom either desire or a sense of obligation would not be felt. In such circumstances where either desire or obligation was absent, the couple could openly arrange things themselves, without the mediation of an *elchi* with an utterance as simple as "Come, sleep with me and I will lie down with you," and they would not hide the resulting tryst (Baliauri 1991: 73). There was no sense of obligation here, and if the partner was tired or did not want to engage in any physical intimacy, they would say as much and not bother to invent any excuses. The resulting form of lying down would emphasize sleeping, with minimal or no signs of desire or respect for the other person. The rules for physical comportment between male and female sleepers, which normally involved restraint and avoidance, were relaxed; boys and girls would lie down somewhat randomly, since sexual desire and gender were not at issue: boys here, girls there, or boys and girls together. None of the usual rules of mutual physical comportment were followed: if closely related boys and girls lay down together and they didn't like each other, they didn't even make a pretense of kissing. The girl arranged her body any which way, paying no attention to where the legs went, either her own or the boy's, and sometimes the couple would even turn their backs on each other; both of these practices were prohibited in normal lying down. They might even fight about the allocation of sleeping space. The boy might say to the girl, "We are too close, get up, why are you lying down here! Get lost, man!"[2] The girl might push the boy away saying things like, "Move aside, you have space there, boy, what the hell is wrong with you? Move, boy, I'm telling you." And they might squabble over space like that, the boy eventually saying, "Shut up girl, or else

if I call out to my uncle, 'She isn't allowing me into the bed' then you will see, who has to get up!" (Baliauri 1991: 72).

(2) *Lying Down out of Desire.* At other times, a boy and a girl might lie down together out of desire (*survilit*). This is precisely the sort of relationship we have been discussing already, the ideal example being at a middle social distance, say, unrelated people living in the same village, people who were neither so close to count as siblings (so desire is possible) nor so distant as to be potential marriage partners (so there is no sense of avoidance or obligation). Here an *elchi* was usually involved initially, and dispensed with later (so that as intimacy advanced it came to be negotiated in the same way as "simple lying down" above). Obviously, this is the primary area where lying down took on a specifically sociable sexual form. In order for sleeping together to express desire, a couple who were supposed to lie down together in an asexual manner sometimes arranged to do so according to the rules of *sts'orproba*, using an *elchi* and following the rules of lying down together, thus expressing desire, even though this was in itself a violation of the rules (Baliauri 1991: 72).

(3) *Lying Down out of Respect (khatrit) for Someone or at Request (perobit).* But a boy and a girl might also have to lie down together, not out of desire but out of respect for another person (*khatrit*) or because they had been persuaded through browbeating or "entreaty" by the *elchi* (*perobit* "at request, pleading"), something we have already seen lovers playfully gesture at above. "Lying down at request" (*perobit dats'ol-adgoma*) is specifically opposed to lying down out of desire: "being forced to lie down with a boy or girl *without desire* out of regard for someone or other considerations" (Baliauri 1991: 189; emphasis added). Obviously, as the name itself suggests, "lying down at request" happened only through the mediation of an *elchi*. This particular form of lying down was most typical of lying down with strangers, with guests out of a sense of hospitality, with potential marriage partners or even with the kin of one's actual marriage partners, that is, relations of avoidance and obligation. Here the form of lying down was not sociable, but emphasized distance, avoidance, showing less desire than respect for the other person.

One particular occasion when this would happen was as a result of conflicts between social obligations related to hospitality and personal desire, primarily when the boy or the girl was a guest in the village and therefore had to be laid down with someone, but was such a person that it was not possible to find someone suitable (*shesaperi*) for them, or if they were the sort of boy that girls in general did not like. The rules of hospitality meant there was a communal obligation to find an undesirable guest a sleeping partner from the side of the host, regardless of individual preferences or desires. This particular kind of obligation was particularly strong between future in-laws, where initially at least an *elchi* was always required (Baliauri 1991: 99–100):

If the girl from the wife's side is not good either in looks or in comportment, the boy from the husband's side cannot refuse to lie down with her, he must lie down with her against his will. So too a girl, no matter how good a girl she is [...], cannot refuse to lie down with a boy of the husband's side, even if she absolutely loathes this individual, with whom they are laying her down. It is clear that they can somehow manage some means to avoid lying down with the other, but they can't refuse openly. That is shameful, and is not acceptable.... What in the world can a girl say? She lies down out of respect (*khatrit*). (Baliauri 1991: 104)

But if all these stratagems failed, and the mismatched couple had to sleep together, there was a great deal of reserve, marking the complete absence of desire:

If nevertheless a boy doesn't manage to find a way out, then he lies down out of obligation (*khatrit*) and falls asleep quickly. The girl, however, when she lies down with an undesirable person, cannot fall asleep early, lest they say "You didn't want to lie down with me and that's why you fell asleep early." They lie down with great reserve (*morideba*). (Baliauri 1991: 104)

The close correspondence between linguistic genres for negotiating "lying down" and the form "lying down" could take is not accidental: each genre foregrounded, i.e., made relevant or even possible, different sexual and sociable potentials of the resulting situation. Desire could come into play in lying down only if each person's desire and autonomy were given explicit linguistic recognition in the prior process of negotiation. If there was no negotiation, then desire and obligation were assumed not to be relevant (genre 1). If the negotiation engaged the person *not as* a willing person who had desire (*survilit*) (genre 2), but as an unwilling bearer of social obligation (*khatrit, perobit*) (genre 3), then that person would go to bed not sexually or sociably, but out of obligation.

The presence or absence of the *elchi* indexed both desire (because the difference between genres 1 and 2 was marked by the presence of an *elchi* who negotiated desire)

TABLE 2.1: Genres of lying down

Linguistic Genre	Form of Lying Down	Sexual	Sociable	*Elchi?*
1. Without Words	Simple Lying Down	No	Yes	No
2. Normal *Sts'orproba*	Lying Down with Desire	Yes	Yes	Sometimes
3. Out of Respect/Entreaty	Lying Down with Avoidance	Yes	No	Yes

and avoidance or distance (the difference between genres 2 and 3 indicates the change from an optional *elchi* who negotiated desire and an obligatory one who forced one to lie down where desire was not present). Paradoxically, the same *elchi* who facilitated social intimacy and desire (genre 2) could also be the *elchi* who expressed social distance and obligation (genre 3).

The Role of Different Genres

The absolutely opposed linguistic genres (1) and (3), neither of which expresses desire, could be played off against one another strategically. One of the reasons why one might lie down with closer kin, or one of one's "regular" *sts'orperis* (neither of which required an *elchi*'s mediation) was to avoid lying down out of obligation (arranged by an *elchi*) with someone one didn't like. Obviously, there was a range of exceptional uses and subterfuges of *sts'orproba* that allowed one to assent to lying down with someone in this way, and yet escape actually doing so. For example, one could arrange lying down with someone to avoid lying down with someone else one did not want to spend the night with: the point is that one could not flat out *refuse* to lie down, but that did not mean one had to actually follow through, even if one had already agreed to do so. Thus, one major benefit of lying down *without an* elchi (either with closer kin or with an existing *sts'orperi*) (genre 1) was to avoid lying down *out of entreaty or respect* arranged by an *elchi* (genre 3) (Baliauri 1991: 73–74, 85):

> When some *elchi* [arranges to] lay a girl down with such a boy as she does not like and out of respect she cannot say no, then she will make a false promise [to do so] and then go to one of her *sts'orperis*. When she arrives she will say: "Help me, this or that *elchi* has laid me down with such a boy and out of respect I told her 'I will lie down with him,' but you help me—either you come to our house, or take me to your house, pretend that you have some business with me." A boy behaves in the same way, if they lay him down with such a girl, who he doesn't like, but he cannot refuse the request, then he goes to a *sts'orperi* girl of his clan and says: "Come and lie down with me, or take that girl to someone else, pretend you didn't know she was to come to me." (Baliauri 1991: 73–74).

Sociable sexuality was thus only possible within certain parameters: for the relationship to be a sociable one, it had to steer clear of culturally recognized actions or relationships with consequences—sexual depravity and marriage. At the same time, *sts'orproba* and "lying down together" could take on different forms in themselves, expressing a continuum of relationships from simply lying down to sleeping (which is sociable but asexual), to *sts'orproba* proper (which is both sexual and sociable, the domain of desire), all the way to expressing the very opposite of true sociability: obligations of hospitality and kinship (with potential sexual others who were also marriageable others, thus avoided: here we have sexuality, kept in check, without sociability). All these nuances of *sts'orproba* assuming different forms depending on the social geography of desire and distance were reflected in both the linguistic and nonlinguistic genres of sexual practice.

As we will see in the next chapter, as a couple became more familiar and intimate, similar changes in linguistic and non-linguistic genres of sexual practice came to mark their increased intimacy, starting with dispensing with the mediation of the *elchi*. Here too a change in terminology occurs, moving from the casual non-exclusive one-night liaisons of *sts'orproba* to the permanent, durable, exclusive relationship of boyfriends and girlfriends, what are called "sworn brothers" (irrespective of gender), among the Khevsurs.

NOTES

1   One of the earliest commentators on Pshavian *ts'ats'loba* (Mamsashvili, *Droeba* 1880, no. 102, p. 2) expresses surprise, which he assumes his readers will share, that Pshavian women are considered more attractive and marriageable the more *ts'ats'alis* they have had.

2   The term for "man" is a Georgian vocative that is used with both men and women.

3

GOING STEADY

———◆———

Khevsur love poetry constantly draws attention to vodka as the currency and symbol of durable romantic relationships between boys and girls. When a romantic relationship moved beyond the casual one-night liaisons between *sts'orperis*, the relationship changed into a durable "boyfriend-girlfriend" relationship, the terminology also changed, and the lovers began to call each other "sworn brothers" (*dzmobili*; the same term was used for both boyfriends and girlfriends). Most love poetry is about *dzmobilis*, and in such love poetry we frequently encounter the figure of a girl, meeting her *dzmobili* after a long wait, with bottle of vodka in hand:

gzashi ro dagkhvda dzmobili, botla ech'ira ch'relia. (Shanidze 1931: 131)

In the road when your *dzmobili* met you, she held a coloured bottle.

qelshi ech'ira gogosa araq'iani minao. (Shanidze 1931: 135)

In her hand the girl held a bottle of vodka.

While in our own culture we might tend to associate vodka with drunkenness, and hence with casual sexual liaisons, the sexual symbolism of vodka in Khevsur romance was all about indexing the temporal dimension of a long-term secretive relationship: stealing, keeping, hiding, sharing vodka, a drink that lasts forever—for a love that would also last forever.

THE SOCIAL LIFE OF VODKA

Among the Khevsurs, vodka served as a general currency of social life. Understanding the very specific, and often opposed, meanings it took on in romantic transactions requires understanding the general ways in which vodka mediated social relations of all kinds. In ordinary Khevsur social interactions, vodka—drinking vodka, giving vodka—was a pervasive sign of casual social relations, as opposed to the dark, viscous fluid that Khevsurs call beer. Khevsur beer, unlike vodka, would go bad after a few days and was not very portable, and moreover it was used to mark more serious social events and rituals within a given community (for more details see Manning 2012b, chapter 7). Vodka, by contrast, was synonymous with visiting, ritual, oaths, exchange, reciprocity—in other words, with social life in general. Vodka was a pervasive medium of gift exchange, and one might even go so far as to say that vodka served as the very social "stuff" out of which relationships were made. Large quantities of vodka were needed for every sort of social ritual event, and it was brewed by the average family 40 times a year at least,

> because without vodka, by local rule, nothing can be done, neither the cost of a funeral, nor weddings, nor reconciling enemies, neither women can become sworn sisters nor men can become sworn brothers, regard cannot be shown for relatives, nor sowing nor harvest and many other customs. Everything requires vodka, beer is required on the other hand for more heavy and serious matters, but even then vodka is also considered necessary. Khevsurs have a good opinion of vodka. (Baliauri 1991: 154)

There were different named genres of exchange that involved vodka. Interestingly, the names of all vodka exchanges seem to draw attention to the *mobility* of the drink, the fact that vodka decanted in small glass bottles is very portable: vodka is a drink associated with motion, visiting, and roads; at times it might be drunk with friends at home, at other times with strangers on the road.

Going with Vodka

Vodka, the portable drink, was always the gift of a party in motion, and visiting others living in other communities was synonymous with bringing vodka: the social motion of people was synonymous with the social movement of vodka. This was called "going with vodka" (*araq'it misvla*). A special one-sided case of this form of exchange was a humiliating self-abasement made in lieu of another, more expensive, payment when one has seriously hurt or wronged another. This was called *araq'it shin misvla* "to go into (someone's) house with vodka," which was to go and kneel before one's opponent, an act that was socially equivalent to a payment of five cows: "This is called 'shin khvets'na' ('begging at the home'). Most Khevsurs will pay the five cows and will not go to a man with vodka, this is a question of self-respect (*tavmoq'vareoba*)" (A. Ochiauri 2005: 124).

Visiting Vodka

When a family had a newborn child, one had to bring "visiting" (*mosanakhavi*) vodka to the home when one went to see the child. If a boy was born, everyone brought good vodka, even just casual friends; if a girl was born, only close relatives brought vodka. Here the strength of the vodka was important: "The visiting vodka for a boy had to be very good vodka, but when visiting a girl no one was interested whether the vodka was good or not, they would say: 'I'm not bringing visiting vodka for a boy, am I? Why do I want good vodka, let them give birth to a boy and then I'll bring good vodka'" (A. Ochiauri 1980: 35).

Road Vodka

Khevsurs were required to bring good vodka as a gift when they went on the road to visit ("going with vodka"), but they were also required to give every stranger they passed on the road a drink of vodka. To not do so would mark them as being stingy. Since gifted vodka had to be good, Khevsurs often carried with them a special supply of weak vodka, so-called "road vodka," to protect the gifted vodka supply from the mouths of strangers (A. Ochiauri 1980: 7, 14–15).

Vodka was, therefore, in ordinary usage a highly versatile drink indexing both serious community events and casual encounters with strangers on the road alike. Vodka was coextensive with social life in general. For girls, however, vodka was the currency of very serious romantic relationships (it was entirely absent from the world of casual relations between *sts'orperis*). But girls crafted very different meanings out of the material properties of the same drink. For girls, the property of vodka that was most important was not only its portability, but its high durability: vodka would not go bad over time, just like the relationships that it maintained. (This portability and durability are things that vodka had in common with love poetry, too.) Vodka could wait indefinitely to be drunk, just as a lover might wait long periods in anticipation of seeing their beloved. Indeed, for girls the material properties of vodka, especially durability, played a role in creating, maintaining, and ending the relationship. While the everyday use of vodka (drinking, gifting, etc.) foregrounded its ability to transcend the village and create long-distance relationships *in space*, including casual ones with strangers on the road, girls instead focused on vodka's ability to create long-term relationships *in time*, to transcend frequent absences, to suture together rare moments of togetherness into a durable relationship. But like everything else about *dzmobili* relationships, the romantic use of vodka to create romantic relationships was cobbled together, parasitic on more general, publicly recognized uses of vodka in other kinds of relationships. To understand durable romantic attachments—*dzmobili* relations—we must first understand the exchanges of vodka and poetry that are at the core of these relations.

THE SEXUAL LIFE OF VODKA

Each bottle of vodka was a romantic history writ large: a bottle might point forward to an anticipated meeting with a lover, or it might become a sad reminder of a break-up. In one poem, a woman abandoned by her *dzmobili* bitterly contrasts the value of her vodka ("the vodka for the forsaken one"), which she had kept for the boy who left her, with the vodka her rival secretly saves up in anticipation of a night spent together (Baliauri 1991: 20). She drinks the vodka she had saved up, which is now no longer the vodka "for the *dzmobili*" (*sadzmobilo*) but the vodka "for the forsaken one" (herself):

gasaoqrebi araq'i	The vodka of the forsaken
maints gulisas atkmevsa.	Still can make the heart speak its secrets.

She drinks this vodka to give herself inspiration to bitterly imagine the way her rival is also saving vodka to spend a night with her newly acquired *dzmobili*:

saidumloda kalai	Secretly the woman
botlit araq'as asmevsa.	Fills up a bottle of vodka.
dghes ertad daaghameben,	Today they will pass the evening together,
ghamitats ertad dats'vesa.	At night too they will lie down together.

Love poetry makes constant mention of vodka because vodka was emblematic of love; a bottle of vodka was a promise. In another poem, a girl denounces a boy publicly in a poem for his aggressive sexual advances. She compares him to a Russian for his lack of shame (*namusi*) in sexual matters, and she hotly disputes his claim that they had exchanged silver rings (a common way that *dzmobilis* mark their affections) and most importantly, that she had brought him vodka in bed, which would imply that she had marked him as a *dzmobili*:

geubna kalebshia	You had apparently said to the other girls
"satite gamitsvalao.	"She exchanged rings with me.
botlai araq'iani	She brought me
loginshi mamit'anao."	A bottle of vodka in bed."
raqel satites gagitsvli,	Whatever ring you might give me,
ra gzashi shameq'arao.	I would throw into the road.
rusivit unamusoo,	You, shameless like a Russian,
qmas git'ekh, aghar vmalao.	I will ruin your name, I will hide it no longer.
kurd-bozvo, unamusoo,	Thief and whore, shameless one,
garq'vnilo ts'aramarao.	Perverted idiot. (Baliauri 1991: 32)

Girls thus appropriated vodka from the general public currency of sociability and re-engineered it for the purposes of romance. One might say in this kind of symbolic piracy that they made maximal use of the material affordances of vodka, that is, the material properties it had that enabled or constrained the possible purposes to which it could be put or the meanings that could be attached to it. First, they "stole" vodka, particularly good vodka, taking it out of public spheres of exchange and circulation so that it could serve as a secret medium of intimacy. Second, they "kept" or "hid" vodka, storing it away in hidden caches, marking the time spent waiting for their beloved and the moment they could give him the vodka; the secrecy of their love was thus symbolized by hiding the vodka. Third, they gifted the boy with vodka in private, so that he, in turn, could drink it more publicly with his friends, incidentally showing that he was the object of someone's love. If girls were abandoned, they could drink the vodka to find inspiration to write bitter poetry of loss, or drink it sociably with another girl, to get rid of the durable reminder of a defunct relationship.

Stealing Vodka

First, the girl had to appropriate vodka from the general currency of exchange (vodka as a collective social expression of a household), and turn it into a private currency (vodka as a sexual expression of an individual): a girl was therefore constantly begging, borrowing, and stealing vodka. She would want this vodka to be the best vodka available. Thereafter, unlike a man bringing vodka on the road (who protected his gifted vodka with watery "road vodka"), she would jealously guard it from the mouths of anyone but the one she chose:

> When a family brews vodka, if they have a young woman in the household, she asks, "Please fill me one bottle!" and tries to ensure that they fill it with good vodka. She asks parents and brothers alike for this. Sometimes even fellow villagers will fill a bottle of vodka for a young woman, uncles and cousins will joke with her, "when I am suffering, then give me some to drink!" But in reality they cannot be given back the vodka she has requested. They say this as a joke. (Baliauri 1991: 154)

Since girls would always have saved-up bottles of good vodka hidden somewhere, a guest might joke with a young girl: "I don't want this vodka, pour me the saved-up bottled vodka of the girls!" Normally, vodka was exchanged between households and travelers as a general medium of exchange, which had to be given freely to anyone one encountered. A girl's stolen, saved-up vodka was absolutely opposed to this public sphere of exchange, remaining instead in its own secret hiding places until she chose to use it, and like everything else in romance, this was done according to her wishes alone.

Saving and Hiding Vodka

Since vodka stored in a glass bottle would keep indefinitely, saving vodka could be a marker both of time passed apart from a girl's *dzmobili* and of the expectation of meeting up again: "Some girls will save up a bottle of vodka for up to a year for their *dzmobili*. This is a sign, that she remembers her *dzmobili* and is saving it for the time when her waiting comes to an end" (Baliauri 1991: 155). Saving vodka measured time spent apart, pointing both to the past (a sign of remembrance) and to the future (in anticipation of meeting once more). Hiding the vodka meant that the relationship was a secret one, that love could only exist hidden in the dark. In the following poem, a woman pining for her lover, who is ill, from the hut where she spends her period of menstrual isolation (another common figure in love poetry), underlines the waiting, the pining, and the secrecy (if they are found out, they will be exiled from their homes), by pointing to a bottle of vodka that measures both:

mtas ikitela vazhao,	Boy from beyond the mountains,
tavis loginchi gdzinao.	You are sleeping in your bed.
shen avadoba miambes,	They told me about your illness,
net'avi mogarchinao!	I hope they cure you!
shentan damidga logini,	They laid me a bed with you,
shen mk'lavze damadzinao,	To sleep on your arm,
sheneb naubreb sit'q'vebi	The words you said then
agharam damacilao!	I will never forget!
vitaic davts'ev, vigone,	Whenever I lie down, I remember,
guls tsetskhli gamichinao.	It sets my heart on fire.
kali var samrelochia,	I am a woman in the menstrual hut,
aghar mivdivar shinao.	I cannot go home.
shens molodinze davmale	I have hidden a bottle of vodka
araq'iani minao.	Waiting for you.
tu eg gagviges bebrebma,	If the old people find out,
ar migvit'even shinao.	They won't let us go home.

(Shanidze 1931: 144)

Drinking Vodka

However, if those future plans were dashed and the *dzmobili* took up with another girl, vodka saved for the *dzmobili* could become vodka for the forsaken one. If a girl saved vodka for a boy in vain, then she would drink it with another girl, never another boy. In one poem, a girl measures the degree of her betrayal and disappointment in the number of weeks she had saved the bottle, so long that mold and mildew appeared in the bottleneck, and exacts revenge in specifying exactly how she will drink it with another girl:

rom mitkhar, rad mamat'q'ue,	When you told me, you lied to me,
shamavkhvebodi satvelsao.	"I will come up in the springtime."
minai araq'iani	I had a bottle of vodka
malodins medga shensao.	Waiting for you.
gatavda shvid k'virai,	Seven weeks went by,
mirdli gaeba q'elsao.	Mold started to grow in the bottleneck.
shavasmev melaniasa	I will pour for Melania [a girl]
sadghgrdzelosa shensao.	A toast in your honor.
davlevdit tito-orolsa,	We will drink a couple glasses,
davaghamdit dghesao.	We will spend all day drinking.

(Baliauri 1991: 155)

Some versions of a popular Khevsur poem, "Night and Day," which I will return to below, draw attention not only to stealing vodka, and bringing it to the boy, but also to sharing vodka in bed, which moves the couple from conversing to kissing, from sharing vodka to sharing spit:

ra shuaghamis dro mavidas,	When the middle of the night comes,
saubar gaishalasa,	Conversation spreads between them,
botlit daghleven araq'sa,	They drink vodka from the bottle,
"guneba shegvitsvalasa."	[saying] "Let it change our mood."
q'ba ro q'bas gamaet'olas,	Cheek is ranged against cheek,
mk'erdi m'kerds deeqalasa.	Breast touches breast.
gaaqshireeben k'otsnasa,	They begin kissing more rapidly,
p'iridgan nerts'q'vis p'arvasa.	Stealing spit from each other's mouths.
adridges natsnauri khq'av,	They have known each other since long ago,
ndobas agharas malavsa.	They no longer hide their desire.

(Shanidze 1931: 144, translation adapted from Tuite 2000)

After they each took a sip, the boy would retain the rest of the bottle and would eventually drink it with other boys in public places. The fact that he had a bottle of vodka that he could share with his friends made public the fact that he had a *dzmobili*, because there was no other way he could have a bottle of vodka. And yet it would be a veiled reference, because he would not publicize who gave it to him.

FROM CASUAL TO DURABLE SEXUAL RELATIONS: *STS'ORPERIS* AND *DZMOBILIS*

The last two chapters dealt in detail with the events leading up to a boy and a girl spending a night together. If it was their first time, the boy or girl would now be initiated into a community of heterosexual practice; they would become *sts'orperiani* "someone who has (had) a *sts'orperi*." Having had at least one, and usually many, *sts'orperis* is a sign of sexual maturity and general desirability for both boys and girls. Once they had laid down with one another two or three times, the *elchi* was dispensed with, and they had a stable, durable, sexual relationship. They would now be *sts'orperis* to each other, and their sexual relations could be less restrained.

But this was still a casual, non-exclusive relationship. From among these *sts'orperis* a girl would eventually choose one boy with whom to form a more intimate, durable, and decidedly exclusive relationship, what was called a *dzmobili* (literally "sworn brother"). Like the term *sts'orperi*, which can mean nonsexual friend or age-mate as well as casual lover, the terminology for this sexual relationship was drawn from a word in the world of non-sexual relationships, the elective relationship formed by ritual between non-kin of sworn-siblinghood (*dobil-dzmobiloba* "sworn-sisterhood and sworn-brotherhood"). In this non-sexual relationship, gender was always marked: two boys could become *dzmobili* "sworn brother" to each other, two girls could become *dobili* "sworn sister" to each other, or a boy and a girl could become respectively *dzmobili* and *dobili* to one another. In the sexual relationship, the "boyfriend-girlfriend" version, strangely, both the boy and the girl were called, and called each other, *dzmobili* "sworn brother." Precisely the relationship where gender was most relevant, the heterosexual version, is the one where gender was neutralized.[1] There were thus strong parallels, and equally marked differences, between the two relationships. Like the sexual symbolism of vodka discussed above, everything about this furtive private adolescent romantic relationship can be said to have been stolen and re-engineered from the materials of more commonly recognized public relationships.

The *Dzmobili* Relationship and Its Rivals

Sometimes the terms *sts'orperi* and *dzmobili* are used somewhat interchangeably (particularly by ethnographers who are outsiders), or even confused; as mentioned, the earlier quotation from Tedoradze clearly mixes up the two kinds of relationships: gifts of vodka do not happen in the context of casual *sts'orproba*. However, in their precise senses they denote different kinds of sexual relationships (Baliauri 1991: 27). *Sts'orperi* denotes someone one "knows" casually, someone one has spent the night with at least once. *Dzmobili* denotes something like "boyfriend or girlfriend," someone with whom one has a durable sexual relationship that is somewhat exclusive; one is still occasionally obligated to have other people as casual *sts'orperis*, but there is only one *dzmobili* at a time. Baliauri describes the general tenor of this *dzmobili* relationship as follows (and also illustrates the ways in which the two terms could overlap; *sts'orperi* is used as a generic term here since it is clear we are talking about something more specific, a *dzmobili*):

> The *dzmobili* is for a Khevsur girl the being she loves most of all. So strong is this love, that it makes her forget everything else. It is possible that a girl would betray her brother, her father, but the *sts'orperi*—never. The secrecy of the *sts'orperi* the Khevsur girl carries to her grave and will tell no one. (Baliauri 1991: 17)

The absolute loyalty of the secret relationship between *dzmobilis* was opposed to public norms in which the girl's loyalty should be first to her real brothers and other kin. This reminds us that desire (*survili*), particularly the desire of women, was seen as an almost sorcerous power, dangerous and destabilizing to public norms of the community. A girl's loyalty to her *dzmobili* knew no limits: she might betray her brother for her *dzmobili*, even if as a consequence she would be exiled or have to commit suicide. Baliauri notes that girls frequently committed suicide for their *dzmobili*, or when their *dzmobili* died. A boy would not do this, but he would mourn and leave off all relations of *sts'orproba* after the death of his *dzmobili* (Baliauri 1991: 18).

Unlike the purely sociable sexual relationship between *sts'orperis*, this relationship was consequential, potentially dangerous, and a constant source of drama. It did not respect any boundaries or loyalties: *dzmobili* relationships could lead to betrayal of kin, destruction of marriage agreements, suicide, or the partners could elope and be exiled or die, and so on. This relationship was rivalrous with *all* other sexual relationships (Baliauri 1991: 22–27). First of all, it was rivalrous with other potential sexual partners of the same type: *dzmobilis* and *sts'orperis*. Both men and women would sometimes leave one *dzmobili* for another. A woman would not choose a man as a *dzmobili* until he stopped lying down with other women as *sts'orperis*, and would sometimes leave him if he did, even if he did so out of obligation (*khatrit*; see chapter 2). At the very least, a couple might spend up to a year apart because one party was sulking over the other having lain down with someone else for whatever reason. In addition, women would often enter into open rivalry with other existing or possible *dzmobilis* for a man's affection. The fact that a boy already had a *dzmobili* was not a problem as long as the girl was convinced of her own comparative worth. If a woman sensed that her *dzmobili* had become interested in another girl, she might swiftly end the relationship, refuse to sleep with him, and start looking for another *dzmobili*. If a woman was jilted, losing her *dzmobili* to another girl, she would insult and spread malicious gossip about her rival, and write anonymous insult poetry excoriating her. Men had to be more reserved in this case, but to be left without a *dzmobili*, especially for a woman, was to be made a subject of mockery.

Dzmobilis also saw their own *dzmobili*'s betrothed as a rival. Since *dzmobilis* could not marry one another, the rivalry tended to be more in the interest of sabotaging the relationship, perhaps in favor of another possible marriage candidate that the *dzmobili* preferred. *Dzmobilis* were very protective of each other: they would not tolerate insults directed at their *dzmobilis*, and so they would not tolerate their *dzmobili* marrying someone who was not worthy (*shesaperi*) of them.

The boy could not show this rivalry openly, but he would attempt to best and humiliate his various rivals in front of his *dzmobili* at every opportunity, in masculine competitions such as horse races or even in simple brawls, the true motive of which was always concealed: if a male *dzmobili* bested a woman's future husband in such a way, she would often break off the engagement. This kind of rivalry could be the secret source of much open enmity and fighting between boys, but they would never openly admit that they were fighting over a girl, which was shameful (Baliauri 1991: 25). Women could show their rivalry more openly, spreading gossip and satirical poetry, or they might even tell their *dzmobili*'s future wife to her face: "You are not good enough [*shesaperi*] for him!"

Night and Day

The stereotypical relationship between *dzmobilis* was one of absolute loyalty built on absolute desire. It was also marked by secrecy:

siq'varuls damalva unda	Love needs to be hidden
mop'arulas tskhvarivita;	Like a stolen sheep;
gamachindes, glovna unda	Once revealed, it needs to be mourned
uk'etias mk'vdarivita.	Like the best dead person.

(Shanidze 1931: 144)

The relationship therefore took absolutely opposed forms by night and by day. By night, it was clearly separated from more casual relationships of *sts'orproba* by being much more sexualized, the intimacy and trust existing between the partners allowing them to dispense with many of the rules of lying down together. A longer version of the poem "Night and Day" cited above gives a clear picture:

dghe-ghame romeli sjobis,	Which is better, day or night,
bich'o, me gk'itkhav amasa.	Boy, I ask you that.

dghes ro ar hkondes ghamei,	If day did not have night,
igits ghmertm daiparasa.	May God spare us from that.
ra dadgas ghamis ts'q'vdiadi,	When the dark of night has come,
bevras ukharis kalasa,	A girl rejoices in her heart,
dzmobiltan ts'asvlas ap'irobs,	She intends to visit her *dzmobili*,
dznelad, rom daishalasa.	It would be hard to keep her away.
daagebs ch'rel khalichasa,	(The boy) spreads a colorful carpet,
daachunchulebs chalasa,	He fluffs up the straw,
kal miva ts'q'nari bijita,	The woman approaches, with quiet steps,
ar gaachkamebs chalasa,	She doesn't make the straw rustle,
ubeshi botlas chaidgams,	She has placed a bottle [of vodka] by her breast,
jalapta monop'aravsa:	Stolen from her home:
bich'i ts'evsa da daishvrinebs,	The boy lies and pretends to be tired,
sdzinav, at'q'uebs kalasa,	To sleep, he fools the girl,
kal maints gamoaghvidzebs,	The girl wakes him up anyway,
ar alevinebs khanasa,	She won't let him waste time,
q'ba rom q'bas gamoakadla,	Cheek touches cheek,
mk'erdi m'kerds daeqalasa.	Breast is pressed against breast.
ertad its'q'eben ch'uk'ch'uk'sa,	They begin quietly chatting,
p'iridan nerts'q'vis p'arvasa.	Stealing spit from each other's mouths.

(Mak'alatia 1984: 160, translation adapted from Tuite 2000)

If the relationship between *dzmobilis* became ever more intimate by night, by day the relationship had to remain secret, kept in constant check and denial. The absence of public expression meant the relationship was always under threat. Aside from visiting relatives, there were countless events, both ritual events such as weddings and funerals, and collective work events such as the harvest, where boys and girls ended up meeting with other unacquainted boys and girls. At such events, *elchis* worked tirelessly to arrange *sts'orproba* between unacquainted boys and girls, trying to determine who was most suited (*shesaperi*) to whom, often without consulting the boys and girls themselves (Baliauri 1991: 135–36, 141–42). Many such events, particularly weddings, involved a lighthearted sociable gathering of the young people (*akhalukhali*), separate from the more serious gathering of the older people (particularly the men, called the *jari*, literally "army"), where, free from the supervision of their elders, they entertained each other, drank, sang songs, and recited poetry, whispered gossip, slander, and anonymous insult poetry, and sometimes ended up fighting.

As can be imagined, *dzmobilis* might well look upon such events not as a romantic opportunity, but as a problem, a gathering filled with a set of potential rivals. In such circumstances, the *elchi*, too, became yet another rival to a durable, but secret, romantic attachment. *Elchis* were allies, but also rivals, of romance: an *elchi* would not be denied in her quest to create new relations of *sts'orproba*, even if it endangered existing secretive relations between *dzmobilis*. This was particularly true where the *elchi* was fulfilling her role of creating *sts'orproba* "out of respect" (*khatrit*) or "by entreaty" (*perobit*) (see chapter 2). Events that involved *sts'orproba* thus became part of a long series of public events at which *dzmobilis* were physically separated or had to avoid each other in public: they might lie together once a month or once a week, but sometimes a whole summer might go by without them seeing each other. A thousand things kept them apart: lying down with other boys and girls; bouts of sulking, either because one's partner had lain down with another or as a result of some other slight; ritual separations, as when boys had to go to shrine rituals where only men are allowed, or when women were sequestered in menstrual huts, as well as when a partner traveled, and so on (Baliauri 1991: 23).

Dzmobilis were only openly *dzmobilis* by night, but by day in the open they had to keep their affections in check, even though some of the various tasks in which they were involved, and the land itself, full of cliffs and gullies, afforded ample potential opportunities for secret meetings alone outside by day, such as when boys and girls tended the cattle in pasturelands far from the village. While the more easy-going Pshavians might see in such secluded spaces a perfect opportunity to engage in their sexual practice of *ts'ats'loba* under a heavy cloak in a meadow, under such circumstances the more restrained Khevsurs were at particular pains to avoid any public expressions of affection or desire:

> Here *dzmobili* boys and girls frequently meet up with one another . . . but they do not under any circumstances either kiss one another or hold hands. Outside of the house, by day, in the fields, the Khevsur male and female neither talk to each other about romantic matters nor ask the other to talk about them. It is not accepted as a rule, it would be a very great shame, as for the boy and girl, so for their entire kin group, if the boy and the girl were to lie down together in such circumstances, even though they are *dzmobilis*. A male shows affection and behaves nicely to a girl when there are people about and at home, but outside, alone, he behaves very coldly, he doesn't even look upon her. If she has even a little self-esteem (*tavmoq'vareoba*), when they are outside a girl will not begin to speak to him of love, not only of her own love, but even that of others. If a girl begins behaving unnaturally and laughing, the boy gives her such a look, that she will never again dare to engage in such behavior. If the boy begins to talk to her softly, then the girl completely loses any love for him in her heart. (Baliauri 1991: 147–48)

For the Khevsurs, the most important reason for mutual avoidance in all these cases was that absence made the heart grow fonder. Distance and self-restraint (*tav-shek'aveba*) produced desire, and desire was lost when a couple lay down together too frequently (Baliauri 1991: 23).

But how did lovers express their love when they were absent from one another? After all, most of their relationship consisted not of nights together, but of days (or even weeks or months) apart. How could desire be expressed in the face of frequently and sometimes lengthy separations of time and space? We have seen part of the answer already, in the lively commerce of vodka discussed above. Another part of the answer lies in comparing this relationship to the nonsexual relationship of sworn-siblinghood on which it clearly was modeled, a relationship in which one also tried to create and maintain durable ties of intimacy despite separations of time and space.

CREATING AND MAINTAINING DURABLE RELATIONSHIPS OVER TIME

As we have already seen, the term *dzmobili* was intrinsically ambiguous; it could mean a "sworn" sexual partner irrespective of gender, or it could mean a nonsexual sworn brother. If there was ambiguity, Khevsurs drew attention to *desire*, using phrases like *sandauri dzmobili* "desired sworn brother" to indicate that more than ritual kinship informed the relationship (Baliauri 1991: 8). Aside from the common vocabulary, the two kinds of relationship were comparable in other respects: they were both durable, elective relationships formed between peers. Because they were elective (freely chosen), they both involved a performative moment of *creating* the relationship between the two parties. And because they were durable, the relationships both involved forms of material exchange by which the relationship was *maintained* when the parties were separated. The main difference between them was that the boyfriend-girlfriend relationship was secretive in both its creation and its maintenance, while the sworn-siblinghood relationship on which it was modeled was publicly recognized throughout.

Creating the Relationship: Oaths and Hints

First of all, both kinds of relationships were elective, based on mutual feelings of "liking": "a *dzmobili* is a person chosen as a result of love" (Baliauri 1991: 27). The girl chose a permanent boyfriend based on liking (*mats'oneba*) and desire (*suruli, ndoba*), just as a boy might choose to become sworn brother with another unrelated boy (or with a girl, or a girl with a girl) based on mutual liking and admiration, based on their own desires to create a durable friendship (A. Ochiauri 1980: 210). The personal sense of absolute loyalty and devotion a woman felt toward her *dzmobili* was no different in kind from the publicly recognized obligations that sworn-sibling *dzmobilis* had to one another.

However, in the same way that *sts'orproba* could express individual desire but could also be arranged out of communal obligation, the most common actual reason for swearing sworn-brotherhood wasn't mutual liking, but rather to create a public, normative relationship of friendship between two unrelated boys who had become enemies. In effect, this "forced" swearing of siblinghood works like a ritual of reconciliation. In much the same way that *sts'orproba* might happen by desire (*survilit*) or out of respect (*khatrit*), here two different private senses of feeling were poured into the same public mold: feelings of liking were given durable public expression, and feelings of hatred were censored and muted by a relationship that denied them public expression.

The secrecy of the sexual relationship and the publicity of the social relationship with the same name point to other differences in their mode of creation. The sworn-sibling relationship (whether out of desire or compulsion) was constituted by a publicly witnessed ritual: the two boys had to drink, in front of witnesses, an "oath of silver" (usually vodka mixed with flakes of silver). The symbolism of the silver is opaque, though one could hazard a guess based on the fact that silver objects were strongly associated with the male shrine divinities that represented the community as a whole (only divinities were permitted to own silver objects such as the sacred cups that were used in shrine rituals); indeed, silver was suffused with associations of masculinity and the world of what was called the *jari* (a word that means "army" and also something like "public"), the community of men who represented the community in religious, political, and military matters. One might then interpret the silver flakes either as being like the witnesses drawn from the *jari*, a way of marking sacredness or publicness, or as being similar to the parallel oaths based on natural substances like blood or breast milk, ingesting the masculine substance of the community or divinity.

It was not enough to drink vodka or beer mixed with silver; the sworn siblings also had to swear an oath. Swearing an oath in front of witnesses made the event a ritual, performative event. When we say that an utterance is performative, we mean that it is language that *performs an action*, a form of social action; social situations and relationships can be transformed publicly by the words that are said: "the performative, which is concerned with language as action, language that in its enunciation changes the world—it brings about a new social state" (Kulick 2003: 139). Swearing an oath publicly is a classic example of a performative utterance, as are, for example, declaring war, finding a defendant guilty, pronouncing a couple husband and wife, signing a contract: in all these cases a linguistic utterance produces a new social state.

The officiating elder would scrape flakes of silver into a horn full of vodka, held by one of the participants, while calling upon the Khevsur divinities to witness. He would call on the two men to help each other, never to betray each other, and so on. Then the two boys would each drink three times from the horn and swear an oath that was also a toast: "From now on you are my brother, my mother will be your mother, my sister your sister. . . ," and so on (A. Ochiauri 1980: 33–34). The relationship was transformed by the attendant ritual act of drinking vodka mixed with silver (without which the words would not be performative, that is, effective or binding) and the performative words that stipulated in what ways the relationship was to be changed, in the same way that saying wedding vows in front of witnesses under the appropriate conditions explicitly stipulates the new terms of the relationship and socially transforms two single people into a married couple.

By contrast, Khevsur girl and boy lovers drank no vodka mixed with silver, swore no oaths, and there were no witnesses. Explicit public ritual performative utterances, overt words and oaths, were replaced by largely incremental, oblique inferences and hints, often through the mediation of an *elchi*. The choice of *dzmobili* belonged to the girl, but (as we have seen) she could not state any preferences outright, instead waiting until she confirmed through inference that the boy shared her desire. A girl might like a boy from the outset and want to be his *dzmobili*, but she doesn't consider him a *dzmobili* as long as he continues to lie down with other girls. Such a situation continues until the girl senses love from the boy. She senses love by means of circumstances such as these: if the *elchi* keeps picking her out from among the other girls to lie down with the boy, or the boy hints or gives her to understand that he likes her the most. Then:

> when a large number of young people are gathered together, the *elchi* will ask both the girl and the boy who they want to lie down with. The girl cannot easily pick a *dzmobili*, she will not say outright who she wants to lie down with, but the boy can openly say: "If I lie down, there, with that girl there, and if not her—with no one." So the girl gleans from various sources whether this boy loves her, or not. (Baliauri 1991: 22)

The decision was the girl's, but only the boy could utter anything resembling a performative utterance, an outright statement of sexual preference or desire. The boy might also act somewhat indirectly if he was not completely sure that the girl liked him back, trying to determine circumstantially what the girl's hidden wishes were. However, unlike the girl, he had the power to tell her directly and openly, in something like a performative fashion, that, for example, he preferred her to all other girls; or to ask her what the *elchi* said about him, whether the *elchi* had lied to her that he preferred to lie down with others rather than her. Or he might say even more explicitly: "I prefer you to all other girls and if you also want to lie down with me, lie down! If not, don't come to lie down with me out of respect (*khatrit*)." Some girls might playfully refuse to answer, while others might answer straightforwardly: "If I didn't like you, I wouldn't lie down with you out of respect" (Baliauri 1991: 23). This was as close as the couple came to an outright declaration of love: the relationship was created out of inference, hints, and perhaps, finally, an explicit statement of preferences, but only the boy could say the words that initiated this, and yet the final choice seems to have belonged to the girl.

While the public relationship of sworn-siblinghood was in the sunlight for all to see, the secretive sexual relationship that was modeled on it was in the shade, or even the darkness. And yet, in both cases, the words that were said seemed to decide the matter and create the relationship: in the one case they were explicit, said before witnesses (both human and divine) at a ritual event of drinking; in the other, they were built up of hints and finally stammered-out confessions of love. Alongside such linguistic expressions of love, vodka also played a performative role in the declaration of love, as we saw above, but not as part of any kind of oath: a girl brought vodka for her *dzmobili* when she visited him at night, which amounted to a performative statement that "you are my *dzmobili*."[2] We saw above that a girl hotly disputed a boy's claim that "she brought me a bottle of vodka in bed," because this would have amounted to a performative act of declaring him her *dzmobili*. So too, if a boy had vodka to share with his friends, this amounted to a performative publicization that "I have a *dzmobili*." Again, as I have emphasized throughout, linguistic and nonlinguistic genres can be deployed separately or in tandem to produce the same social effects.

Maintaining the Relationship: Waiting and Exchange

"Am I in love?—Yes, since I'm waiting." (Barthes 1978: 39)

Barthes (1978: 40) sums up the Western lover's predicament in the act of waiting: "The lover's fatal identity is precisely: *I am the one who waits*," and if anything this was even more true of the Khevsur lover. Khevsur lovers were constantly kept apart. All social relationships, in Khevsureti and everywhere else, involve moments of both presence and absence; however, the absences are felt more keenly in romantic relationships as agonizing, pining, *waiting*. One might put it this way: a casual *sts'orperi* was really only a *sts'orperi* when spending the night together, and was otherwise nothing; a *dzmobili* was not first and foremost the person one habitually spent the night with, but the person one was *waiting for*. A slightly different variant of the same poem quoted above, detailing a night spent together (from Tedoradze 1930: 139–40; translation is Tuite's 2000) expands on the theme of doubts felt by the boy as he waits:

vazhasats molodini akv,	The lad as well, full of eagerness,
ar utsdis p'uris ch'amasa,	Cannot take time to eat his meal.
ts'ava, gaigebs loginsa,	He goes and readies the bed for her,
gaibunbulebs chalasa.	Lays the sheets, fluffs up the straw.
gulshia gulis misnada;	Heart is working its magic on heart;
tana k'i pikrobs amasa:	At the same time, he is thinking
"k'i ara mamivides, ra,	"Could it be, she will not come,
rom rait daishalasa?"	Or that something has gone awry?"

The lover (*dzmobili*) is a lot like one's sworn sibling: they are both relationships in which the time spent together, face to face, is the exception rather than the rule; both are people whose next visit might be days, weeks, or months away. Somehow a sense of continuous presence must be constructed symbolically against the brute fact of long periods of absence. Each relationship must be confirmed, remembered, and renewed by reciprocity: constant visiting and exchange of gifts. Part of the purpose of forming sworn-sibling relations, and all this resulting to-ing and fro-ing and gift exchanges between sworn siblings, was precisely to widen the sphere of potential sexual relations of *sts'orproba*:

> Let's say that a girl likes a boy and she doesn't have any means to become closer to him, then the girl sets up things so that either her brother or male cousin becomes a sworn brother with the boy she likes and after that she will have the possibility of visiting and getting closer to him . . . girls also become sworn sisters with women, both because of liking one another and also because of the love of a boy. This happens when a girl likes some boy in the other village, or they both do, and they have no means of going back and forth, then the girls become sworn sisters and they acquire a pretext for going back and forth, which leads to the boy and the girl becoming closer. The sworn sister would serve as an *elchi* for the other sworn sister, when she came as a guest with [a gift of] vodka. (Baliauri 1991: 211)

When visiting a sworn sibling in another village, boys and girls brought *sadzmobilo* ("for the sworn brother") or *sadobilo* ("for the sworn sister") gifts of vodka for their sworn brothers and sisters (Baliauri 1991: 211). The party in motion always brought a gift of vodka. The party who was being visited always returned this gift with a *sadzmobilo/sadobilo* gift of a different kind: if a boy, then a copper pot, a short sword, or a calf; if a girl, she might give a gift of something she had embroidered with her own hands (Baliauri 1991: 211). Such gifts were always given openly, for all to see.

The gift exchanges between sexual *dzmobilis* were very similar. First, since the girl always went to the boy, and never vice versa, the girl was *always* the party in motion when "visiting" the boy, and this explains immediately why she always "came with vodka," because vodka was the gift brought by the party in motion. The boy was always the stationary party, so he never gave the girl vodka. In other respects, however, the boy gave the girl appropriate *sadzmobilo* gifts, and the girl also gave the boy gifts other than vodka, too, which they kept as mementos. A poem addressed to a girl draws attention to the gendered exchange:

sadzmobiloshi magartva,	He brought you a *sadzmobilo* [gift]
sam manatian arghani,	A three-ruble accordion,
shents shegenakha botlai,	You in turn saved for him a bottle
araq'iani, tsamtsami.	full of vodka.

(A. Ochiauri 1980: 125)

The kinds of gifts exchanged were in general the same in both the nonsexual and the sexual relationships; the important difference was in *how* they were given. While the gifts between sworn siblings were given openly, the gifts between boyfriends and girlfriends were given secretively and indirectly. A girlfriend, in addition to saving her boyfriend bottles of vodka, would sew and embroider gifts for him (secretly, often when she was not supposed to be working). Her boyfriend would carve wooden objects for her own use, and give her silk scarves, silver rings, or accordions. All of these were given indirectly, secretly, the girl giving the boy things by the hand of the *elchi*, the boy through some relative (Baliauri 1991: 64–65). Such objects were kept as durable reminders—in fact, carefully preserved to be carried to the grave.

Certain gifts not only acted as personal reminders of a secret relationship, but also afforded the possibility of partial public disclosure of the existence of such a relationship. For example, a boy who shared his vodka with his friends was also indirectly publicizing that he had a girlfriend who gave him that *sadzmobilo* vodka. Between boyfriends and girlfriends the list of such *sadzmobilo* gifts, gifts that openly indexed the existence of a romantic secret, included things like silver rings. Exchanging rings too, like bringing vodka, could serve as a semi-performative gift: the silver ring was worn publicly, but its significance was secret. If asked, they would say the ring was a gift from a deceased relative and they were keeping it as a reminder. Keeping the gift was a sign of devotion, but giving it was a test: the boy might take a ring off his finger and give it to the girl, saying, "You will keep it, you know, you won't keep it, you know" (that is, maybe you will keep it or maybe you won't). Sometimes a boy would test a girl in a casual relationship by offering her or asking from her a ring, to see if she would assent. If she gave such a ring in a casual relationship, he might then give it to someone else, which would be insulting to her (Baliauri 1991: 123). Sometimes a boy would test a girl by making a secret mark on a gifted ring, so he would recognize it if she gave it, in turn, to someone else. If he saw it on another boy's hand, he would become angry and would sometimes challenge the other boy by throwing a cup of vodka or beer in his face, if they were at a drinking event. The ensuing fight would be brutal, but no one would know precisely why they were fighting. Sometimes they would be forcibly reconciled by being forced to become sworn brothers, but it would not be really resolved until the girl somehow got the ring back from the other boy. Upon getting it back, the girl would smash the ring with a stone, and send it back to the boy who gave it (Baliauri 1991: 67–69). The situation of the twice-given ring was possible for girls, too, but they had fewer ways to ensure the return of the ring. The situation could similarly degenerate into a fist fight between the girls and threats directed at the boy, which, however, would not be taken seriously by the boy (Baliauri 1991: 70). Gift exchange, then, afforded not only a means of maintaining a relationship, but also a means for ending one: if giving a durable gift created or maintained a social tie, destroying a gift ended it. In this sense, a girl destroying a ring and drinking vodka with another girl were the same act, equivalent to a performative linguistic "break-up" statement that ended the relationship.

NOTES

1   One possible reason for this might be that the term *dobili* "sworn sister" also refers to a kind of female demonic consort of the shrine divinity, which we will encounter in chapter 5.

2   There is some evidence that this kind of oath was used, perhaps without witnesses, in the forming of sexual relations of sworn-siblinghood in the region. The earliest accounts we have of this sort of sexual relationship in Pshavi, in the nineteenth century, define a girlfriend (*ts'ats'ali*) as "sort of like a sworn sister," "a pretend sworn sister" (*vitom dobili*), differing from a true sworn sister in that the relationship was an erotic one. These early accounts state that the relationship was formed ritually in an identical way in both sworn-siblinghood and romantic cases, by "the oath of silver," drinking vodka with silver flakes (*Droeba* 1880, no. 102, pp. 2–3).

4

INVISIBLE LOVE POETRY

———————

K HEVSUR SEXUALITY was "obscured in the mists of secrets," as the ethnographer
Sergi Mak'alatia wrote in the first half of the twentieth century: "The Khevsur
will not reveal its rules to outsiders, and for this reason it is extremely hard and dangerous for an investigator to collect correct data about it locally" (Mak'alatia 1998 [1925]: 6).
Perhaps for this reason, Mak'alatia, like virtually all other ethnographers of this tradition, myself included, availed himself of evidence from love poetry for precisely
the most intimate and secretive scenes of Khevsur sexuality. Without these linguistic genres of love poetry, we would probably never know anything about Khevsur
romance in general, or even that it existed. Moreover, without the circulation of love
poetry that publicized the most intimate aspects of personal lives, acting both *infor-
matively* to report on things one could not witness or experience, allowing participants
to compare their experiences with those of strangers, and *performatively* to censure
bad lovers and praise good ones, Khevsur romance could not have existed as a "community of shared practices."

   Students of sexuality always confront the same epistemological problem—how can
we know what really happens between lovers when they are alone? This is a meth-
odological problem for all sexuality research, one which, as Cameron and Kulick
(2003: 106) point out, tends to skew analytic attention away from discussions of how
language expresses sexual desire in intimate situations toward linguistic enactments
of sexuality in other more accessible domains, since "few people would agree to the
recording and analysis of their naturally-occurring sexual interactions." But this is a
problem not only for ethnographers, but for members of the culture, too, who might
want to know whether what they are doing and feeling corresponds to a broader sense
of "what is normal" or "what is permitted" or "what other people are doing or feeling."
Some of this information ("the rules" of what was permitted) was freely available: boys

taught boys, and girls taught girls, these rules. Some of it ("what really happens") was only a matter of inference or hearsay, if that.

For example, when a Georgian colleague and I were doing fieldwork in the neighboring valley of Pankisi with a Pshavian man named Gabriel on very similar Pshavian practices of romance, he began with a list of rules of touching that are certainly no secret. They are publicly known norms, part of "what everyone knows" as members of a culture, a community of shared practices. But what happens between two lovers in private, to what extent the norms are actually followed, is generally not observable either by ethnographers or by members of a culture, and here Gabriel could talk only about his own experiences:

> GABRIEL: They had freedom [to touch] the chest. Both had their bodies alongside one another, they were not allowed to touch one another with their bodies and they freely touched each other's chests; they could kiss each other too, they could hug each other too, they could caress each other too.
>
> COLLEAGUE: And to what extent was there this, that is, in the youthful period, that is, self-restraint?
>
> GABRIEL: Self-restraint, as it happens now I myself underwent this . . .
>
> COLLEAGUE: This process.
>
> GABRIEL: I have undergone this process. Here I think, that it is a belief, a belief that the doors to everything carnal there are already locked to you. Well, that's the way it was with me, I don't know how it was with others.

Gabriel not only expresses doubts about how things went with others, but also, in turn, encounters doubts expressed by other younger Pshavians about whether he obeyed the rules himself:

> GABRIEL: Nowadays some people don't believe me and they ask me: "Was there really, Gabriel, such things?" "There were," I answered. "Have you experienced them yourself?" "I have experienced them," I said. "Then, how did you restrain yourself, man?" "Well, I restrained myself without a problem." I don't know.

When we (rather stupidly) asked Gabriel about intimate scenes between boys and girls, specifically, what they talked about when they lay down together alone, Gabriel surmised reasonably enough that "probably they would talk about love, other [everyday topics] wouldn't be there, like sheep, cows, fields, nothing like that." Otherwise, like ethnographers Mak'alatia and Tedoradze, he relied primarily on evidence from love poems to reconstruct things he had never experienced himself. For example, he adduced evidence from poetry that, for example, occasionally two women would lie down with one man:

GABRIEL: Sometimes two lay down together.

COLLEAGUE: Two women.

GABRIEL: Two women, the man lay down in the middle. There is a poem:

> or kalt sho, vt'rialebdi,   Between two women, I turned
> sagrekhelshi t'arivita   Like a spindle in a spindle-spinner.

Notice the metaphor!

Pshavians like Gabriel often turned to poetry for evidence about intimate moments between others where their own personal experience failed them; ethnographers, in turn, simply reproduced whole poems to cover the most intimate phases of romance. When it comes to intimate scenes between lovers, the ethnographer Tedoradze is representative in that he simply reproduces poems such as "Night and Day" (discussed in the last chapter) and adds that "this poem so well describes Khevsur *sts'orproba*, that I don't think it's necessary to write anything more" (Tedoradze 1930: 140). Poetry about romance, of which there is a great deal since both Khevsurs and Pshavians are noted for their oral traditions of poetry, precisely the most *public* of all indigenous linguistic genres, is paradoxically the largest source of information, both for ethnographers and members of the culture, for the most *secret and intimate* moments of romance.

The Khevsur poet "K'undza" (Gamakhela Ch'inch'arauli) once said: "A good poem is like a bird: whence it flies and where it is flying, no one knows" (Gogoch'uri 1974: 38). The formal properties of poems (rhyme, meter, etc.) make them into durable, bounded objects, easy to memorize, repeat, and recite again and again in new contexts across space and time. By virtue of the indefiniteness of its address (including both intimates and strangers) that results from its potentially limitless circulation, love poetry not only *reports on* or publicizes intimate scenes, making them available to indefinite others, including strangers, but also can act reflexively *within* those intimate scenes, allowing lovers to threaten the possibility of public sanction for private misbehavior (see also Manning 2014a). In my own fieldwork among the Pshavians of neighboring Pankisi, my Georgian colleague and I collected the following poem from an older Pshavian woman named Babulia which depicts intimate romantic negotiations of Pshavian *ts'at'sloba*, of precisely the sort that, as we have seen above, can either get you thrown out of bed or elicit a poem of denunciation:

BABULIA: Here, this one is about a *ts'ats'ali*.

COLLEAGUE: Well, well, we are really interested in *ts'ats'alis*, especially, Paul is interested; that's why he came all the way from America, that he could record that sort of thing.

BABULIA [reading the poem aloud]:

p'at'ara davts'ev kaltana,	I lay down with a little girl,
gavkhsen mdzivian saq'elo;	I opened her beaded collar;
kalma khelebi shemt'atsa:	The woman grabbed my hands:
"ras shvebi, dzaghlis nasheno!	"What are you doing, you offspring of dog!
khelebs ubeshi rad miq'op,	Why are you sticking your hands in my bosom,
agremts shav mits'am dagpeno!	May the dark earth cover you!
its'ek da kheli ar gadzra,	Lie there and don't move your hands,
aghar gamikhsna saq'elo! . . .	Don't open my collar again! . . .
me arai makvs sasheno!"	I have got nothing for you!"
avdek, gamovts'q'e menatsa;	I got up, I got angry myself;
"ra makvis shentan sapero?	"What do I have that is good enough for you?
'ts'ukhelis vits'ev kaltana,'	'Last night I lay down with a woman,'
mtel kveq'anaze gavpeno!"	I'll spread the news across the whole world!"
chokhis k'altaze gameba:	I tied my chokha [coat] about the waist:
"sad mikhval, mits'is damq'relo?"	"Where are you going, wretched of the earth?"
avdek, davuts'ev iseva,	I got up, I lay down next to her again,
gavkhsen mdzivian saq'elo.	I opened her buttoned collar.
mopereboda isitsa:	She too showed affection:
"sad midiodi, shavbnelo?"	"Where were you going, evil one?"

Over half a century earlier, the Georgian ethnographer Sergei Mak'alatia collected a shorter, but very similar poem in Khevsureti (1984 [1935]: 161):

ts'in-ts'in ro davts'ev kaltana,	The first time I lay down with a girl
mashin movdzie saq'elo,	I searched for her collar,
shaishal-gadailaqa:	She got angry:
"ras scha, she viris nasheno?!	"What are you doing, you, born from an ass?!
k'ats'rit ra chamomit'ane	Why are you putting your fingernails
sirmit shak'ruli saq'elo!	On my collar, braided with gold!
an dedas ra movat'q'uo,	How will I deceive my mother,
an bnelchi rogor davk'ero?	Or sew it back in the darkness?
memre gamoval, vidzakheb,	Then I will come out, I will call out,
mtels kveq'anaze magpeno!"	I'll spread the news about you across the whole world!"

"nu ut'q'vi, chemo kalao,   "Don't say anything, my girl,
nems-nach'ers menav magtsemo."   I myself will give you the needle and thread."

In both poems, very similar in spite of being separated by the better part of a century and at least a couple of high ridges and deep valleys, intimate negotiations take place against the awareness of broader publics who might sanction bad behavior. In both these poems, there is the same kind of intimate scene of sexual transgression, where the boy attempts to open the collar of the girl. In each poem, which have completely different outcomes, one of the partners (in the first, the boy, in the second, the girl) gestures at the possibility of composing a poem publicizing the event to humiliate the other, causing the partner to assent to their wishes.

The poem *reports* this event, making secretive details of intimacy available to a wider public, one that includes both strangers who have had similar experiences, such as other Khevsurs and Pshavs, and in fact an open-ended list of strangers including ethnographers, and now, you who are reading this. It is precisely the circulation of love poetry, then, that makes possible a *shared* culture of romance, a community of shared practices—publicly shared ideas about what is and what is not possible. While the explicit rules of what is possible were generally taught by word of mouth within a community, it is the violations of the normative order—aspects of bad behavior—that are generally made public by poetry.

But poems like this not only make public, by reporting on, representing, and revealing, aspects of romantic life that would normally remain hidden, allowing members of the culture to compare their experiences with those of others, and allowing ethnographers to become aware of the existence of these practices. Poems like this one also *act* performatively, intervene in romance, and produce results. Poetry produces a normative order by making public violations of the rules, ruining someone's public persona or name, so that even the threat of composing a poem about bad behavior might be enough of a sanction to prevent bad behavior from happening in the first place.

At the same time, poetry, as a genre, represents a form of linguistic expression bound by formal constraints such as rhyme and meter. In this respect, the very form of Khevsur love poetry, where expression of sentiment is crossed by formal constraint, is very much like the form of Khevsur sexuality in general, where individual desire is crossed by self-restraint. One might say that a poet who subjects her powerful sentiments of love to the constraints of formal expression produces an image of a lover whose desires are similarly subject to self-restraint. Abu-Lughod (1986: 245; see also Caton 1990: 29–31, 110–13) makes a similar point for Bedouin love poetry: "By channeling such powerful sentiments into a rigid and conventional medium and delimited social contexts, individuals demonstrate a measure of self-mastery and control that contributes to honor."

The formal constraints of poetry such as rhyme and meter also serve to make poems more like bounded durable objects that can be memorized, repeated, and circulated, transcending time and space. In this sense the production and circulation of love poems were comparable to gift exchange in general; in fact, poems did not merely resemble other gifted items, but were counted among them. A poet, composing a poem of praise addressed to a specific person, could even demand within the text of the poem itself a countergift, what was called a *salekso* ("for the poem"): a gift in exchange for the poem, an item of clothing, a horn for drinking vodka, or even a drinking horn full of vodka (Gogoch'uri 1974: 70–85).

The similarity between poems praising the lover, which are composed only by girls for boys, and gifted bottles of vodka saved for the lover is particularly striking: they are both things girls do for boys, seeking through both means to give the relationship a greater extension in time and space than would otherwise be possible. But at the same time as love poems express individual desires, they place them in check, expressing them according to the forms (e.g., rhyme, meter) and norms of the genre, in much the same way that a Khevsur lover expressed desire while bound by self-restraint and *namusi*. The figure of the author and object produced in a Khevsur love poem is always an embodiment of key Khevsur normative concepts of good, desirable persons. The boy is *desirable* (*dghiani*) because he is like a "good servant": brave, warlike, masculine, with a good sword and a fine steed, the kind of boy who would willingly sacrifice his life for the community, not the sort of boy who would chase women or compose love poetry. The girl who composes this poetry is *namusiani*; she keeps her desire in check, is modest (*moridebuli*), and she does not directly disclose her identity or desires.

THE INVISIBILITY OF KHEVSUR LOVE POETRY: THE ABSENCE OF THE LYRIC MODE

Because of these formal aspects of self-restraint, Khevsur love poetry is difficult to recognize *as* love poetry in our sense. Aside from the poetry of censure, probably the most interesting for contemporary audiences, there is little "lyric" poetry, that is, poetry, usually cast in the present tense (hence I discuss all poems below in that tense), which focuses on the expression of personal, emotional feelings. In fact, Khevsur poetry is so seemingly hard to find, and once found, so stoic and stern, that the folklorist Ak'ak'i Shanidze, who pioneered the study of Khevsur poetry, assumed that love poetry was incompatible with the heroic, warlike nature of the Khevsurs and that only the neighboring, more easy-going Pshavians composed love poetry:

> Love poetry is relatively less well represented [in the Khevsur poetic corpus].
> In this branch the Khevsurs sink down below the level of Pshavs. But they

sink down below them not because they were not able to say poems about love as beautifully as the Pshavians,—no, this branch of poetry is not so attractive to the warlike nature of the Khevsurs. (Shanidze 1931: 013)

Shanidze is repeating a local ethnic ideology in which the Khevsurs and Pshavians are treated as absolute opposites because of relatively minor differences of customs (as we have already seen). This local ethnic binarism becomes a set of stereotypically opposed temperaments in the hands of folklorists like Shanidze, explaining the putative lack of lyric sensibility among the Khevsurs because their "warlike nature" preferred "epic" poems about dead heroes to "lyric" poems about love. Ethnographers like Mak'alatia have also characterized the temperaments of the Khevsurs in darker, more serious shades than the Pshavians (Tuite 2008): the male Khevsur is "daring," "bold," "arrogant," and "proud," while Khevsur women "lack feminine tenderness and carry themselves with a masculine manner"(Mak'alatia 1984: 106). While Khevsur women have some of the same virtues, like boldness and pride, as men, "because of their work and heavy social conditions the Khevsur woman has a sad and dejected manner of speaking" (1984: 106). Meanwhile, Pshavian men and women alike are "bold, uninhibited," "amiable and respectful . . . affectionate and flirtatious . . . [and] enjoy having fun, poetic improvisation and entertainment" (Mak'alatia 1934: 90–91; translation based on Tuite 2008).

Shanidze's theory is basically that the very different temperaments of the Khevsurs and Pshavians were directly reflected in their favored forms of poetic expression: the warlike Khevsurs preferred epic poetry celebrating heroes dying in battle, the more carefree Pshavians preferring lyric poems including love poetry. But as I will show, Khevsur women composed a lot of poetry about romantic themes; however, they composed it as a kind of epic "praise poetry," praising the living lover as if he had the same virtues as a hero fallen in battle. Therefore, Khevsur poetry seems very unlike the poetry we typically understand as love poetry, a kind of lyric poetry about expressing individuality, individual emotions, and individual desires, which is the form it took among the neighboring Pshavians. Khevsur poetry does not passively index naturalized "temperaments," but actively enacts desirable properties of the author and the object, sexual self-restraint and modesty, in its very form. Khevsur love poetry (composed only by women) is unlike neighboring Pshavian lyric poetry (composed by men and women alike) in the way in which it displays the *morideba* (modesty) and *namusi* (sexual shame or self-restraint) of the female author by erasing both her identity and any overt expression of her desire. The boy, in turn, is not praised as an object of the poet's individual sexual or romantic desire, as in some Pshavian lyric, but is portrayed in a sociocentric manner as being *dghiani*, a generally likeable, heroic boy, with a good sword, a good horse, and plenty of enemies.

In this process of erasure of desire, the desiring subject is also erased, and the author disappears entirely into her work, which makes it very different from the poetry of the neighboring Pshavians, whose love poetry is easily recognizable as an expression of the feelings of the author for her lover. To fully understand Khevsur romance, we need to understand why Khevsur love poetry does not look like anything we would recognize as love poetry, and why the greatest authority of Khevsur poetry decided it did not exist because love was not an emotion befitting the warlike Khevsurs.

To understand the strangeness of Khevsur love poetry we need to be a little more honest about our own Western social preferences and ideas about what love poetry should look like. Khevsur poetic genres include a good deal more epic poetry about dead heroes than lyric poetry about love, and we are apt to sympathize more with lyric poetry than with epic poetry, since within our own society lyric poetry seems to be closer to what we believe to be the "essence" of poetry. We tend to view poetry as a genre that foregrounds authentic emotional expression and the individual, whereas epic poetry—poetry about dead heroes—seems antiquated in that it seems to glorify those who have made the ultimate sacrifice of their individuality to become part of an undifferentiated collective. Lyric poetry, by contrast, glorifies not the submersion of the individual within the collective, but precisely the conflict between individual desires and collective norms, as Adorno puts it: "The 'I' whose voice is heard in the lyric is an 'I' that defines and expresses itself as something opposed to the collective" (Adorno 1991: 39–40).

We are likely, therefore, to allow our own conception of what poetry really is to lead us to seek examples of lyric expression as a means of individual protest against an oppressive collective situation: we sympathize with the lyric voice of the lover partly because his or her plea is much broader; the political conflict between the individual and the collective is writ large in the lover's personal plight. As a result, the repertoire of Khevsur love poetry seems a bit disappointing, especially when compared, for example, with the neighboring Pshavs, whose poetry is much more often cast in the lyric mode and thus much more recognizable as love poetry.

Articulating Desire in Pshavian Lyric

Perhaps the most famous and most critically celebrated example of Pshavian lyric is the poem "Let me be turned into a silver cup," by the Pshavian poetess Khvaramze (who lived c. 1840–90), a poem that was first transcribed and printed in the nineteenth century, after her death, and has become so popular that she is now recognized as one of Georgia's first and finest female poets. Khvaramze's poetry all revolves around her own personal tragedy of unrequited love, returning again and again to her tragic inability to be near, to touch, her beloved. In this poem, Khvaramze fantasizes about being transformed into a series of objects that would allow her to become closer to her beloved. As Tamila Gogolauri comments, "each wish has as its justification and its only goal—proximity to the beloved" (Gogolauri 1996: 17). Georgian folk poetry frequently involves fantasies of transformation, most often into a bird, which would allow the lover to visit her beloved (and other poems by Khvaramze make use of this trope), but the first stanza of this poem focuses instead on her wish for transformation into a series of objects made of silver or gold (cited in Gogolauri 1996: 21–22):

vertskhlis tasadamts maktsia,	Let me be turned into a silver cup,
ro ghvinit agevsebodi,	That I would be filled with wine for you,
daperili mkna ts'itlada,	Let me be burnished redly,
shamsvamdi, shagergebodi,	You would drink me, it would befit you,
an mkna vertskhlis satite,	Or make me into a silver ring,
ro khelze chagedebodi;	That you would wear me on your hand,
ana mkna okros burtvai	Or make me into a golden ball
k'altashi chageshlebodi;	In your lap I would lie;
an vertskhlis pulad maktsia	Or let me be turned into silver money
jibeshi chageqrebodi!	I would collect in your pocket!

All of these things are objects that would bring her physically close to her lover, but they are also all made of gold or silver, precious metals of course, but also metals that are metaphorically, and perhaps cosmologically, associated with men: men are likened to "golden buttons" in the sacred esoteric "cross language" (jvart ena) used by "oracles" to give voice to the words of the gods; only men can drink from the silver cups kept in the sacred precincts of the shrine.

In the second stanza, she moves from objects that are made of gold or silver, which are associated with men both metaphorically and metonymically (they are all objects that physically touch the man's body), to a series of objects from everyday life that, unlike her, are allowed to touch him physically: a field to be cut by his scythe, a rose for him to smell, a silk shirt for him to wear and wear out:

an sheni namglis q'ana mkna,	Or make me a field for your sickle,
ro pkhaze shagech'rebodi;	That I might be cut on your blade;
ana mkna vardi q'oili,	Or make me a rose flower,
ro p'irze dageqrebodi;	That I might be strewn on your face;
ana mkna mois p'erangi,	Or make me a silken shirt,
ro gulze dagadnebodi!	That I might melt on your chest!

Finally, moving from metaphoric and metonymic masculinity to identity, from inanimate objects to animate, she wishes, as she does in other poems, simply to become a man, his brother, and then, more daringly, his lover:

an sheni dzma mkna mots'ile,	Or make me into your brother, by your side
arodes dageq'rebodi;	I would never abandon you;
an sheni nandauri mkna,	Or make me your lover,
guls javrad chagech'rebodi!	I would cut you painfully in the heart!
dzalian dats'ukhebuli	Filled with longing
gzazedamts shageqrebodi	Let me meet you on the road.

At the end of the poem, instead, she moves from fantastic transformations to a more potentially realizable fantasy: she wishes to encounter him by chance on the road, with no one else around.

Khvaramze's poem seems to be a more satisfying lyric expression of unrequited love than the Khevsur praise poems that erase the lyric subject, which probably explains its appeal to Georgian urban audiences, and perhaps also to you, the reader. Here we have a clear lyric expression of a set of individual desires that are so impossible to realize within a collective normative order that she is forced to imagine magical transformations into entities that could make her closer to her lover. Her desire is so strong that she expresses desire not only for the physically impossible, but also for the culturally impermissible: to encounter her lover alone on the road, she as a woman, he as a man.

The Erasure of Desire in Khevsur Love Poetry

From a Khevsur perspective, such an unrestricted lyric expression of individual desire as Khvaramze's, opposed at all points to the collective order, would be considered dangerous. The Khevsurs used the term desire (*survili*) to denote a particularly intense, uncontrolled, maddening, one-sided longing, which was almost like a dangerous form of sorcerous possession: "a young person (especially a girl) who has fallen into desire disturbs community traditions, loses any sense of proportion and the boundaries of self-control" (Gogoch'uri 1974: 106–7). For Khevsurs, desire was to be given limited expression and kept in check within the boundaries of "rules," for example the rules of lying down. Individual desire was to be balanced by other virtues of self-control, shame, and restraint, which preserved one's own autonomy and that of others.

A similar kind of self-control was displayed in poetry, where the expression of desire was restricted not just by obvious formal features like rhyme and meter, but also by the way in which desire, and even the lyric desiring subject, was itself *erased* from the poem. The female Khevsur poet not only erased her own identity as well as that of her addressee, except for a few hints (so that this dangerous desire was kept secret), but also phrased her desire not as an individual expression of emotion from her own perspective (the lyric mode) but rather in the form of praise for her lover from a generic, sociocentric perspective. Just as she established her lover overtly as having desirable masculine features of self-control, for example, she implicitly showed that she had corresponding feminine features (*namusi, morideba*) precisely by erasing herself.

ANONYMITY: ERASURE OF THE AUTHOR OF LOVE POETRY

Among the Khevsurs, girls were the active authors of love poetry, boys the passive objects, addressees, or audiences; desire was expressed for boys by girls, but at the same time as they composed love poetry, they actively erased themselves from their poems. It needs to be stressed, however, that anonymity was not characteristic of all Khevsur poetry; only certain kinds of poetry of blame or censure (*shairi*) and certain kinds of love poetry were anonymous.

In fact, Khevsurs frequently composed their names into their poems. There were many conventional ways of doing this. The beginnings of Khevsur poems frequently include a traditional address or invocation where the poet speaks to his or her instrument—the three-string lute called a *panduri*, the accordion, or another instrument. Like almost everything else in Khevsur life, instruments were gendered with respect to who could use them: anyone might use a *panduri*, but only women could play the accordion, so if an invocation is to a *panduri*, we might assume the author is male, but if it is to an accordion, the author is certainly female. Compare these two otherwise similar conventional invocations; the first author might be male or female, but the second is certainly female:

dauk'ar, chemo panduro,	Play, oh my *panduri*,
angelozivit qmiano!	Having a voice like an Angel!
	(Gogoch'uri 1974: 100)
idzaxe, chemo garmono,	Cry out, my accordion,
angelozivit qmisao!	With the voice of an angel!
	(Gogoch'uri 1974: 103)

The address to the instrument, which already indirectly indexes the gender of the poet, is also a place where sometimes poets identify themselves by name as well (Gogoch'uri 1974: 88–89):

dagik'ar, chemo panduro,	I play you, my *panduri*,
alq'ebma gaigha zhriali	Your strings make noise

| k'iden gamotkvams leksebsa | Gas'para Eristviani |
| gasp'ara eristviani | Again composes poems. |

If it occurs at the end, this section of the poem will sometimes imagine a speaker who asks the identity of the poet (Gogoch'uri 1974: 89):

| melekses tu ra ik'itkhavt, | If you ask who the poet is, |
| grankhais gamotkmulia, | It was composed by Grankhai. |

Love poetry, on the other hand, is the most typical example of Khevsur poetry that is anonymous by design (Gogoch'uri 1974: 121).

> ... [W]e can scarcely find one example in a love poem where a female author directly names herself. She always uses some sort of secret word (password) or a hint, which would only be understandable to her beloved. This is why the love poetry of women is almost completely anonymous. (Gogoch'uri 1974: 121)

Here is a fairly typical example of this kind of love poem (from 1915 or before). Both the opening and the closing identify the author, but only in the the most general terms ("a woman alone," "if someone asks who the poet is, it is a Khevsur woman far away"). The poet also makes veiled reference to the man she is praising, but again in the most indirect way imaginable ("one from Arkhot'i"). Other than this, the poem makes reference to the generic sadness of the author because of the separation, and engages in some very generic praise of the addressee:

samshabats gatenebada,	It is dawn on Tuesday,
martuai-or kalio.	I am a woman alone.
tkvens dushmans aisetai,	May your worst enemy
me gavatene ghameo.	Spend the night alone as I did.
chemi dzmobili mamgonda,	I remembered my dzmobili,
tsremli chamamdis tskhvareo.	A bitter tear fell.
veghartsagh vkhedav tvalita,	I can see you nowhere,
arts mamdis naubario.	Nor does any word of you come to me.
sada khar, arkhot'iano,	Where are you, one from Arkhot'i,
khutmet'is mtvare mtskhralio.	Fifteen full moons have passed.
sts'orpertan namusiano,	Restrained [namusiani] with your sts'orperis,
magt'k'ivis kali, zalio.	You worry about your womenfolk.
mak'etis saimedoo,	Loyal to kin,
dushmantan niaghvario!	Destroyer of enemies!

bevrjel ats'ite chachnuri,	Many times you have made your sword red,
aiskha siskhlis tsvario.	You have shed drops of blood.
melekses turas ik'itkhav,	If you ask who the poet is,
shorad qevsuris kalio.	It is a Khevsur woman far away.
	(Mak'alatia 1984: 108)

There were many reasons for this kind of anonymity. We have already seen that maintaining the secrecy of the *dzmobili* relationship was a central norm of the relationship. In addition, the genres of poetry that figured most in women's repertoire, *leksi* and *shairi* poetry, and particularly that thematic subgrouping called *sakalvazho* poetry ("poetry about girls and boys"), all dealt with contemporary life and living people and was often potentially highly consequential in pragmatic terms, particularly satirical or insulting *shairi* poems that could lead to insult and fights, which would be shameful. Such *shairi* poems, also called *saseno* poems (poems of reproach, rivalry, or insult, but we might translate literally as "poison poems"), which form the largest and most interesting portion of the Khevsur *sakalvazho* poetry corpus (we have seen a fair number already), had to be anonymous because they had potentially very powerful negative social consequences. Such poems typically kept both the identity of the author and the addressee anonymous, and they were often performed out of the limelight rather than openly in the *akhalukhali* (the gathering of young people), since their primary pragmatic purpose was to express bitter rivalry (*senva*, literally "poisoning") and start fights, which was shameful:

A fight frequently would follow *saseno* poems. If a boy offended a girl in some way with a poem or by saying something else, young men close to her would not tolerate this and the matter could end in a fight with short swords. Out of fear of this women frequently hid their annoyance, they would not disclose the fact to their male friends and relatives. Often such an enmity resulted, that one clan would be incited against another clan over women. This was very shameful. They would reproach her: "Because of your tongue such an event happened, that a clan was incited against another clan and people have cut one another." In spite of this, boys and girls would not let it rest and would tell each other *saseno* poems on the sly. When they would compose [such a] poem, they would conceal their own identity, and often the identity of the poet to whom their own poem was a reply was also completely unknown, and even the speaker could not figure out [whom they were replying to], so they too would compose their reply poem in such a way that [showed] they did not know whom they were talking about. *Saseno* poems said about women annoyed all the women, if they recited it in an *akhalukhali. Saseno* poems by women also annoyed all the boys, and they too would without fail reply with a *saseno* poem. (A. Ochiauri 1980: 30)

Among the Pshavians, and even more so among the Khevsurs, public performance of poetry (*leksoba*) was considered shameful for women, but women were free to compose poetry and recite it, just not "publicly"(Gogolauri 1996: 5–8). Pshav and Khevsur women composed poetry freely and performed it in limited public events; nevertheless, such poetry circulated widely but at the same time somewhat anonymously. Little is known of the authors and their addressees (Gogolauri 1996: 6; Gogoch'uri 1974: 94), except in those cases where a woman reclaimed her anonymous poetry as she grew older. In the late nineteenth century Grigol Apshinashvili wrote in the Georgian newspaper *Iveria* about Pshavians (among whom men as well as women composed love poetry, unlike the Khevsurs):

> Women take part in the composition of *leksi* and *shairi* poetry too, but not as openly as men, reciting poetry publicly like a man is very shameful for a woman in Pshavi. While a woman is young, she composes poems secretly, when she gets old, then she no longer is ashamed as much and often teaches poems she herself has composed to young girls and boys. (Cited in Gogolauri 1996: 5)

This need for secrecy, more extreme among the Khevsurs than the Pshavs, and the modesty that it enacts, provides a simpler explanation for the seeming absence of love poetry from the Khevsur corpus collected by Shanidze. As Gogoch'uri (1974: 107–8) points out, the very fact that love poetry was so secretive and strongly gendered as *exclusively* part of the female repertoire would explain why Shanidze, an outsider male, would have had trouble collecting it directly from female informants: it is very unlikely that Khevsur women would have sat down with a male stranger and agreed to recite their love poetry to him (Gogoch'uri 1974: 108). The same problem does not exist for Pshavian love poetry, which can be recited by men and women alike. The apparent disappearance of love poetry from the Khevsur repertoire is actually a by-product of the female author disappearing from the limelight of public performance.

REPLACING INDIVIDUAL DESIRE WITH
DESIRABILITY IN PRAISE POETRY

Khevsur love poetry is essentially a branch of praise poetry. In indigenous terms, all Khevsur poetry was classified in terms of its function: poetry of praise (*keba*) or poetry of blame, censure, insult, satire, scorn, or derision (*senva* "bitter rivalry; poison", adjective *saseno*). The dead could only be praised, while the living could either be praised or blamed. Certain genres, for example epic or heroic "songs" (*simghere*) that recalled the exploits of "good servants" who died for the community, the world of predecessors, only had the function of praise. Other poetic genres such as the *leksi* and *shairi* (*leksi-shairi*) were by contrast addressed to the living, the everyday world of contemporaries. *Leksi* can be used for praise or censure, while *shairi* are more strongly associated with blame. For those recently dead there was both poetry of praise and poetry of lament, while those long dead were either praised or forgotten entirely:

> Of old the Khevsurs had rules such as the following: they would say poems
> to living warriors and praise them, they would recall the dead with eulogies
> and give them respect. In this way they would give cheer to the young, who
> occupied themselves with protecting their rules. (A. Ochiauri 2005: 309)

From a pragmatic perspective, all Khevsur poetry was ultimately addressed to the public persona, the "name" (*sakheli*) of an individual: making or breaking a person's name. In the case of heroic poetry, living men, hearing of the fame of these dead men, reflected on their own lives and thought, "I wish I could make such a name and then die. No one will know of my death and they will always remember such people with names" (A. Ochiauri 2005: 66). The primary function of heroic "songs" was "making a name" (*sakhelis kna* [Gogoch'uri 1974: 192–93]), that is, creating fame for a departed hero, establishing that man's life as a model for imitation by the living. By contrast, poems of blame, satire, and censure (*shairi, senva, saseno*) could destroy the name of living persons, and they were feared for that reason (Gogoch'uri 1974: 23–25). A bad deed, publicized by "becoming a *shairi*" (*shairis gakhdoma*), had powerful effects on the name of the person who was the subject (Gogoch'uri 1974: 24). We have seen already, and will see again, examples of the use of poetry to publicize offenses against the normative order in romance.

Another way in which the Khevsur girl "disappears" from her love poetry is the way she frames the love poem as a praise poem. Poetry that expresses the love of a girl for a boy takes the form of praise poetry, rather than the lyric expression of the author's emotions: "the older love poetry of Khevsur women is mostly praise, rather than the lyrical expression of experiences, the emotional universe of the woman in love is not expressed" (Gogoch'uri 1974: 120). In the same way that a Khevsur girl hid her individual identity by composing anonymous poetry, as discussed above, she also erased her lyric subject position, praising her lover not from the egocentric perspective of her own "emotional universe," but instead from a much more sociocentric perspective. She was concerned with how he embodied the attributes of a good servant (*k'ai q'ma*), the way he was likeable or praiseworthy (*dghiani*) in general. For example, in the poem adduced immediately above ("It is dawn on Tuesday"), we find that he is restrained (*namusiani*) with his lovers, loyal to his friends and relatives, a terror to his enemies, brave in battle. In other such poems—after a conventional opening address to the instrument, here an accordion (an instrument played only by women, which indexes that the poet is a woman)—we also find praise not only of personal virtues of the lover, but very often, for example, we find praise for his dress and accoutrements, including his horse and sword:

abechav, chemo garmono,	My poor dear accordion,
naoch'istavad tsvriani,	All your folds are wet,
dushmani[s] k'arebze malaghebs	The thunder of hooves of my *dzmobili's* horse
dzmobilis tskhenis dgriali.	At the doors of his enemies emboldens me.
tskhen unda gq'vandes, dzmobilo,	You should have a horse, oh *dzmobili*,
iorgha, gulit mqriani,	A swift-footed palfrey,
zed edgas k'azmulobai	On it should be horse tack [saddle, reins, bridle etc.]
ch'reli, sru nasevdiani.	Of many colours, covered with engravings and inlays ["nielloed"].
	[...]
ts'elze gbav "kist'iseuli"	At your waist hangs "Kistiseuli" ["The Kistian style one"—the name of his short sword]
ch'reli, su nasevdiani,	Of many colours, covered with engravings and inlays,
nalesi zumparazeda,	Sharpened on the sharpening stone
samsalasavit pkhiani.	Extremely sharp.
okros araq'chi naghebi	Decorated with gold leaf,
khanjari nasevdiani,	An engraved and inlaid short sword,
oms egre mogats'adinebs,	Makes you thirst for war,
mtvrals rom pshaurad ghriali.	Just as bellowing like a Pshavian makes a drunk thirsty.
raqel k'argia vazhk'atsi,	What a good lad,
dushmaniani, mt'riani,	With many enemies,
khan gaigonos kebai,	Sometimes let him hear praise,
khan sit'q'va ginebiani.	Sometimes words of cursing.

(Mak'alatia 1984: 159)

In such poems the girl gives a one-sided expression of her love, not by foregrounding her individual feelings for her lover, but by praising him in much the same way that heroic poems praise dead men as ideal models or paragons of masculinity: we are more likely to hear about the terror of their enemies than the love of their lovers. In this way, girls' poetry about boys largely resolves itself into classifying boys as "good servants," that is, objects of praise, or "bad servants," that is, objects of derision: as ideal masculine figures interested in battle or effeminate figures interested in women:

k'ai q'ma q'malsa chakhedavs,	A good serf looks at his sword and says,
"net'ar, gamich'ris tu ara?"	"I wonder, will you cut for me, or not?"
tsudai—kalis ubes:	A bad one—to a woman's bosom:
"net'ar, shamikhvevs tu ara?"	"I wonder, will you embrace me, or not?"
	(Shanidze 1931: 013)

Here the opposition between masculine "heroic" or "epic" poetry and feminine "love poetry" seems to break down, as the two forms converge in the treatment of their male object. Women especially praise living men in "love poetry," and men praise dead heroes in "heroic poetry," true. But what do women find praiseworthy in their lovers? Khevsur women, in general, are attracted to living men who are *dghiani*, who have the same virtues or attributes as dead "good servants," men who are heroic, gallant, brave, attractive, self-controlled, well-dressed, and indifferent to girls. Since a valiant "good servant" will also have a worthy steed, such poems often lavish praise on horses as well as men. Men, too, in the very act of seeming indifferent to women, concerning themselves with dueling; war; and other heroic, public matters, made themselves attractive (*dghiani*) in the eyes of women. Indeed, men deliberately sought out duels ("good servant" behavior), not merely *because of* matters of love (jealousy, betrayal), but also *to* attract a lover ("bad servant" behavior) (Baliauri 1991: 17). Khevsur love seems as one-sided as Khevsur love poetry, but such an assumption would seriously underestimate the role that matters of romance played for men.

The folklorist Shanidze explained the difference in Khevsur and Pshavian poetic repertoires by reference to their innate temperaments: the Khevsurs expressed their warlike temperaments in their preference for epic poetry, while the Pshavians expressed their relatively lighthearted nature in love poetry. But both Khevsurs and Pshavs have love poetry; one might say that the Pshavian love poetry is more obviously lyric, in that it directly expresses the author's desire (*survili*), while Khevsur poetry is invisibly lyric, since it expresses the author's self-restraint (*namusi*) by erasing that desire. Thus, because of the way the conventions of love poetry force the identity and the concrete desire (*survili*) of the female author to be erased and elided into the generic desirability of the male object of that love, Khevsur love poetry becomes invisible as such, and comes to resemble praise poetry. Whereas a Pshavian love poem, such as that of Khvaramze, represents the speaking subject's egocentric *desire* directly, a typical Khevsur love poem instead praises the way that the object is sociocentrically *desirable* (*dghiani*). Thus, love poetry itself disappears invisibly into a large corpus of praise poetry directed at dead heroes, just as male approaches to romance, their effort to be *dghiani*, makes them imitate dead heroes, behave in the manner of the "good servant," rather than actively seek out lovers, in the manner of the "bad servant." Poetic expression and sexual expression show the same tensions between desire (*survili*) and self-restraint (*namusi*). However, the corpus of anonymous "boy and girl" (*sakalvazho*) poetry also includes "*shairi* poems" of censure, which makes up the larger and more interesting part to read, a kind of poetry that plays a crucial role in romantic scandals, to which I turn in the next chapter.

5

DEMONS, DANGER, AND DESIRE: THE "ARAGVIAN" SEXUAL REVOLUTION

THE KHEVSUR IDEOLOGY of sexuality represented desire as a dangerous, almost magical force that was destructive both for individuals and for collective norms. Such destructive desire was also strongly associated with women. In the first chapter we saw that Khevsurs located desire within a cosmological framework of myth: desire itself was not created by God, but came to be the moment God created both boys and girls, who desired each other but had no way to express this desire; they could only pine for each other, so they perished from desire. God then weakened this strictly (hetero) sexual desire by transferring it from sexual others to other kinds of desire: desire for things such as drinking horns, tobacco, and clothing. He also instituted the practice of *sts'orproba* and its rules to give heterosexual desire a delimited means of expression. The association of destructive desire with femininity also probably referenced this cosmological framework: Khevsur cosmology was sharply dualistic, divided according to gender; all of creation was created either by a masculine God (or children of god) or a feminine Devil (or demons). Since the normative, collective order was overseen by male shrine attendants and meetings of the all-male *jari*, and was instituted by masculine divinities, it is easy to see how anything that was disruptive of this order, for example individual sexual desires, would be associated with feminine demons and spirits.

A good example of this association of desire with femininity comes from another portion of Khevsur cosmology: demonology. It is common in many societies to create imaginary demonic or monstrous others who display equally monstrous sexualities that are somehow an inversion of the normal human condition of sexual desire. Western vampires, for example, display a peculiar sexuality whereby drinking blood takes on an erotic value paralleling sex between humans. In other regions of Georgia there is a female goblin called an *ali*, who seduces and destroys young men; if captured and domesticated by cutting her wild tousled hair and trimming her fingernails, she can become an unwilling wife who always seeks her lost hair and nails like a hidden treasure. If she finds them, she becomes free and exacts a terrible revenge for her marital abduction. This spirit seems to be exploring, on the imaginary plane, anxieties about the dangers inherent in the common practice of marital abduction (Manning, 2014b).

For the Khevsurs, the demonic sexual other *par excellence* was the *dobili* ("sworn sister") (see also Manning 2014a). Every male shrine god (there are only male gods) had a set of female demonic consorts, his "sworn sisters." Male shrine gods did not marry their consorts, since marriage was for humans alone; they instead engaged in something very like *sts'orproba* with these beautiful female demons. These demons, who had their own special shrines, were placated by humans with sacrifices that were in every way the inverse of those used for male divinities: instead of sheep, goats were sacrificed (A. Ochiauri 2005: 81), and instead of silver cups, clay cups were used (A. Ochiauri 2005: 373). These demonic powers could take the form of small children, beautiful or old women, as well as monstrous or animal forms (snakes, pigs, birds, or in one case a "mist-colored horse"). They typically came out to "play" at dawn and dusk (A. Ochiauri 2005: 81, 191, 233, 336).

These creatures were said to be particularly dangerous for women and children, perhaps expressing indirectly the rivalry between real human *dzmobilis* and the future spouse of their lover. With men, however, like the *ali* of the plains, they engaged in all manner of licentious sexual behavior that was diametrically opposed to all other sexual practices: they were promiscuous (allowed in *sts'orproba*, but not marriage); they always engaged in sexual intercourse (allowed in marriage, not so much in *sts'orproba*); lying down with a *dobili*, even in a dream, made a man ritually impure (as in marriage but not with *sts'orproba* [Baliauri 1991: 63]); they were completely fecund, every sexual act producing children (children are allowed in marriage, forbidden in *sts'orproba*), but they produced only more beings who were like or worse than themselves, and consequently, they destroyed their own young (Mak'alatia 1984: 236–37).

As in most cultures, Khevsur cultural identity—the cultural sense of self—was defined at its boundaries, by reference to *alterity* or "otherness," that is, to real or imagined *others* who did not share their customs and norms. Khevsurs explored many of their anxieties about desire by reference to cosmological origins in myth and by imagining monstrous feminine others whose insatiable sexualities were the inversions of normative human sexuality. This is a kind of extreme cosmological alterity. But otherness was also explored on the historical, human plane, where some sort of collective norm was violated because of individual desires; these events also produced historical narratives of scandal and drama which, like myths and monsters, indicated the dangers of desire to the collective order.

Even as they told myths that located their norms within a divine cosmology that included demonic others, Khevsurs were also aware that their sexual practices and other norms were not widely shared by nearby human others. The Khevsurs were surrounded by other peoples: the Chechens and Ingush to the north, the Tush and Kisti to the east, the Mokhevians to the west, and the Pshavians who dwelled in the lower parts of the river valleys to the south. Of all these groups, only the Pshavians had anything like the sexual customs of the Khevsurs, and the Pshavians were the only others with whom the Khevsurs were likely to intermarry. Even so, the Khevsurs imagined the Pshavian sexual practices of *ts'ats'loba*, which were for the most part very similar to their own *sts'orproba*, to be in many ways familiar, and yet at the same time strange, inversions of their own practices.

Although the Pshavians were imagined as being "the opposite" of Khevsurs in certain ways, the Khevsur imagination of absolute sexual alterity on the human plane was summed up instead in the figure of the Russian. All local groups that did not share the norms of the Khevsurs could be characterized by the term *kochriani*, which meant, in everyday language, "those who do not have the customs of the Khevsurs"; in the divine language (*jvart ena* "the language of crosses") that was used, for example, by the spirit mediums called *kadagi* ("oracle") in order to give voice to the gods, this same term simply meant "Russian." At the time these sexual practices were still current, Khevsurs were under the rule of the Russian empire or, later, the Soviet Union, in which the dominant population was Russian. As a people living in strongholds high in the mountains, Khevsurs initially experienced Russian rule as an occasional incursion into their traditional life, and in general most customs like marriage were practiced according to traditional law. As Russian rule moved from occasional encounters to a continuous presence in everyday life, however, Russian "law" (*k'anoni*) became an external force opposed to the "rules" (*ts'esi*) that defined the Khevsurs. Russian law included religious and civil regulations of customs pertaining to sexuality, in particular marriage.

In addition to this external set of norms imposed by force, summed up with concepts of "Russian rule" and "Russian law," Khevsurs imagined and encountered individual Russians as beings exemplifying a kind of almost nonhuman sexuality, essentially embodying a sexual shamelessness equivalent to dogs. It is probably significant that the most common word for "prostitute" among the Khevsurs was the Russian borrowing *mat'ushk'a* (literally "little mother, mama" in Russian, where the term had no such negative meanings or connotations). Russian rule would eventually turn Khevsurs into Russians, it was thought, so to talk about Russian rule was to talk about the impending doom of Khevsur rules and Khevsur communal identity, and to compare Khevsurs to Russians was to compare them to whores, dogs, creatures with no sense of honor or shame (*namusi*), who lacked any concern for name or fame (*sakheli*) or shame (*sirtskhvili*). Particularly in the sphere of desire, violations of the rules of the Khevsurs, whatever their source, represented a potential threat to Khevsur identity. By not containing their desires as they should, Khevsurs would lose their identity and become others, "become Russians."

Even within the Khevsur community the Khevsurs were also aware that their own norms showed some internal variation in this area, as in many other things. The Khevsurs were a *very* small group of people, numbering a handful of thousands, living on either side of the main range of the Caucasus mountains, which divided their village communes (*temi*: groups of villages usually occupying a single valley) into two broad groups: those that lived on "this side" (*piraket*) of the Caucasus (the southern flanks, closer to the plains of Georgia adjoining Pshavi, mostly in tributaries of the Aragvi basin, including Khakhmati), and those that lived on "the other side of the mountains" (*mtis iket*), further from Pshavi and the plains of Georgia, on the borders of Chechnya (Figure 5.1). According to Baliauri, the Khevsurs who lived beyond the mountains (e.g., the district containing Shat'ili) accepted that the norms of those who lived on "this side" were always correct. If there was a conflict that could not be resolved, or where the rules were unclear, in "far" transalpine Khevsureti, they always sent emissaries to "near" cisalpine Khevsureti to ascertain what the authoritative rules and norms were, whereas the Khevsurs who lived on "this side of the mountains" had no interest in anyone else's norms because they believed their own practices were authoritative and that they were the best conservators of tradition (Baliauri 1991: 157).

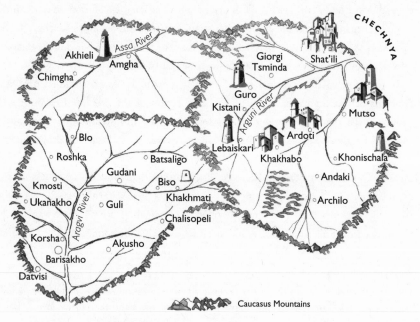

FIGURE 5.1: Detailed map of the villages and districts (*temi*) of Khevsureti. Courtesy of Lisa Gronseth.

As we have seen, individual sporadic violations of the norms of sexuality occurred here and there, and, especially when marriage was also involved, these violations were a source of a particular kind of historical narrative of scandal, producing ephemeral arguments and conversations, gossip, and poetry of censure (*shairi*). Here I am interested primarily in more concerted challenges to the normative order of sexuality, where whole generations of Khevsur boys, and in particular girls, rose to challenge the normative order of sexuality, advocating both for more permissive practices of *sts'orproba* and also more permissive rules of marriage that would allow sexual partners of *sts'orporba* to marry one another based on mutual desire rather than marriage by compulsion or force to strangers.

Around the time of the beginning of the First World War (in which the Khevsurs participated as soldiers, as subjects of the Russian empire against Germany), right before the Russian Revolution (1917), two major revolutionary challenges emerged to question the traditional order of *sts'orproba* and marriage. From around 1913–15, young people in a small corner of Khevsureti began to experiment with the form of lying down in *sts'orproba*, which led to a scandal across Khevsureti. This was called "Aragvian (*araguli*) *sts'orproba*" because it was innovated by the young people of the Aragvi region, so named because it consists of a set of villages in "near" Khevsureti closest to Pshavi, at the headwaters of the Aragvi river that flows into Pshavi; the residents of which area are called "Aragvians" (*Aragvelebi*) (Baliauri 1991: 156–73).

Around the same time (1914–17) in the same general region, young women announced, often by means of poetry, that they had no intention of marrying strangers by compulsion, and would henceforth only marry those they themselves desired, usually their *dzmobilis*. This particular innovation was in part clearly related to the former change in sexual practices, but it was also occasioned by the introduction of Russian law, and specifically marriage law and Orthodox Church marriage, neither of which corresponds to Khevsur customary law or religion. Particularly important was the fact that the Russian marriage law and religious practice combined to make divorce a much more difficult and shameful affair; for Khevsur women in particular, this meant that they would not be able to escape an undesirable husband as they had in the past, simply by returning home or living with their relatives. Marriage to strangers in the face of such a strict marriage law became more ominous and potentially dangerous (Baliauri 1991: 34–40).

It is surely no coincidence that these two events—a revolutionary new form of sexual practice and an equally revolutionary demand to choose marriage partners—occurred around the same historical period. This was also the time when our two main Khevsur ethnographers (Natela Baliauri and Aleksi Ochiauri) themselves violated the rules of marriage and became exiles from their own communities (1914). To understand how a change in the customs of lying down was related to a change in marriage, we first need to understand the external problem of Russian law in relation to Khevsur customs of marriage. We also need to understand the specific changes in *sts'orproba*, and how these related to and affected marriage.

Russian Marriage

Russian colonial administrators and priests considered Khevsurs to be lapsed members of the Orthodox Christian faith, which was the Russian state religion, and hence sought to "restore" them to Orthodoxy. Khevsur marriage ritual did not involve Orthodox church weddings ("writing the cross" before a Orthodox priest), and Khevsurs found the Orthodox ritual to be shameful. The change in ritual during this time meant endless complications: in particular, as discussed above, Khevsurs found that Russian marriage laws made divorce, which had hitherto been relatively easy for either a boy or a girl, much more onerous, shameful, and difficult. Previously, although the boy and the girl who would be married were often virtual strangers, they could also divorce easily; the woman could return to her relatives and live with them (though she would likely not be able to remarry). However, after the change, boys and girls became much more interested in finding out more about their potential marriage partner, because leaving them would become more difficult.

The problem was that the pool of potential marriage partners, according to Khevsur rules, could not include anyone who was already well known to one: excluded were people of the same clan or village, and especially anyone with whom one was acquainted sexually, that is, a *sts'orperi*, or even worse a *dzmobili*. To marry one's erstwhile sexual partner would change how one viewed that person, and how one viewed *sts'orproba* itself: the pair would no longer be classified as virtual siblings, and hence this was regarded as a sign of sexual depravity. After the girls of near Khevsureti announced (presumably through poems as well as face to face) that they would no longer "marry by compulsion" (*dzalit*), this meant that the ideal marriage partner could now be someone one already knew, including people of the same surname, people from the same village or village commune, and especially one's existing lovers (*sts'orperis, dzmobilis*). As we have seen, the fantasy of a marriage to one's existing romantic partner had occurred before, but it was an idle fantasy, or worse, something that could lead to exile or suicide if the partners actually acted on this fantasy and eloped; now it became a central demand occasioned by the changes in Russian marriage law. And boys and girls did, indeed, begin to elope with their lovers (including our main ethnographers of Khevsur romance!), producing immense tensions, exiles, and even the death of one or the other of the lovers. Since marriage relations typically formed connections with people from outside one's own area (exogamy), it was comparatively cost-free to alienate people who were already strangers, but the same move could now create great conflicts within individual communities and villages.

It was actually comparatively easy to dissolve a proposed marriage partnership with a stranger to make way for a marriage partner one actually desired. (*Elchis* often played a key role in this activity, too.) The strategems could be as simple as pretending to have a dreadful illness, or claiming that the shrine divinities themselves opposed the marriage. If this failed to dissuade the potential spouse, a girl might steal off to hide somewhere, in the woods, with a distant relative. Her relatives would search for her, thinking perhaps she had killed herself or had fallen off a cliff into the water and drowned. She would find a way to inform them that she was not dead, but that if they didn't let her have her way, she would indeed kill herself: if her arranged marriage had not proceeded too far, then she was now free to marry someone else (Baliauri 1991: 35).

The Aragvian Way of Love

At around the same time, the sexual practices of *sts'orproba* also began to change, beginning in a small area of near Khevsureti, specifically the Aragvi region, which forms the only passage from Khevsureti to Pshavi, and spreading from there. Since *sts'orproba* was a relationship that took place not only within a village, but also between villages and communities while visiting, this new form of sexual practice soon spread, as lovers from different communities encountered the new practice and either adopted it themselves and taught it to their lovers, or rejected it, at the same time rejecting their erstwhile lover. And as the practice spread, word of the practice spread too, through gossip and poetry, producing a general sense of scandal and conflict within and between different communities.

What were the "Aragvian rules" of *sts'orproba*? Some things remained the same, including the fact that the girl went to the boy at night, initially with the mediation of the *elchi*. In addition, as elsewhere in Khevsureti, there was an absolute absence of force or compulsion, particularly of the girl by the boy; the girl remained absolutely free (Baliauri 1991: 158). No one would be compelled to adopt these new rules, so if they became familiar with them, they would be seen as having desired to do so.

The differences lay primarily in the rules of what was allowed in "lying down." As we have seen before, the Khevsur "rules" of lying down were very specific about exactly how the bodies were to be arranged with respect to one another, exactly who could touch whom where, and so on. In Aragvian lying down, these rules were relaxed, possibly even dispensed with. The girl allowed the boy to touch her wherever he wished, and she herself would open his shirt and kiss him on the neck and chest. The boy, if the girl allowed, could kiss her on the face and neck, place his head on her chest, open her *paragi* (beaded collar) and embrace her in this way. Absolutely no attention was paid to the placement of the lower body, and they could lie together however they liked, embracing each other with their whole bodies (Baliauri 1991: 158). Sometimes the girl would even lie *on top* of the boy, which was sometimes singled out as being particularly scandalous. Other changes were brought in too. In the relationship between *dzmobilis*, for example, the use of affectionate "pet names" for one's lover became common, a practice that for some reason other Khevsurs found to be particularly strange and newsworthy (Baliauri 1991: 160).

Of course, one could not lie down with just anyone at any time in this way. Just as there were variations in the rules of how lying down was arranged and what could be done, depending on factors such as kinship distance, relative acquaintance, and whether it was "out of respect" or "out of desire," so Aragvian rules could be used only with certain others. Initially, it would happen only within the community with one's existing lovers, if they were of like mind, and if they were not, even proposing it often ended the relationship entirely. One could not engage in this new style of lying down with real kin, or with potential affines (marital kin, as when one visits one's future spouse and is laid down with his or her relatives). Precisely those people with whom one lay down "without desire," that is, siblings and future in-laws, were banned. Clearly, Aragvian rules emphasized and maximized "lying down" as an expression of erotic desire, and were appropriate only for those relations where such desire was in general felt to be appropriate.

So what was so scandalous about Aragvian *sts'orproba*? Aragvian rules maximized the linkage of lying down with sexual desire. Since the rules of *sts'orporba* were designed to give *limited* expression to desire, this change produced a sense of lack of self-control, and the accusation of depravity became possible. Girls might censure other girls who followed these practices as follows (Baliauri 1991: 159):

> "You whore! I am not disgraced and shamed like you, am I? Your and my womanhood are not of the same kind, you who lack name and shame! Men know me, *sts'orperis* do not laugh at me in their heart like they do you!"

To which the girl who follows these practices might reply with irony, defending her autonomy against these voicings of communal norms:

> "Why, you are a good girl, aren't you? No one is asking you about my affairs, little sister. Do you really think it bothers me what you think, you poor thing? Your talk and the barking of a dog are all the same to me."

But the problem went further than simple accusations of depravity, which, as we will see, were easily and often disputed, since the new rules amounted to little more than a relaxation of some of the old rules. More significantly, when one adopted these new rules, one could no longer proceed with the fiction that *sts'orproba* and *dzmobiloba* was really just some sort of sibling relationship. The two practices became more and more an unambiguous expression of eroticism, which was vaguely linked with "depravity" but which moreover directly gave a lie to the idea that the lovers "look on each other like brother and sister." If boys and girls looked on each other with this kind of desire, then the rules of their relations could no longer proceed under the assumption that their meetings were purely siblinglike: desire became potentially consequential (leading to marriage, for example), and the fictional magic circle of sociable sexuality could therefore collapse.

This could have pervasive effects on the rest of social life, particular the freedom and autonomy of girls. Since the general freedom of girls to move about as they wished in Khevsureti was predicated on the imputation of generally siblinglike innocence with respect to her own desires and the desires of others, the existence of a new set of genres of expressing sexual desires more directly meant that not everyone was equally trustworthy or self-controlled. Such a situation, it was felt, would have the negative consequence of disrupting the freedom and autonomy of movement that characterized girls, and boys too. Just as a family would restrict the movement of a girl from the house if she had many suitors who might marry her by abduction—with or without her implied consent, marital abduction could be equivalent to what we would call rape, kidnapping, or simply elopement—so too would they do so for more general reasons. As word of this new practice became widespread, communities often became conflicted on the issue, often split between generations or households, and families would begin to restrict the movements of their girls. To explain these restrictions, they would often invoke the stereotyped figure of the Russians and Russian rule to explain her new loss of autonomy:

> They [parents and brothers] would say to the girl: "Now such a time has come upon Khevsureti that, even boys are not allowed to go out anywhere, let alone girls. The Khesvurs have turned into Russians, who can be trusted? These days boys and girls have become Russians. Those alive today are mingled together like goats and she-goats, they have lost all sense of name [*sakheli*] and shame [*sirtskhvili*]." (Baliauri 1991: 159)

If indigenous accounts saw the main negative result of these practices as being a general increase in Russian-style depravity, they also emphasized that the principal consequence of such depravity would be that the girls could lose their freedom and autonomy because of the lack of trust in the self-control of others that would result.

The second negative consequence was that this new form of desire would lead to the desire to marry whomever one wanted, and specifically one's existing lover. As a result, this same period was characterized by a general disruption of proposed marriage partnerships by *dzmobili* relations, as *dzmobilis* became rivals of marriage partners in a new way, namely as potential, if scandalous, marriage partners themselves. This jeopardized the way in which these two relations were kept apart, and romance thus became no longer sociable, something pursued for its own sake, but consequential, a prelude to marriage. When one couple eloped, for example, in the period where these new practices of lying down became connected to new ideas about marriage partners, the older generation again blamed the changes on the advent of Russian law and Russian mores:

> According to others, however, although they [the couple that eloped] were not related, it was all the same: the rules of Khevsureti [*khevsuretis ts'esi*] was being destroyed by [Russian] law [*k'anonit*], which no one approved of. The people were outraged anyway. They heard poems composed by women, saying that "we will get married to people even from our own clan [*gvari*, surname] and whoever we ourselves want." The old people blamed this matter on the Russians and even in laments they bewailed the fact that they had fallen into the epoch of the Russians, that Khevsureti was ruined, girls and boys were ruined, Russian ways have come among us, girls sleep with boys shamelessly and then intend to marry them. They lie to the people saying "we are *dzmobilis* and how could we get married?," girls have become sluts, and so on. (Baliauri 1991: 42)

Thus, according to the traditionalist argument, this was all going to lead to a complete collapse of Khevsur identity and norms (virtues of self-control, shame, etc.), so that everyone would become shameless Russians. Emancipating desire, by combining erotic desire with choice of marriage partner, could lead not only to the eradication of *sts'orproba* in general (Baliauri 1991: 160), but also to the loss of autonomy and freedom of women in particular. The general freedom and autonomy of men and especially women to come and go and do as they pleased hung in a precarious and paradoxical balance: if the young people did as they pleased (sexual autonomy), then they would lose their more general freedom and autonomy. The virtues of Khevsur women—that they were bold, daring, proud, free, autonomous, and willful—would be lost. Khevsur women would become like Russians ("sluts, whores"), and as a consequence they would end up like Georgian women of the plains, shut into their houses with restricted mobility.

The entire conflict, then, turned on different interpretations of autonomy and freedom. As we will see in the case studies of these scandals, Khevsur girls in particular presented their cases always in terms of these same virtues and ideals of freedom and autonomy, too. Conversations about these new norms therefore resulted in a kind of antinomy, an unresolvable contradiction between two arguments that are both equally rational, because both sides proceeded largely by championing a different interpretation of the same basic Khevsur ideals of autonomy and freedom. Even if some interpretations saw these new rules as being evidence of depravity (lack of shame and self-control) or Russian domination (loss of Khevsur freedom), which amounts to the same thing, the arguments that Baliauri has her nonfictional characters voice typically explore an internal contradiction and a deep ambivalence between desire and self-restraint within the norms and ideals of Khevsur culture and notions of person, rather than external contradictions between Russian and Khevsur norms (an argument, usually easily dismissed, that the Aragvian norms directly represented in themselves a "Russian" form of fornication).

Baliauri presents cases showing the consequences of the spread of this form of relationship across Khevsureti. Each revolves around a conflict between individual desire and communal norms, much like a Greek drama with individual hero and communal chorus. Some of these antiheroes, followers of new practices, were boys and others were girls, some involve hearsay or even imagined conversations linked to events, others involve exchanges of satirical *shairi* poetry, but all are stories built around real historical events with real historical individuals. But these antiheroes are no straw men or straw women, nor are they simply villains. We have no reason to believe they were other than real historical persons, but lest their arguments be dismissed on the basis of moral failings, the characters are idealized: the women are beautiful, proud, free, and hard-working, the men gallant and attractive; they are not in themselves bad people, but they always meet their exclusion by the community with defiant proclamations of their own autonomy, countering the derision and condemnation they receive with real arguments that make sense in the same terms that the arguments mustered against them do.

KHEVSUR GIRLS' LOVE STORIES: THREE CASE STUDIES

Mariemi's Story

The story of Mariemi, a girl from Datvisi, one of the centers of the Aragvian innovations, begins in a typical way: Mariemi was a very pretty, bold, and happy girl, who at the same time was a follower of the new Aragvian rules of lying down. Everyone loved her, many men wanted to marry her, but the moment gossip spread about her that she lay down with boys in the Aragvian style, she was shunned by these suitors, except for the local boys who themselves engaged in this practice. Mariemi paid no attention to the gossip spread about her. In addition, she cast off her existing future husband

and betrothed herself to another boy who was from both her same clan and her same village (a straightforward violation of the marriage rules of exogamy). Her brother and male cousins did not interfere with her lying down with boys in this way, since they themselves lay down in the Aragvian style; the opposition came instead from her sisters and female cousins. Her sisters no longer spoke to her and demanded that her parents eject her from the house (Baliauri 1991: 160). While they were making this request, Mariemi played the *panduri* or the accordion and recited poems. She was the oldest of her siblings and beloved of her parents, so her parents refused the request of her sisters, on the grounds that she was not actually engaging in depravity.

But other relatives intervened as these rumors spread from village to village, in particular an elderly aunt from the father's side, who heard the rumors and strongly opposed her niece's behavior. She came to her brother's house, and began to speak to Mariemi's parents with words of bitter reproach and warning, advising them to marry her off to her existing husband before something shameful happened: "What this girl is doing is nothing Christian. We also were girls once, we also had *sts'orperis*, we boys and girls lay down and we got up together, but this is not the rule, that a girl lie down on top of a boy" (Baliauri 1991: 161). Mariemi's father paid no attention to his sister's warnings, and they continued to fight. Mariemi looked upon this behavior of her relatives, the cursing and abuse directed at her, said nothing and laughed, and when her aunt had calmed down and become bored with the topic, Mariemi got up and reached for her brother's short sword, which was hanging high on the wall, and whacked her aunt in the face with the sheathed flat of the blade. Her mother, shivering from fear, fell on the girl to hold her back, but Mariemi managed to get in a few more whacks anyway. The aunt managed to flee, but this obviously created a rift between the relatives.

A cousin came to intervene and remonstrated with her for the shameful act of beating old women with swords: "First, how are waving short swords around a woman's affair, and secondly waving them at old women? . . . Are you crazy? Waving a short sword about is shameful, you are a girl, aren't you? You aren't a boy, are you, that you take up a sword?" Mariemi laughed at their fear and at her cousin's words and told them "with a smile, but still with an angry intonation" (Baliauri 1991: 161):

> What are you saying, my little brother, what? That my father's sister reviled and rebuked me pointlessly and with hearsay, from such a conversation not only a person, but even a rock would split open! [. . .] Who asked them [referring to her kin] for their opinion about my "lying down"? How is it their business, with whom and how I lie down and get up? Who asks them for advice, whether it is good or bad what I am doing? I know my own affairs and those senile old people are not being asked. About my depravity or lack

thereof I don't ask anyone anything, I have done nothing wrong and I will do nothing wrong, nor can anyone even make fun of me for that, I am Mariemi.

Her cousin laughed while Mariemi said her piece, and then finally replied at length. The following are some excerpts:

> Mariemi, you are too bold and proud, it's not good, but I no longer want to anger you either. [. . .] In Khevsureti Khevsurs are together in *sts'orproba* like brothers and sisters. Although by doing this no one is doing anything bad, but in itself such lying down together is not good. [If things continue in this way] they will no longer give permission for young people to come and go together, and they will begin to be suspicious. For example, if I had heard that my wife were to have engaged in such lying down, I too would have suspected her of fornication in my heart, I would have left her, even if I know, that by doing that they do nothing wrong . . . my uncle's wife and father's sister are right when they say that *sts'orproba* needs to be done according to the rules of *sts'orproba*. As long as Khevsureti is called Khevsureti, so long must everything be done according to its own rules, that we may remember the fame and shame of the ancestors.

The conversations in this story read like a set exchange of speeches between two orators: Baliauri here, as in many places, recreates conversations based presumably in part on hearsay, and she makes each character say the kinds of things that would be expected in that situation in order to illustrate the positions of each actor. Unlike her imagined conversations before, each speaker speaks at length and gives their whole position. Her cousin expounds upon the need to maintain a traditional order, in part to maintain the freedoms of the Khevsurs, while Mariemi, the epitome of personal autonomy, expounds upon the law of autonomy from her own personal perspective: "I am Mariemi." In the end, Mariemi got her way and married the one she wanted, a boy with whom she had engaged in Aragvian practices for a long time.

Nanuk'i's Story

While the practice of Aragvian lying down was spreading through social networks, being learned and transferred from commune to commune, rumor of it was spreading faster. The distant region of Arkhot'i, along the Assa River in northwestern Khevsureti (where Baliauri herself is from) learned of the practice first from an older woman, Mamida, a woman who had married into the Arkhot'i commune[1] but was herself from the Aragvian region. She returned from a visit to her father's house there with stories about these practices: "In Aragvi they have adopted a complete new set of rules for *sts'orproba* and they even change names for their *dzmobilis* and *sts'orperis*." Upon hearing these scandalous tales the Arkhotians laughed, joked, and composed derisive poems about these new practices (Baliauri 1991: 167–68).

The first girl in Arkhot'i to actually adopt these practices was named Nanuk'i, a girl who, like all the others in these stories, was beautiful, good, and hardworking (Baliauri 1991: 168–70). Her father had many relatives in the Aragvi region, and so she frequently visited them, and she was laid down with local boys there as part of the general custom of visiting. Among so many *sts'orproba* partners she presumably came in contact with one who was following the new rules, which she learned and then wanted to bring to her partners in Arkhot'i. This provoked surprise, because up to that point she had been against the practice. As word got out, Nanuk'i was shunned and left alone, without *sts'orperi* or *dzmobili*.

Once, at a wedding in her village where the bride was from the Aragvi region, among the young people there was singing, dancing, and poetry as usual. Amid this general merriment, however, Nanuk'i sat alone; no one wished even to sit near her. When time came for the *elchis* to arrange "lying down" between the guests from Aragvi and the hosts from Arkhot'i, no one wanted to lie with Nanuk'i. This presented a problem for the *elchis*, who always worked tirelessly to see that no one was left without a sleeping partner. They asked everyone, who would like to sleep with whom, and then they laid down all of them with whomever they wanted to sleep with. All except Nanuk'i: the local Arkhotians refused to sleep with her, citing her adoption of strange Aragvian customs.

The *elchis* replied: "Nevertheless, Nanuk'i is no less a woman than the others, true, she has adopted a different custom of lying down, but by doing that she is still not doing anything wrong. Let someone lie down with her and tell her that that Aragvian lying down is forbidden." While they might have laid her down with the Aragvian guests, when they asked Nanuk'i, Nanuk'i herself wanted to be laid down with her own people. They finally found a boy to lie down with her, but in the middle of the night he got up, wrapped himself in his cloak, went out, and lay down outside. This was noted by all, although he said nothing, but it was assumed that he avoided her because of her new practices. Nanuk'i herself was defiant: "I get angry when someone lies down with girls who are better than me, when they lie down with those that are worse than me, I'm not even aware of it. Their *sts'orperis*, in terms of looks and breeding, none of them can best me. I will be their equal and better, not just in Aragvian lying down, but whatever I must learn! By doing that [Aragvian lying down] I have done nothing bad and am not doing anything bad, nor do I have less conscience and shame than them!" One of Nanuk'i's female relatives was asked by her friends about Nanuk'i's comportment and advised to warn Nanuk'i to leave off this "devilish" Aragvian *sts'orproba*. Nanuk'i's relative replied that she had herself warned Nanuk'i about this many times, angering her, but that Nanuk'i always replied in the same way—in a manner that bears a striking resemblance to the way in which Mariemi defends her position above:

> Who asked you? It is none of your affair, I am doing nothing wrong with my practices of lying down and have never brought them to anyone else's door. I am Nanuk'i. I do not concern myself with others and I do not have the same ideas about conscience and shame as others. However I might lie down, I am doing nothing wrong, I will not lie down any other way—my self, my wishes. Leave me alone from now on, I will tell you nothing more. (Baliauri 1991: 170)

Ashekali's Story

The news of this scandalous genre of lying down soon spread to neighboring regions, and the practice found early adopters in each region too. Where there is scandal, there is censure, as well as poetry of censure publicizing these scandalous events. The tale of Ashekali, of the village of Batsaligo in the district of Khakhmati, adjacent to Aragvi, differs from the stories of Mariemi and Nanuk'i in that it doesn't take the form of a reconstructed conversation, but rather a poem, which is like a skeleton that Baliauri fleshes out with a back story (Baliauri 1991: 166–67). Ashekali's story otherwise begins in a very similar way to Mariemi's, illustrating a conflict between generations of the same family. Like Mariemi, Ashekali was in every way a desirable girl until she adopted Aragvian practices, at which point she came to be avoided as a sexual partner by her peers in the community. Her relatives began to fight with her: "Girl, from where did you bring in that behavior and lying down? What is making you crazy, girl, why do you not lie down and get up according to Khevsur rules?" Ashekali's constant critic was her grandmother, Shukia, who had raised Ashekali since her mother died when she was young. Initially Ashekali, like Mariemi, patiently endured verbal harangues and censure, but eventually she could no longer endure it and they fought. The fight reached the point at which she seized her grandmother and dragged her out into the cowshed, beat her savagely, and locked her in. This incident of intergenerational savagery became the topic of a *shairi* poem of censure:

leksia akhal natkvami,	A poem freshly composed
shamaiarna gzanio,	Has made its rounds on the road,
shamaiarna k'orshani,	Has made its rounds from door to door [reading *k'arshani*],

gadaiarna mtanio.	Has crossed the mountains.
dzvels aterivit gaitkva	Like Ateri of old,[2]
tatarat ashekalio.	Ashekali of the Tatarat lineage made a name for herself.
berdeda ts'amauktsevav,	She knocked over her grandmother,
shukia ghulelt kalio,	Shukia, a woman of the Ghulelt [lineage],
sadzrokhes gadmautravis,	She dragged her into the cow-shed,
magra dazhjara k'ario.	She shut the door firmly.
	[. . . .]

[Ashekali addresses her imprisoned grandmother:]

"mzeze nu dakhol mk'dario.	"Don't go out into the sunlight, dead one.
vertsad chaidev sagdzali,	Nowhere can you put aside food for the road,
vertsad gaghbande jghanio,	Nowhere can you sew up your torn shoes,
sadaraisa iknebis,	Wherever they may be,
veras ikmodes skhvanio."	Others can do nothing for you."
chaedga ashekalasa	Ashekali had placed for her
qal-erobian jamio:	A bowl of flour mixed with clarified butter:
"sadac ro magshivdeboda,	"When you get hungry,
amait'ane, ch'ameo!"	take it, eat it!"

Ashekali's remarkable behavior had made her famous, but not in a good way. She had, in the terms discussed in the last chapter, "become a *shairi*"!

Lastly, news of these practices spread even farther than the practices themselves, eliciting more poetic responses. In the more distant parts of Khevsureti, beyond the mountains, the practices did not spread as much as word about them did, which provided a fertile field for poetic composition of derisive poetry. A poet from Lebaiskari in far Khevsureti composed the following poem (Baliauri 1991: 172–73):

q'inulobit chaviare	In the ice I descended
dilas k'ist'nis-ch'alaio.	In the morning along the riverbank at Kist'ani.
gavigone, gamik'virda,	I heard, I was surprised by,
qvesurt anabanaio.	The news of the Khevsurs.
ais ikna k'ai vazhi,	This one here was a good boy,
vinc shaiba daniao.	Who was attacked with a knife.
ais ikna k'ai kali,	This one here was a good girl,
vinac soplis sharaio.	Who is now the main road of the village.
aghar indobt ertmanetsa,	You no longer trust one another,
isk'i upro balaio.	But this is worse.

sanakhvad gvejavrebis	It makes us angry to see
tsudi qevsurt kalaio.	A woman of the Khevsurs gone bad.

According to Baliauri, the Argavian sexual revolution was an experiment that lasted only a few years: for a while, in almost every village there appeared one or two practitioners at least, but the conflict and negative reactions swirling within the Khevsur culture of circulation spread faster and farther than the practices themselves, and ultimately this attempted sexual revolution failed. In the process, however, Khevsur identity and key notions of personhood were put to the test. Often the very ideals of Khevsur identity, such as autonomy and freedom, which Khevsur rules were supposed to protect and which were threatened by these new practices, became the basis for arguments by followers of these new practices that they should be allowed to do as they pleased. Even though these new sexual practices emerged at the time of a historical and structural conflict between new Russian rules of marriage and Khevsur traditions, the actual new practices seem to have emerged out of the tensions internal to the existing genres themselves: a latent potential or affordance to challenge existing norms, emerging from latent tensions or contradictions within the norms themselves.[3] Khevsur notions of personhood and desire, and particularly notions of freedom and autonomy, were deployed again and again on both sides of each narrated conflict: desire, after all, is the very basis for autonomy, but it is also the destabilizing force that must be kept in check in order to preserve it.

NOTES

1   Arkhot'i is the name of *temi* (region) along the Assa River in Figure 5.1, including the villages of Akhieli, Amgha, and Chimgha.
2   This may well be the same character as the "Eteri" mentioned in the myth of desire in chapter 1.
3   I thank Perry Sherouse for this point.

6

INTELLIGENTSIA AND PEOPLE: A LOVE STORY

IT IS A REMARKABLE FACT, one that demands explanation, that we know *any-thing* about the private sexual lives of a few thousand Georgian mountain people, and that we probably know more about their romantic lives than we do about the remaining population of the country of Georgia. In this chapter I ask two related questions. First, how did the entire Georgian nation, by the mid-twentieth century, become aware of, interested in, informed about, and finally begin to romanticize a people they had hardly been aware existed in the early nineteenth century? Second, how did the sexual lives of these same people, a few thousand people living in the high mountains of Georgia, come to the attention of the entire Georgian nation? In this chapter, then, I begin a detective story, covering the different genres of an emergent Georgian print culture that allowed the most intimate scenes of Khevsur romance to become part of Georgian public discourse.

Part of the answer to this question of how we know anything about the Khevsurs or their private lives has to do with the emergence of print culture, specifically the newspaper. The advent of the newspaper in Georgia in the 1860s came along with a new taste for genres of realistic reportage, such as ethnography, which described the ordinary lives of peasants, including Khevsurs (see Manning 2012a). Ethnography also involved a specific kind of verbal realism, quoting the words of the peasant and painstakingly transcribing both conversations with peasants and peasant verbal art (folklore) as realistically as possible. These new genres, whose home was the new medium of the newspaper, also created new kinds of imagined addressees: the public. Texts written for the newspaper were addressed to a public of *strangers*, an anonymous audience who were imagined as abstract contemporaries, other ordinary people more or less like oneself who had shared concerns about the issues of the day. Georgian newspaper correspondence was not only written *for* strangers; it was also written *by* strangers, more or less anonymously by writers using pseudonyms. This completely new form of discourse fostered a similarly new kind of "imagined community" of readers and writers of the newspaper—the "public"—and people held conversations with one another exclusively through this medium. This "public" was imagined as consisting concretely of members of a new social formation called the intelligentsia, a newly emerging social class who defined themselves through the newspaper, both as writers and as readers. The intelligentsia was imagined as a largely urban, educated class that was defined in opposition to the largely rural, uneducated peasants. The discourse of the urban intelligentsia, "the public," revolved around these rural peasants, "the people," because the intelligentsia saw themselves as having a defining historic mission to overcome this divide between the public and the people. This would be accomplished by "getting to know" the peasants, who were just then being emancipated from the servitude of serfdom, by describing the peasants in the pages of the newspaper, as a prelude to enlightening them.

If the newspaper took the form of an abstract conversation between intelligentsia-strangers, much of the correspondence written for the newspaper from the 1860s onwards took the form of concretely described conversations between members of the intelligentsia and peasants. By the 1880s the intelligentsia began to devote more and more ethnographic attention to marginal mountain-dwellers like the Khevsurs, at a time when Khevsur culture was still thriving in the form described in the first five chapters, part of a developing "romance of the mountains." As a result of the development of the newspaper and the intelligentsia, the voice of the Khevsur became a kind of narrated figure, a "quoted voice," subsumed within ethnographies and realistic depictions of village scenes and always encompassed by the "quoting voice" of the intelligentsia author (these terms are drawn from Inoue 2006).

This new "romance of the intelligentsia and the people" is part of the answer to the first question raised at the start of the chapter. The rest of the answer has to do with the extension of education to the peasants: under socialism, some members of the peasantry received education and become part of the intelligentsia themselves, so that the "quoting voice" of the intelligentsia author and the "quoted voice" of the peasant came to reside within one and the same person.

I will illustrate this transition by telling two stories about Khevsur women, both named Natela, who both happened to have been married by marital abduction: the first Natela is an object of ethnography and also desire, a (possibly fictional) character written about, a "quoted voice," and reported in an ethnographic sketch written by an intelligentsia writer as a typical Khevsur peasant girl; the other is a real Khevsur woman named Natela (Baliauri), who, as an ethnographer writing about the lives of the Khevsurs, herself became a member of the intelligentsia and who is the source of much of the material discussed in the last five chapters. Since Natela Baliauri is both a Khevsur woman and an ethnographer of the Khevsurs, in her writings two perspectives are juxtaposed—the quoted voice of the Khevsur object of writing, and the quoting voice of the intelligentsia writing about the Khevsurs—so that her "double-voiced" ethnographies allows us a much more intimate perspective on Khevsur life than would be otherwise possible.

GENRES OF REALISM AND ROMANCE

The mission of the first Georgian newspaper, *Droeba* ("Times," 1866–85) was strongly tied to a specific set of social concerns: the desire of the intelligentsia, or reading public, to "get to know" (*gatsnoba*) the recently emancipated peasants of Georgia. This newly emergent Georgian urban reading public were uncomfortably aware that they no longer *knew* their rural kin, the peasants, who they supposed, unlike themselves, were defined by being not only poor, but also unenlightened, backward, and illiterate. The intelligentsia defined their historic mission to overcome this social divide by both getting to know, and then enlightening, the peasants.

This mission was expressed in a related set of aesthetics, namely, that the best way to get to know the rural population of Georgia, it was felt, was through realistic genres of representation. Realism included both realistic fiction (e.g., novels) and nonfictional works such as ethnographic sketches. Both these genres, fictional and nonfictional, had in common the fact that they presented rigorously realistic, almost photographic, "pictures" from "everyday life," objectively and empirically describing the material conditions of the peasantry. Realism, as a genre, was defined as having real life, specifically the everyday lives and material conditions of the peasantry, as its central object. Realism was characterized by a detached objective authorial stance that was strongly opposed to the aesthetics of romanticism that dominated the previous generation of mostly aristocratic writers, a sensibility that privileged the lyric expression of the writer's sensibility and moods and that typically found expression in poetry, for example, extolling the beauty of the landscape without any reference to the peasants living there, or their plight.

The various genres incorporated within a single issue of a newspaper all embodied these two related programs, one aesthetic, the other political: using realistic description to "get to know the peasants" in order to transform the lives of the peasants for the better. Realism, then, was understood as a kind of "civic aesthetics" (affirming the social role of literature), a "social realism" that was strongly tied to the "social question," which described the abject condition of the peasants in the period of the Emancipation beginning in the 1860s, when the peasants were released from bondage and servitude to feudal lords, becoming free but at the same time being materially indebted to their erstwhile masters. In effect, by critically reporting on the lives of the peasants, the intelligentsia hoped to transform their lives for the better. Realist writing was critical realism—a form of social action.

Unlike Western newspapers where the addressee of the newspaper, "the public," is understood to be overlapping with or identical to the object discussed by the newspaper, "the people," in Georgia at this time this was not the case: "the public"—the intelligentsia, the people doing the talking—and "the people"—the peasantry, the people being talked about—were completely separate groups. The defining mission of public discourse was how to cross this social divide so that the intelligentsia could recognize in the peasants, and the peasants recognize in the intelligentsia, that they both belonged to the same family. In short, newspapers in this period depict a kind of (unrequited) love story between the intelligentsia and the people.

This love story was imagined as a set of reported conversations between these alienated lovers. The ethnographies in Georgian newspapers of this period are *dialogic* in the sense that contemporary ethnographies are, in that they are composed of two kinds of conversations: on the one hand, the conversational encounter with the native informant or peasant of the encounter "in the field" (as we say in Western ethnography) or "in the village" (as Georgian ethnographers say); on the other hand, "the writing of the ethnographic account addressed to an audience of readers" (Bauman 2004: 160). If the entire contents of an issue of *Droeba* represented an intimate conversation between the "quoting voices" of intelligentsia-strangers hiding behind pseudonyms, the voices of the people of Georgia, also understood to be Georgians, could be found only as "quoted voices," transcribed according to the conventions of realism in genres such as pictures, sketches, folklore, and ethnographies, as well as in stories and novels illustrating their plight. Reported conversations with peasants addressed related concerns deriving from the aesthetic of realism, not only of knowledge ("how do you know what the peasant said?") but also of form ("how did the peasant speak?"). The space of the newspaper, then, was a place where the Georgian urban intelligentsia both addressed their literate intelligentsia publics and narrated the plight of their illiterate other, the Georgian peasant, who was always mired in the mud of real villages. This often made the plight of the Georgian peasant more compelling and more real to the concerned readers of the the city who were reading the peasants' anguished words.

The conversation between the intelligentsia and the people in the pages of the newspaper is part of a tale of estrangement, but also a love story. By the 1880s, the Georgians had fallen in love with the mountain people in general, and with the Khevsurs in particular. The Khevsurs became the ideal peasant for the intelligentsia public, since they illustrated different and opposed dimensions of the social question: on the one hand, the harsh material conditions of the mountains dictated that the Khevsurs lived lives of almost unbelievable poverty and squalor compared to other Georgian peasants, so the reader could be concerned with the material plight of the Khevsurs, and hope to improve it; on the other hand, the Khevsurs, who fought battles wearing chain mail and swords, lived a picturesque, exotic life of unchecked romantic freedom from an intrusive Russian imperial state, a chivalric, poetic world very different from the prosaic everyday life that characterized other peasants, or indeed, the bureaucratized and stifled life of the writer under imperial autocracy. Khevsurs were both the ideal peasant other and a kind of idealized proxy for the self. By talking about Khevsurs, Georgian intelligentsia could engage in exacting exercises of realistic description, with plenty of material poverty, but they could also covertly engage in a romantic idealization of the same exotic, chivalric *free* peasants, and imagine Khevsureti as a kind of imaginative *elsewhere*, a Georgia free from Russian imperial autocracy. As a result, the mountains became the object of a hybrid aesthetics that could be called "romantic realism." Georgian writers also increasingly imagined the mountains as places of romanticism and exoticism, another kind of imaginative *elsewhere* characterized by free expression of sexual desire. The conversation between the intelligentsia and the people thus became an intimate, romantic conversation between intelligentsia and peasant, rather than a cold, realistic conversation about peasants between intelligentsia strangers. The relationship moved from being purely platonic to one fraught with erotic overtones, as Georgian readers began to elide themselves into the lyric subject positions of narrated Khevsur lovers.

THE STORY OF NATELA: A KHEVSUR ROMANCE OF THE NINETEENTH CENTURY

By the 1880s, this eroticization of the general romance of the mountains was becoming commonplace. In one of the earliest writings on Khevsur life, *Some Pictures from the Daily Life of the Khevsurs* (by V. Barnovi, a well-known Georgian writer), which was published in serialized form as a feuilleton in the pages of the Georgian newspaper *Droeba* in 1878, what begins as a commonplace realistic sketch of "pictures from peasant life" becomes instead infused with sexual overtones between the intelligentsia male and the peasant girl. In considering this one single literary encounter of a member of the intelligentsia with the strange world of Khevsureti, we see how the Khevsurs are initially imagined in the cold, hard light of neutral realism, but this changes as the author begins to develop an infatuation with a Khevsur girl named Natela, who is a recurring figure in his narration. With this change, the reader is drawn from viewing the Khevsur realistically, within a cold, detached, objective, ethnographic sketch of mountain customs, to viewing them in the warm light of romance: they are pulled into the world portrayed in the picture and experience a kind of desire themselves.

The figure of Natela infuses the otherwise dry ethnographic frame narrative with an exciting narrative subplot of local romantic drama. Not only a figure involved in a local romance, she also serves as a figure of erotic desire for the readers. Natela thus plays two separate roles in this text as a character. On the one hand, she is a Khevsur girl, a member of an unfamiliar and somewhat exotic group of mountain-dwelling Georgians, an ethnographic figure of the exotic "native" within a realistic ethnographic sketch of Khevsur life. Since she is a peasant character, the specifics of her life can illustrate the ethnographic realities of peasant life in general. On the other hand, she is a beautiful young woman. As a female character, she can again play two roles. On the one hand, in a strictly gendered role, she can illustrate the ethnographic plight of Khevsur women and elicit sympathy, concern, and demands for reform. On the other hand, her gender can be sexualized, as an attractive female other to the male character of the narrator; she can become an object of desire for the narrator and, by extension, the readership. As a character animating this ethnographic sketch, she gives the narrator cause to wonder and license to explain certain aspects of the culture of the Khevsurs; but she also serves as a comely figure, allowing readers' imagination to animate this discussion with their own erotic desires.

The account begins with a general travel narrative, a series of picturesque travel notes in which the landscape is the central figure of description. Then, slowly, a single feminine figure, Natela, appears in this landscape and comes to dominate the attention of the narrator. We meet her at the very end of the first installment, where the two travelers find her standing under a tree, watching her herd of cattle grazing in a nearby meadow. As Barnovi's travel companion, Gabriel, engages her in conversation, asking her the whereabouts of her father, Aluda (who is their host), and talking about other things, Barnovi, the narrator, occupies himself with "looking her over. Her clothing, comportment, and she herself taken as a whole left some sort of unforgettable impression on me" (*Droeba* 1878, No. 220, p.2).[1]

As indeed it had to, the next installment (1878, 221) begins with a lengthy description of Natela that fills a long newspaper column. This realistic description begins with ethnographic details, specifically her clothing, the strikingly distinctive Khevsur dress for women, followed by a paragraph for her exotic head-dress and accessories, and then the woman herself. At this point the narrator's detached realistic description of the native turns into self-evident infatuation, and the narrator imagines that Natela is flirting with him:

> The woman herself was of middle stature; her face shone entirely in shades of white and red, though a slight trace of unkemptness was noticeable on her (this trace made her still more beautiful in my eyes); a proportionate chin, clean lips, clean nose; thick, dark, chestnut coloured eyebrows and eyelashes divided her round and full face. As a decoration of the same face imagine on her cheeks two attractive dimples, which beautified her when she smiled. As she talked Natela

glanced up several times and lit up her speckled, lively, almost smiling eyes at me, although right away she concealed them from me with a forest of lush eyelashes. This portrait almost drew me and I was staring at her transfixed, she, perhaps because of this, from time to time blushed. (1878, 221.2)

Since this is a realistic ethnographic description, "pictures" taken directly from "life," the narrator is at pains throughout to chronicle key ethnographic differences between Khevsurs and the plains Georgians who are his readers, particularly those that relate to gender norms. Natela's freedom of movement and boldness, as an ethnographic figure, allow him to illustrate those differences. As we have seen, Khevsur women were in some respects quite free in their movements compared to Georgian women elsewhere. This freedom of movement was balanced by principles of gender segregation, as when they were confined to menstrual or birthing huts. These matters are here and there described from a purely realist or critical perspective typical of the activist approach of critical realism. For example, elsewhere in the same installment, the fact that Khevsurs and Pshavians both practice isolation of menstruating women and women giving birth in separate tabooed buildings (respectively menstrual huts [*samrevlo*] and birthing huts) is given a reasonably accurate ethnographic explanation in terms of local notions of purity:

Apparently they consider a woman giving birth to be extremely impure, so that not only touching her, but even passing near her is a breach of purity for them; "mixture, mixing up" (*shereva*) (as they call coming close) appears a great disgust and misfortune. Because of this as soon as a woman's time of birth comes, at that time they lead her out from the house and they house her in a hut, here they give her food and water. Here the woman gives birth alone; neither a grandmother for her nor a midwife. The woman giving birth must remain three days at least in the hut together with her child.

Immediately afterwards, the narrator adopts the voice of an intelligentsia activist reformer and condemns the practice as a backward "harmful custom," part of the "social question," something that the state needs to abolish:

The unfortunate consequences of such a custom are clear: Sometimes a woman cannot take care of herself and child and they both die, sometimes the straw bed catches on fire and they are burnt ... Then the woman giving birth goes over from the hut to the *samrevlo*, they burn the hut. The *samrevlo* is a cleaner and stronger room. Here, I think, the woman giving birth remains again forty days alone. Women go out into the *samrevlo* also during menstruation.

This is clear, how harmful is such a search for purity and throwing a woman giving birth outdoors in such a time of need. Apparently the government has forbidden this custom many times. But, you know, that which the centuries have planted in the heart of a people, good or bad, rooting it out in one fell swoop is extremely hard. (1878, 221.3)

Natela illustrates other ethnographic aspects of gender as well. After they take their leave from her, the travelers return to the ethnographic problem of her engagement in outdoor agricultural activities alone, such as herding cattle alone, which from the perspective of a plains Georgian could only be an invitation to sexual misconduct. The factual absence of sexual misconduct in the face of the (implied) possibility of rape or abduction is explained ethnographically by the narrator's more knowledgeable companion Gabriel in terms of local customs of blood vengeance:

"Who knows how much they work; aside from house work they work side by side with the men in outside work too; in gathering hay, in carrying it, reaping, and how beautifully they reap! On the threshing floor and in everything else...."

"Doubtless guileless people live here; a woman walking in a meadow alone...."

"Yes, here the people all have the same customs and if anyone dares to try anything, he soon will taste the cold iron of a sword. Look, one brave lad is following her around, I think she also likes him, but, inasmuch as parents don't want it, he can't do anything about it." (221.3)

In a subtle shift, Natela moves from being a local girl whose main function is either to provide an illustration of Khevsur gender roles or to serve as an object of desire for the narrator/reader. She is a local girl who has a story of her own, assuming the role of a star-crossed lover in an embedded narrative chronicling the growing romance between her and a local boy. This embedded narrative of local romance marks the beginnings of a covert sexualization of Khevsur life, the romanticization of the Khevsurs, which becomes a dominant motif of interest in the Pshavs and Khevsurs in later works. Natela, as well as her star-crossed suitor, Gagai, reappear at a feast in a later chapter:

At the end of the feasting table sat our woman Natela seen amongst the cattle; her beauty was now even more strongly captivating. I noted, that she was looking very often toward one corner of the table of the young men.... I looked in the direction where Natela was contemplating. There sat a young boy dressed in clean clothing.... His appearance, movement, talk clearly attested to his yearning. Silently he kept looking over with excited eyes toward the woman.

"Here's that boy that I was telling you about then! You see, how he and Natela look at each other?" Gabriel, who was sitting by my side, whispered to me. (226.2)

Their flirtation at the feast leads, in the final installment of the serial, to her (apparently willing) marital abduction by the boy. The seemingly idle mention of the ethnographic detail of menstrual huts above turns out to be a crucial element in her abduction, which is foreshadowed by the author in his otherwise neutral ethnographic description: one of the elements of harm introduced by menstrual isolation, it seems, is the way it affords the possibility of marital abduction. Weeks later, the author and his companion, Gabriel, are taking a walk at sunset, passing near the menstrual huts described earlier, when they chance to overhear the whispered conversation between the boy (Gagai) and the girl (Natela) as they negotiate the abduction:

"Who are you? Why are you there?" A gentle voice was heard.
"It's me, I am Gagai." He called out from outside.
"Oooh! What do you want here? Go, they will kill you." The girl said with a trembling voice.
"Look here, come here for a little bit . . ."
"No, my love, I can't come; they will slaughter us."
"No one is here. Didn't Mamidura tell you just now? . . ."
The boy went into the veranda. The creak of a door was heard, the woman came out. Two dark shadows embraced each other, the gentle sound of kissing barely reached us . . . (1878, 227.2)

And with her (apparently willing and successful) abduction, the lovers depart and the feuilleton comes to an abrupt end. What began as a neutral realistic exposition of "scenes from peasant life" has become a love story, but to narrate *realistically* the most intimate details of the conversation of the lovers, the author presents himself as having overheard them by chance while on an evening walk.

THE STORY OF NATELA: A NATIVE ETHNOGRAPHER
OF THE TWENTIETH CENTURY

This representation of romantic life in the story of Natela is also important because it contains the first minor mention of something like the custom of *sts'orproba*, under the Pshavian name *ts'ats'loba*, embedded within a specimen of local poetry (1878,

226.3). However, there is no ethnographic explanation of what this relationship is, and it seems to play no role in the flirtation between the boy and Natela, or in the subsequent abduction. Such a silence is not surprising. By the 1880s and 1890s there was an immense explosion of realistic genres in the Georgian press that made the life of the mountaineers their theme, whether they were transcriptions of native poetry (such as the poetry of Khvaramze in chapter 4), melodramatic novels with romantic protagonists set in ethnographically realistic mountain settings, or ethnographies that covered the daily life and ritual life of the mountaineers. By 1892 it was already clear that the "mountains" and their inhabitants, "our mountain people," had become a central object of interest defining a "new direction" in Georgian literature:

> This new direction is the study of our mountain people, their customs, traditions, beliefs, ideals, poetry. This direction also has another side, that is, our poets and novelists have turned the life of these people into themes for the practice of their own talents. (Ch'reladze 1892 1.1)

However, even though these writings transformed the mountain people into the exotic objects of realistic description and also the heroic subjects of romantic novels, a true "romance of the mountains," they provided very little reliable information about the ethnographic details of the romantic lives of these same mountaineers, particularly customs like *sts'orproba* and *ts'ats'loba*. It was not until the 1920s and 1930s that there was an explosion of ethnographic (Mak'alatia 1998 [1925], 1934, 1984 [1935]; Tedoradze 1930) and novelistic (Robakidze 2004 [1932]; Javakhishvili 1994 [1926, 1934]) descriptions of the practice. So it was only long after the mountains had already become associated with romance and romanticism in general that the specific character of mountaineer romance came to light.

The first Georgian to publish extensive ethnographic descriptions of these sexual customs was Sergi Mak'alatia (whose separate writings on the subject began in 1925 and figure as sections of his full ethnographies of Khevsureti and Pshavi in the 1930s). The preface to his 1925 work drew attention to precisely how scarce previous Georgian writings on these customs were. While much of the public life of the Khevsurs, their ritual life, and so on, were well described by Georgian ethnographers by the end of the 1880s (e.g., Barnovi's account from 1878 contains very reliable guides to many such customs), none of these writers, Mak'alatia complains, even mentions the existence of sexual traditions such as *sts'orproba*. Indigenous writers such as Vazha Pshavela, who do mention it and were in a position to give a full description, he argues, refrained from doing so because the material seemed shameful or scandalous (see also Tuite 2008). According to Mak'alatia, the silence stems from the fact that the sexual life of the Khevsurs is difficult, or even dangerous, for an outsider to study, and for insiders, perhaps, shameful to discuss with outsiders. His fellow ethnographer Tedoradze summarizes the strangeness and secretiveness of the similar Pshavian customs as follows:

> Pshavian *ts'ats'loba* is completely strange and incomprehensible to outsiders. In this respect in their intimate life there are many secrets the revealing of which means to them insulting the will of the ancestors. To this end they are matchless keepers of secrets in the conservation of old customs and for this reason is it more difficult to release them from the chains of fanaticism. (Tedoradze 1930: 165)

Given this secrecy, it appears that none of these more intimate descriptions and imaginings of Khevsur romance would have been possible without the rise, at the same time, of *indigenous* ethnographers. Behind all these ethnographies and depictions of this hidden aspect of Khevsur life is a single figure: the native ethnographer Natela Baliauri (1896–1988), who not only wrote her own manuscript on the topic (finally published posthumously in 1991), but whose family also served as hosts and consultants for many visiting ethnographers who would later write on the topic. In fact, the most noted ethnographer of the group, Sergi Mak'alatia, became related to Natela affinally (his brother Nik'o, a teacher, married Natela's sister, Melano, an ethnographer herself). And it was Mak'alatia himself who was the first to publish a full description of the practice of *sts'orproba* (Mak'alatia 1998 [1924]). This story "about love" cannot be told without telling the story of the conditions of possibility of its telling, the story of the creation of an indigenous elite. In the case of Natela Baliauri, this story is *also* a story "about love."

Natela Baliauri's account of *Sts'orproba in Khevsureti* (1991) is unique because it provides an insider's perspective on a set of rituals and relations that are not easily accessible to outsiders. Her ethnography provides a unique look at the inner, intimate face of the group, and as such it is really the sort of ethnography that could have been written *only* by an insider (on these points see also Manning 2007). And yet, for all the intimate insider knowledge upon which this account is predicated, it is written from the detached analytic perspective of third-person objective reportage that is typical of genres of realism. Seldom does one find the pronoun "I" of autobiographical voicing in the text, even in those places where, almost certainly, the account is autobiographical.

After all, certain scandals narrated in her book—such as those involving, say, marital abduction or violations of rules of exogamy—clearly resemble actual events from her life. The very fact that she is writing on this subject is, after all, the result of her own exile from the community for violating its rules of marriage. Here are the brief details of her life, related by her daughter, also an ethnographer:

[N. Baliauri] was born in 1896 in transalpine Khevsureti, in the village of Akhieli in the *temi* of Arkhot'i. At 18 years of age she married an inhabitant of the same village, Aleksi Ochiauri, and since they broke the rule forbidding a boy and a girl from the same village marrying each other, they were forced to disappear (into exile). Thus they appeared in in the Pshavian village of Shuapkho, where they settled permanently. (T. Ochiauri 1995: 4)

In essence, her husband, Aleksi Ochiauri, abducted her (I do not know if it was what we would call a "willing" elopement) in much the same way as Gagai abducted Natela in Barnovi's account above. However, since they were both members of the same community, their marriage was impossible, and they were exiled to neighboring Pshavi, where both became native ethnographers of the region. This was made possible by new progressive educational programs after the Socialist Revolution, which allowed Aleksi and Natela to enter a *rabfak* (worker's faculty, an educational program designed to allow workers to enter higher-education programs) and to acquire a higher education, which led to their becoming both members of the intelligentsia and noted ethnographers of the region.

Due to their status as exiled insiders, and to their location on the boundary of Pshavi and Khevsureti, the household of Natela Baliauri and Aleksi Ochiauri became the host household to generations of ethnographers, folklorists, philologists, and archeologists who worked on Pshavi-Khevsureti (K'alandadze 1995); it was also the center of a small circle of mountaineer ethnographers and linguists in the 1920s and 1930s whose numbers included the ethnographers Giorgi Tedoradze and Sergi Mak'alatia. In the texts of these other linguists and ethnographers, Natela and Aleksi occupy a shifting hybrid position, figuring now as members of the educated intelligentsia, now as members of the folk, now as collaborators, now as local informants. In the latter role they are sometimes represented as Pshavians (of Shuapkho, their place of exile), but at other times as Khevsurs (from Akhieli, their natal village). As exiled Khevsurs in Pshavi, they were also liminal to two worlds, partial outsiders both to the Khevsureti about which they spent the rest of their life writing, and to the world of the educated elite, as village intelligentsia, marginal products of the socialist *rabfak* education system (see also Manning 2007).

As noted, the peculiar quality of Baliauri's ethnography—the absence of first-person narration, which aligns the "I" of the "quoting voice" with the "I" of the "quoted voice"—can be traced to the fact that she inhabits both these worlds, the native's and the ethnographer's, but strives to keep them separate. On the one hand, she tells stories of private dramas, the stories behind poems, which no outside ethnographer could possibly know, often cast in a rigorously realistic transcription of Khevsur dialect that makes the book formidably difficult to read. On the other hand, like outsider ethnographers, she erases herself from the text and reports with a neutral voice, a "voice from nowhere" cast in an equally neutral standard Georgian. It is in her use of reported speech, the imagined conversations in her ethnography, that her hybrid position becomes clearest. Without any explanation whatsoever, Baliauri populates her ethnography of intimate practices with fluidly and freely imagined private conversations, each of which is both strangely intimate (including pillow talk between the boy and the girl) and at the same time rather generic: a model of a typical conversation that *would* happen at a given juncture in the developing relationship. In fact, as we have seen, she often indicates that these are "typical" and not "real" conversations throughout by putting in gaps such as "insert name here."

The dilemma of Barnovi, the outsider ethnographer, is to tell us *how he knew* (realistically) what Natela and Gagai said to each other in private. He uses the device of "overhearing" the conversation. Natela Baliauri's dilemma as intelligentsia ethnographer is quite different: how to separate an overly intimate connection between ethnographer and native. If Natela Baliauri as a *native* ethnographer feels confident enough to report typical conversations between natives, that means she must have had some such experiences herself, or heard reports of them from close friends. But because she is speaking as an *ethnographer*, she is naturally reticent about divulging her own experiences as such; she does not want to report from memory *her own* intimate life, rife with scandal, as a native, for who would want to share such things with strangers? She is faced with a dilemma: how to represent the situation ethnographically, based on intimate materials that can only be known biographically. So she blends her own omniscient "quoting voice" with generic narratives featuring the "quoted voices" of anonymous characters. Some of these *must* point to events from her own experience, including things she herself once said, but by presenting them in a neutral third-person account, she decontextualizes and depersonalizes them. The conversations she constructs are thus indexical of her knowledge of the terrain of intimacy as a member of the culture, but at the same time specific connections to specific persons, herself included, are erased, as these intimate others become ideal types, or strangers encountered through her professional identity as an ethnographer reporting on a culture: they are intimate and yet anonymous.

The very intimacy and adolescent banality of the conversation are what make this ethnography, otherwise so stern and often downright prudish, so touching. I argue that this is how Natela Baliauri avoids and detaches her authoritative "intelligentsia voice" from her own messy autobiographical involvement with romantic scandals very similar to the ones she recounts of others. At the same time, by so doing, she protects not only her "objective" professional identity as objective ethnographer, but also her "native" identity as Khevsur girl. As a Khevsur girl, she erases herself from her ethnography to display modesty, in much the same way and for the same reasons that I have argued a Khevsur love poet erases herself from her poem. And why not? After all, in all honesty, who of us would relish writing an ethnography of our adolescent traumas, crushes, and errors of judgment without some shift of perspective from the self? How strange and yet so understandable, then, to have in front of us a text that is so very historically reflexive and autobiographical, in that it describes the very customs that defined the life course of the author, but with the autobiographical connection erased: the text presents itself as decentered, non-reflexive, the autobiographical moment surviving only in traces, in intimate conversations attributed to anonymous speakers. Natela, the ethnographer, in quoting herself, erases every sign of Natela, the Khevsur girl, even from her own story.

NOTE

1   In subsequent references to *Droeba*, only the year of the serial, along with the issue and page number where applicable, will be given, e.g., 1878, 221.2.

7

ECHOES OF LOVE LOST: SOCIALIST
NOVELS AND FILMS

A S I SHOWED IN THE LAST CHAPTER, the Georgian fascination with *sts'orproba* is part of a long pedigree of Georgian fascination with all aspects of Pshav-Khevsur culture—a more general "romance of the mountains." From the late nineteenth century onward, Georgian ethnographers and writers have found in the remote mountainous regions of Georgia, particularly the regions of Khevsureti and Pshavi, a fragmentary ethnographic image of a romantic and exotic lost Georgian world; it comprises a numerically small group of Georgians, whose vanishing customs exhibit lost chivalric ideals that putatively once belonged to Georgia as a whole, thus representing an image of a lost totality that continues to inform the present. Fragments of this lost totality, appearing in ethnographies, novels, films, and everyday life, circulate in a complex, multi-genred, and interdiscursive space of citations. These are strange, exotic customs belonging to another time and place, reflected in a set of fragmentary images that also contain gaps, voids, and blank spaces that seem to invite being filled by the imagination and animated with personal fantasy and desire.

This work of the imagination seems to move in different, even opposed, directions: on the one hand, a prurient, almost pornographic, interpretive tendency that focuses on finding or filling in gaps and silences in the original account with steamy and salacious sexual details; on the other hand, a somewhat defensive reading that treats the absence of sexual details in the accounts as an absence of sex in the original, resulting in a platonic, romantic, chaste, chivalric reading of Khevsur romance. (We have already seen these tendencies illustrated in the discussion of Georgian beer ads in the Introduction, above.) These opposed tendencies stem from the ways in which Khevsur romance is repurposed as it circulates within the horizons of the nation: as a national tradition, it becomes respectable, platonic, chivalric; as an erotic tradition informed by diverse repressed private desires, it takes on the opposite properties, becoming ever more eroticized, even pornographic. Khevsur romance, since it can never be observed and can only be known through second- or third-hand hearsay, quotations, and representations, is a kind of black box, the outer dimensions of which—i.e., what was officially allowed and what was forbidden—are visible, but whose specific content—i.e., what actually happened between two lovers—is known at best only indirectly, if at all, thereby becoming a fertile field for the imagination. Was this a purely platonic love of absolute restraint? Or was it an absolutely libertine form of fornication? Such doubts and questions exist not only for ethnographers and other contemporary Georgians, but also for the very people who practiced it, who constantly express similar doubts about how things went with others.

The alterity of the practices of Khevsur romance is magnified by these absences. The practice is exotic and strange in itself, but it is also distant in space and time, belonging to *there* and *then*, an "elsewhere" to the "here" of normative Georgian sexuality. It presents itself as a hieroglyphic that needs to be deciphered and translated. The *citationality* of this practice, the fact that it now lives only as a reported sexuality, not a practiced one, allows it to serve too as an imagined or fantasized sexuality, a field of unrealized and unrealizable potentials for the framing of desires. Thus, as it drifts further and further from directly experienceable reality, it comes to have what Patrick Galbraith, in another context, calls a sort of "virtual potentiality" in which "the threat of real-world relational interaction is effectively removed from the fantasy, as is the potential for any real-life consequences" (Galbraith 2009). Virtual sexuality is a bit like the imaginative version of the sociable sexuality that I have argued *sts'orproba* represents: both represent a "play form" of sexuality removed from any real-life consequences, but in sociable sexuality this play happens in the flesh, while in virtual sexuality it happens in the imagination.

Sexuality thus not only involves real sexual practices but also centrally involves the circulation and citation of genres of representation of real and fantasized sexual practices. Much of what constitutes sexuality is not fact, but fancy, of course; however here, cited fact drives fancy forward, and fancy proliferates in the empty spaces in the cited facts.

In these final two chapters we see a general gradual movement from the creation of citable texts—products of realist nonfictional descriptions of Khevsur romance, which explain how we ever found out anything at all about the topic—to the circulation of these textual fragments and the fictional or imaginative "filling in" of the gaps. The circulation and citation of these texts produce a sense of the "real": these practices are not merely an idle sexual fantasy; they really happened at some time, somewhere, making fantasies about them perhaps more compelling. The gaps in these texts instead produce a "virtual potential" that removes the consequentiality of this reality, making Khevsur romance an open erotic world into which writers can write their readers, populating the gaps of Khevsur romances with virtual points of entry.

As we have seen in the last chapter, early socialist ethnographers were bedeviled by the empirical problem presented by the secrecy of indigenous romance. Presumably largely through the help of indigenous mediators like Natela Baliauri and her husband, Aleksi Ochiauri, in the 1930s a small circle of Georgian ethnographers flourished, all of whom made a point of including the sexual practices of the highlanders (which had been more or less invisible to earlier ethnographers) along with other aspects of indigenous social life. When these ethnographers turned to romantic materials that they could not observe themselves, they became in a sense folklorists, making much greater use of indigenous poetry as the main source for the disclosure of intimate scenes unknowable to outsiders—just as Khevsurs and Pshavs do themselves. But when their informants or poetic sources failed them, they seemed willing to rely on their imaginations and surmise to fill in the gaps in the account of "what really happened."

As Mak'alatia notes, what few fragments were written by outsiders before this time seemed to focus in on prurient speculation on the specifics of sexual practices, postulating widespread "abnormal" sexual practices of *coitus interruptus*, for example. Mak'alatia (1998 [1925]: 6) quotes a certain N. Khudanovi as saying: "In Khevsureti one rarely finds a young person, who from the age of thirteen doesn't have a lover, but not a Platonic one, but a so-called '*ts'ats'ala*' [sic], and despite the existence of such a relationship, between them pregnancy is a rare occurence, [since pregnancy] is considered to be very shameful and therefore among them the sexual act is completed abnormally." Mak'alatia also cites another early commentator (a certain Barisakhoeli, "one from Barisakho") who describes the custom as having a similarity to sworn brotherhood: "The Khevsurs have the vile and abominable custom of '*ts'ats'loba*,' according to which a girl and a boy declare sworn-brotherhood to one another, they both drink beer from a single bowl and then they are no longer ashamed to lie together somewhere in the '*ch'erkho*' [upper masculine floor of the Khevsur house] or the hayloft. This form of sworn-brotherhood they only have among themselves and never with outsiders, which is strictly forbidden."

Given that the few descriptions of these customs in the period before the Socialist Revolution were so strongly condemnatory (as well as completely confused), and tended to engage in the prurient reduction of romance to sex, it is perhaps not surprising that insiders, like the famous Pshavian poet and ethnographer Vazha Pshavela, or later, Natela Baliauri, would have been either loath to discuss the matter or defensive about it (on Vazha Pshavela's attitudes toward Khevsurs, for example, see Tuite 2008). Therefore, while some writers tended to reduce the custom in question to speculation about what was not reported, filling in the silences and gaps with essentially pornographic speculation about sexual practices like *coitus interruptus* based on inference from low pregnancy rates, other writers, and particularly indigenous ones, sought to read the custom as being more or less platonic (asexual), as a form of eroticism without sex.

These tensions remind us that Georgian ethnographers and others are concerned to reconcile the strangeness, even the potential scandalousness, of this Khevsur tradition with the fact that Khevsurs had become the best and most traditional Georgians. How to reconcile this local ethnographic sexual practice with the emergent sense of a Georgian national tradition? If silences and gaps in the narrative provoke a prurient suspicion that illicit sexual relations must have been widespread, but remained hidden because of practices like *coitus interruptus*, in other respects the reserve and restraint of the tradition reminded Georgians of classical poetic exemplars of Georgian romance. Frequently they would align this local tradition with the best traditions of classic medieval knightly Georgian love poetry, the kind of platonic love (*mijnuroba*) depicted in Rustaveli's twelfth-century poem "The Knight in Panther's Skin," which forms the centerpiece of Georgian national imagining and the Georgian literary tradition.

Rustaveli's poem is a sort of "chivalric" love poem, and contains an oft-cited definition of different kinds of love, related to different forms of poetic expression. On the one hand, there is *mijnuroba*, which takes two forms. The first and highest kind is a heavenly love that cannot be expressed in words, the second a kind of platonic, courtly love in this world, modeled on the otherworldly love, and likewise concealed, secretive, expressed in pining, and the proper topic for poems such as Rustaveli's:

> 21. But far is it [the first mystic love] beyond the understanding of even the wisest men; it makes the tongue weary and brings fatigue to the ear of the listener. My theme is rather the earthly passion that visits us mortals—which has yet some likeness to the mystic when there is nothing wanton in it, only silence and longing. (Rustaveli, 1977; Stevenson translation)[1]

Mijnuroba is sharply contrasted with desire or lust (*sidzva*):

> 24. Love [*mijnuroba*] is a thing rare and fine, hard to comprehend; it can in no way be likened to the desire [*sidzva*] of the flesh. Love is one thing, desire another; and deep indeed is the chasm that stretches between them. Let them not be confounded—give ear to my words! (Stevenson translation)

> 25. The lover must be constant, not lewd, impure and faithless; when he is far from his beloved he must heave sigh upon sigh; his heart must be fixed

on one from whom he endures wrath or sorrow if need be. I hate heartless love—embracing, kissing, noisy snogging. (Rustaveli 1912; Wardrop translation, modified)

Linking mountain romantic traditions to Rustaveli's account of love was part of a more general tendency to see in Khevsureti and Pshavi a "living museum" in which one could meet in the flesh the Georgians that Rustaveli described in his poem a thousand years earlier. It also afforded a vocabulary for assigning Khevsur sexuality to Georgian traditional forebears, producing an image of a national culture that had not changed for a millenium. Vazha Pshavela, for example, himself a noted Pshavian poet frequently compared to Rustaveli, redeployed the Rustavelian distinction between *mijnuroba* and loveless fornication onto "old" and "new" versions of Pshavian romance when he claimed that the "breeze of contemporary life turned even *ts'ats'loba* into fornication," whereas "in the old days, as the old folk say, it was apparently a kind of Rustavelian love [*mijnuroba*]." By translating the Pshavian term *ts'ats'loba* into medieval Rustavelian romantic terminology (*mijnuroba*), Pshavela connects the local tradition to the national one, even as he claims that this tradition has degenerated in the contemporary period. While one reading of Khevsur romance fills in the gaps of the existing account swith speculation about physiological or pornographic details of the encounter, this second reading sees in the same absences of detail simply an absence of sex.

By the 1920s and 1930s, there were a wealth of new accounts by non-native ethnographers that gave a clearer idea of these traditions, although they bore some of the signs of these opposed tensions in "reading" the factual gaps in Khevsur romance. For example, the ethnographer Tedoradze more than once compares the Khevsur lover to one of the knightly characters of Rustaveli's epic poem (implying a sympathetic "romantic" platonic or chivalric reading of Khevsur romance) (1930: 134, 139). He characterizes *sts'orproba* in general terms in a way that would imply that its "beautiful" essence is nothing less than *mijnuroba*, sharply opposing it to fornication and "snoggery" (*simt'lashe*, recalling Rustaveli's word, *mt'lashi-mt'lushi*, which I translated as "snog" since it implies something like wet, noisy kissing associated with lust (*sidzva*): "Khevsur *sts'orproba* in itself means love (*t'rpiali*, *siq'varuli*), solely a spiritual connection between two young people of the opposite sex. All forms of fornication are forbidden and no snoggery has any place in their love" (Tedoradze 1930: 131).

For Tedoradze, writing at the very end of the period in which "free love" was considered to be "progressive" under socialism before the Stalinist cultural revolution of the 1930s, which reaffirmed conservative models of sexuality and romance centered on heterosexual marriage, the essence of these practices (both Khevsur and Pshavian) is pure, chaste, and "beautiful" (he freely uses the Rustavelian term *mijnuroba* and variants [1930: 159, 161] to translate it) and also represents a "primitive form" of a potentially progressive "free love" in the "hidden sexual sphere" (157; also 136, 159, 165): "In short, Pshavian ts'ats'loba has a peculiar originality: its joyful appearance, beautiful sexual experiences, which is expressed in a true free love" (165).

On the other hand, this essentially positive reception is balanced by prurient and moralizing concern for the way in which this chaste, "knightly" (rainduli), "spiritual" (sulieri) love must necessarily lead to its opposite. As discussed above, both Mak'alatia and Tedoradze engage in the same speculation about the kinds of "abnormal" sexual activities engaged in by the Khevsurs and Pshavians: given natural impulses and the low rate of pregnancy, both seem to agree, it is clear that the "abnormal," "unnatural," and even "harmful" practices of "uncompleted sexual acts," which are explained with Latin phrases in Latin type (coitus interruptus and onanismus coniugalis, i.e., mutual masturbation), must have been widespread (Mak'alatia 1934: 119; 1984: 162; Tedoradze 1930: 159–60).

How to reconcile these opposites? Mak'alatia (1934) generally follows the outlines of Vazha Pshavela's analysis that these practices once were more chaste, but have nowadays degenerated into harmful and unnatural sexual practices, quoting an older Pshavian woman who claims that the women of today "have become Russian" (i.e., shameless) (1934: 120). Mak'alatia cites families that advertised their daughters for marriage as not having engaged in ts'ats'loba (1934: 120). In contrast to his relatively tolerant description of the 1920s, his ethnographic descriptions of the 1930s (particularly of Pshavi), perhaps reflecting the new cultural politics of Stalinist sexual conservatism, contain sharp condemnations of this general decay of a once-beautiful chaste custom into a harmful custom of fornication that exerts a negative influence on social life as a whole (1934: 119–20, 122–23). Tedoradze, by contrast, offers us this remarkable reconciliation between what for him are startlingly opposed qualities. The fact that Khevsurs and Pshavians were untroubled by the way they have made fornication into a local custom, and the lack of any expected negative social or psychological effects, is explained by the fact that they were unaware that it should have any:

> The Pshavian boy in love has a sound mind and his creative talent in the expression of feelings gives remarkable artistic pictures. It is, however, strange, that the uncompleted sexual act, which has almost turned into the rule in Pshavian ts'ats'loba and Khevsur sts'orproba, does not exert such harmful influence on men, as would be expected as a result of the aforementioned sexual anomaly. It is possible that this can be explained to a certain extent by the fact that Pshavs and Khevsur have absolutely no conception about the bad consequences of these unnatural phenomena and for this reason the harmful influence on their psyche is relatively lighter than on other people. (Tedoradze 1930: 160)

Around the same time as Georgian ethnographers were describing Khevsur romance, Georgian modernist writers also chose to take the theme of mountain romance as the topic of their works (for a parallel discussion see Manning 2014a). Like the ethnographies, these modernist fictional writings quote extensively from recently published volumes of folk poetry (Shanidze 1931); they realistically transcribe the voices of the Khevsurs, using authentic Khevsur dialect in their imagined conversations; and they appear, to varying degrees, to be based at least in part on actual ethnographic fieldwork, as well as on careful readings of existing ethnographies, using ethnographic fact as fuel for their imaginations. But at the same time, these otherwise realistic modernist novels display a tendency to rewrite the relationship between the intelligentsia and the "people" from being a *reportive*, realist one (i.e., the stance of the ethnographer outsider neutrally describing the practices of the people and their conversations) to being a *romantic* one (i.e., the male member of the intelligentsia falls in love with the female member of the "people"). Modernist novelistic renditions of native romance seek to overcome the gulf between intelligentsia and folk, city and village, narrator and narrated, by romantic or erotic means. It is the man who acts as narrator—he comes from the plains and either desires or consummates desire for the female figure (a Khevsur). Here the lovelorn relationship between the intelligentsia and the people, the reading public and the narrated people, takes on a directly erotic form.

Both narratives under discussion, Grigol Robakidze's story *Engadi* (1932) and Mikheil Javakhishvili's novel *Tetri Saq'elo* (*White Collar*) (1926, revised 1934), have more or less the same structure: a Georgian outsider, a member of the intelligentsia (a vicarious erotic proxy for the male Georgian reader), enters a Pshavian or Khevsur community for some reason. Along the way, he befriends a local man who becomes his sworn brother, and this leads to his acquiring a lover, a *sts'orperi* or *ts'ats'ali* (the two become interchangeable). Whatever the rest of the plot involves, for example the fateful confrontation of tradition and modernity, village and city, a central tension in the plot is the Georgian man's struggle and frustration with the incomprehensible rules, the desire crossed by constraint, of *sts'orproba* or *ts'ats'loba*. In the case of Robakidze, the narrator spends a great deal of time trying to "decode" the relationship, as if it were some sort of hieroglyphic whose true importance was its hidden meaning, rather than a sexual practice to be pursued straightforwardly for its own sake, as his lover constantly reminds him.

This erotic re-imagining of native romance in these fictional narratives takes opposed forms in each story. Because the details on what could happen sexually between a boy and a girl when they are alone are somewhat sketchy, with more blanks than there are facts, these blanks and voids become spaces of potential that could be freely populated by the imagination. While *White Collar* frames *ts'ats'loba* (the term *sts'orproba* is also used) salaciously and sexually, *Engadi* turns on the restraint imposed by this chastely framed tradition (in this case, Khevsur *sts'orproba*). Both authors reinterpret the nature of the rules to make the relationship permeable to outsiders, allowing outsiders to engage in it and thus to allow outsider Georgian readers to imagine themselves vicariously participating in it. It is precisely this "opening up" of the tradition to outsiders that allows the novels to become sites of vicarious participation, of eroticism. In particular, the characters (the male outsider and the female Khevsur) display a kind of virtual potential: the characters themselves are permeable, so that the Georgian readers can imaginatively and erotically identify themselves with one or the other character as desiring subject and treat the other character as the sexualized object of desire.

In *Engadi*, the general incomprehensibility of Khevsur *sts'orproba* to the rest of Georgia is a major trope of the narrative. In one important scene, the non-Khevsur hero finds himself enjoying, and yet enduring, this relationship with Mzekala, a local Khevsur woman:

> [Mzekala] came, lustful and immaculate. Our caresses turned into torture. "Why can't what happens between men and women happen between us?" I asked her, lying by my side. "Am I not your *sts'orperi* and you—mine!" she answered me. "Is this not torture?" I cried out. "Is it torture?" she answered me. "Isn't it sweet?" "This" was without a doubt sweet, but also so torturous. What man could endure this fire?
>
> Mzekala informed me of many things about *sts'orproba*.
>
> "Sometimes the *sts'orperis* don't have enough strength," she told me, "but this is shameful, it is a shame." "If they were to marry?" "There can be no marriage, it is forbidden." "Then I cannot marry you?" "No!" "Is this not torture!" "Is it not sweet?" (216)

As this literary depiction of *sts'orproba* shows, the incomprehensibility of this framing of desire arises from the way that it colonizes a space of erotic license ("sweetness"), limited by self-restraint ("torture") and opposed to both marriage and intercourse.

In Javakhishvili's *White Collar*, too, a woman (Khatuta, the sister of Jurkha, our hero's sworn brother) comes to the man at night, but their encounter goes somewhat differently. When he sees the woman carrying a sword (*khanjali*) in the darkness, he calls out:

"Khatuta . . . Is that you? . . . Is it really you? . . . What in the world do you need that *khanjali* for, woman?"

"So that you do not touch me . . . I came for *sts'orproba* . . . I came to Jurkha's sworn brother."

I came close to her, but I encountered the sharp blade and I stopped.

Now I understood. I remembered the whispers of the previous day, Khatuta's shy singing, Jurkha's warning, and stories I had heard in the past about a strange Khevsur custom—cruel, delightful, and destructive *sts'orproba*—*ts'ats'loba*—a strict custom expressive of the highest brotherly love—even today I do not know whether it is savage or superhuman, divine or satanic: a Khevsur has a woman lie in bed with a guest who is a relative or a sworn brother, but in the morning this woman must rise again still a virgin.

I snatched the sword from her coat and put it aside.

Khatuta noticed and told me:

"Give it to me here. This is not the rule!"

"What time is it for rules?"

I couldn't open her buttons and I tore them with force. (Javakhishvili 1994: 580)

In both stories the heroes confront a custom that is seemingly a unity of opposites: pleasure crossed with restraint. Robakidze's hero behaves with restraint, while Javakhishvili's dispenses with all restraints, opening the girl's shirt by force (compare this with the male protagonist of the poems discussed in chapter 4). Similarly, Robakidze's hero ultimately accepts not only that he cannot have sex with Mzekala but also that he cannot marry her, whereas Javakhishvili's hero ultimately does both with Khatuta: in the unequal conflict between tradition and modernity, the village and the city, urban modernity (symbolized by the titular "white collar" of the urban professional intelligentsia hero) wins in the end. While Robakidze's account is often credited with being the more realistic ethnographic representation, Javakhishvili's is the more popular, presumably not only because it was published more accessibly, or because of the frankly erotic content (his *ts'ats'ali*, for example, performs *ts'ats'loba* in the nude), but also because it refashions the tradition with literary artifices that domesticate this exotic tradition: he adduces a concern for virginity not found in indigenous tradition but which is a major concern for Georgians. In addition, the hero eventually transforms this strange relationship that involves neither sex nor marriage into one that includes both, one that his Georgian readers can accept as normative, taking Khatuta to the city as his wife and abandoning his Khevsur friends as they prepare to fight a losing battle against the Soviet forces.

The circulation of these frankly erotic novelistic readings of Pshavian and Khevsur ethnography came to form the basis for an indigenous Georgian erotic literature, such that citations of *ts'ats'loba* and *sts'orproba* from these novels produced a kind of virtual potential for sexual fantasies *taking place in Georgia* for a whole generation. According to informants from the late socialist period, the generally somewhat impoverished repertoire of erotic and pornographic representations from that time included not only the usual late-socialist prized Western imports of (sometimes photocopied!) *Playboy* magazines and pornographic videos, but also indigenous forms of ethnographic eroticism, mediated by pseudo-ethnographic novels like Javakhishvili's, which included fantasies about some place in Georgia where otherwise unimaginable sexual liberties of various kinds were possible. One of my friends from this generation explained it as follows:

> I remember really well, that my classmate Temo, when we were like 14–15 years old, that would be 1980–1981, drew our attention to one episode from Mikhail Javakhishvili's novel "White Collar," where, if my memory serves, the main hero (who is the narrator) says: "That night my *ts'ats'ali* so *ts'ats'aled* me, that the second day I couldn't stand up straight." Temo's interpretation of this passage was "You see, that is, either she gave him a hand job or a blow job." From this I and my classmates soon came to the conclusion, that in reality there was much more sexual liberty in the mountains, that *there* anal and oral sex and so on was a normal activity, that the activity of being a *ts'ats'ali* [noun], *ts'ats'loba* [verb], refers precisely to these kinds of activities, that so called legends, that the *ts'ats'alis* place a sword between them, are simply lies. I and my classmates were not alone in having these notions, many people of my age and older have expressed similar ideas.

For Georgians of this background, the Pshavians were libertines for whom anything was possible, *except* vaginal intercourse: Pshavian romance becomes an absolute inversion of Georgian normative sexual expression (heterosexual vaginal intercourse in the context of marriage), and the ambiguous eroticism of the literary model of *ts'ats'loba* is concretized as being essentially pornographic. More generally, the social life and circulation of this citational sexuality have come to reside essentially in its almost algebraic quality: incomplete propositions with variables. Its virtual potential for sexual fantasies, what *drives* its continued circulation, derives from this real indexical linkage to some objective reality that is also always distant (*there*), combined with incompleteness, gaps, lacunae, and absences—all of which can be filled with conjecture and subjective fantasy. It is thus driven and sustained by its citationality.

FIGURE 7.1: Imeda (Tengiz Archvadze), the artist (wearing his white-collared shirt), draws pictures of Shat'ili in the film *Ballad of the Khevsurs* (National Archives of Georgia).[16]

SOCIALIST FILMS

The most picturesque village in all of Georgia is the Khevsur fortress village of Shat'ili, in the farthest part of mountainous Khevsureti, a stone's throw from Chechnya. Shat'ili remains today one of the most recognizable symbols of Georgia, but it is also a tragic symbol of a lost world. The population of Shat'ili, along with that of the rest of Khevsureti, was forcibly resettled in the plains at Stalin's order in 1952. Mountain villages like the picturesque Shat'ili, emptied of living Khevsurs, became museums of an unchanging traditional life as if frozen in a photograph. We have, then, a definitive moment after which Khevsur romance moved from being a real, living tradition to something that, like the rest of the ethnographic life of the Khevsurs, existed only in circulating fragments: citations, memories, images, and descriptions.

The emptied villages of Khevsureti provided occasional sets and stages for a series of socialist films about the life of the Khevsurs, and yet the forced immigration of the Khevsurs to the plains in 1952, effectively the end of Khevsur communal life, haunted these films about the region. In the decade or so after the forced immigration, the Georgian film industry produced four films set in this region, which is rather a lot for a socialist film industry in a small republic that produced at most a handful of films in any given year.

The first such film, the late Stalinist film *They Came Down from the Mountains* (*Isini Chamovidnen Mtidan*, 1954), is also the most macabre misrepresentation of the depopulation of Khevsureti. Here the villages of Khevsureti are represented in typical Stalinist socialist-realist style as being already rife with modernity and socialist civilization, and Khevsurs are represented as already modernized socialist citizens who willingly come down from the mountains to engage in higher eduction as metallurgists: the mountains come to modernity.

The most reflexive of the films is *A Meeting in the Mountains* (*Shekhvedra Mtashi*, 1966), which deals with the making of a (fictional) film about Khevsur traditional life. The romantic comic misunderstandings of the film revolve around the female romantic lead, a well-known actress and popular singer (Lali Mindeli, played by popular acress Leila Abeshidze, who also starred in *They Came Down from the Mountains*), trying to get into her role as a Khevsur woman for the film, passing herself off to a handsome engineer she meets on the road while mounted on a horse and in full Khevsur costume as a real Khevsur woman named Mzevinari. The remainder of the movie, which takes place both in modern downtown Tbilisi, the capital of Georgia, and in mountainous Khevsureti, revolves around her managing her dual identity, sometimes appearing on stage and screen as herself, Lali Mindeli, and sometimes in her assumed role as Mzevinari, who she pretends is really the twin sister of the popular actress.

But the most important film made in Georgia about the Khevsurs is without a doubt the film *Ballad of the Khevsurs* (*Khevsuruli Balada*, 1965), which came out in the period of destalinization under Khruschev (for a parallel discussion of this film see Manning 2007). It also focuses on the relationship between socialist modernity and traditional Khevsur life. Here the forced immigration of the Khevsurs is represented as a benevolent act of the socialist state, an "evacuation to safety" (*gakhizvna*), and the Khevsurs are depicted as returning to a Shat'ili that has now become a model socialist village outfitted with all the amenities of socialist modernity.

The original screenplay (written by Giorgi Mdivani in 1956) was envisioned as a filmic reworking of Javakhishvili's *White Collar* (see above) with, naturally, a good deal of censorship of the specifically sexual scenes. However, in 1957, the daughter of the novelist, Ketevan Javakhishvili, denounced the writer of the screenplay for deviating so far from the original plot that it could not be considered to be based on this work, and that the screenplay should not be used (K. Javakhishvili 1957). Mdivani wrote an angry letter insisting that he had never intended to replicate the plot of the novel of the great author Mikheil Javakhishvili, but only the "motifs." This letter ends with a strongly underlined section, evidently written with great emotion, claiming that, therefore, no one could accuse him of being a criminal (Mdivani 1957). Since the author of the novel had, like many other writers, been imprisoned and shot during the Great Purges of the Stalin period (1937), a danger that would have still been hanging in the air since Stalin had died only a few years earlier in 1953, Mdivani's fears about the potentially grave consequences of criticism of his manuscript can be better understood. The decision was made not to shoot this particular script (or Mr. Mdivani!) and Mdivani rewrote the script in 1964 as an entirely independent work (Mdivani 1964).

The resulting film, now renamed *Khevsuruli Balada* ("Ballad of the Khevsurs"), resembles the novel in that its main argument situates romance within a frame narrative of the (now benevolent) confrontation of Khevsur tradition and socialist modernity, the village and the city. The film covers three historical periods: first, a more or less completely idealized contemporary socialist modernity after the "evacuation" and "return" of the Khevsurs (circa 1965); second, the presocialist period of intact Khevsur tradition; and lastly, a middle period some time in the 1920s and 1930s where the bulk of the narrative occurs, and where tradition and modernity confront each other within the context of a star-crossed romance between Imeda (played by Tengiz Archvadze, a popular actor who also starred in *Meeting in the Mountains*), a modernized Khevsur boy who returns to Khevsureti as an artist, and a traditional Khevsur girl, Mzekala (played by Sopik'o Ch'iaureli, one of Georgia's most popular and respected actresses). The bulk of the film, told retrospectively by the aging hero, the artist Imeda, to a visiting Georgian doctor, is simply a tragic love story. As a boy, Imeda's father is killed in a duel, and the orphaned boy is taken to live in Tbilisi by a wandering member of the intelligentsia who is first to arrive on the scene. The boy learns to write and paint. Now an adult, he is introduced by a childhood friend who comes to Tbilisi to his natal village and, more importantly, to Mzekala. He falls in love with Mzekala, but he runs afoul of another of Mzekala's suitors, Torghva. In a duel, Imeda manages to kill Torghva. The lovers flee on foot into the snows of the Khevsur winter, pursued by Torghva's brothers. Imeda's sworn-brother, Aparek'a, strives to lead the pursuers astray in the snow, but to no avail. The brothers, who are mounted, eventually track the lovers down and, while attempting to kill Imeda, kill Mzekala instead.

Modernity and Tradition: Frame Narrative and Framed Narrative

A constant concern of any socialist film about tradition is how to represent the traditional life of some group (in this case, the Khevsurs) in a traditional setting without thereby undermining the claims of the state that socialism had already

brought the amenities of modernity to everyone. In this film, the romantic traditional life of the Khevsurs is framed as the traditional past, a lost world, within a
present-tense frame narrative of an encompassing socialist modernity. Like many
socialist films from the period, this film begins with some obligatory showcasing
of the technological achievements of socialist modernity. The original literary
script by Mdivani is quite explicit about this, developing a (completely fictional)
representation of contemporary (circa 1960s) socialist Khevsureti where modernity is rife, where there are working telephones, an airport, automobiles, and
a resident population. The script also makes very specific mention of the real
achievements of socialist technology, which could be seen in the Tbilisi airport,
such as Soviet jetliners (e.g., the Tupelov TU-104, the world's first successful jet-
liner, and the Ilyushin IL-18, one of the world's most popular planes of the period)
(Mdivani 1964: S2121–14).

If the main argument of the *frame* narrative (taking place in the 1960s, the
present) is about the benevolent achievements of socialist modernity, the main
argument of the *framed* narrative (taking place in the early socialist period, the
1920s–30s) is about traditional romance. Here traditional social relations among
the Khevsurs are presented as if characterized by extremes—love and violence
are everywhere, often in tandem. In a sense, the Khevsurs are more savage, more
backward, more violent, and the social institutions that are employed to charac-
terize this are the blood feud and dueling, which are each presented as a social
curse that animates much of the narrative: Imeda's father is killed in a blood feud,
and his dueling weapons adorn Imeda's wall in Tbilisi as a reminder of his past;
Imeda kills Torghva in a duel, and his relatives, seeking blood vengeance on Imeda,
accidentally kill Mzekala instead, bringing the film to a tragic end. The pervasive
theme of blood feud and dueling represents the overt nature of negative social
relationships, but positive ones are recognized as well, between men in the form
of the ritual of sworn-brotherhood (between Imeda and his friend Aparek'a), and
between men and women in the form of open flirtation and romance, where the
highly elective character of romance is stressed. The boldness of Khevsur women
is constantly emphasized, reflecting their sense of autonomy and freedom. Imeda's
first encounter with Mzekala happens at a spring, where she and some other bold
Khevsur girls, mounted on horses, flirt with him, demanding he give them water
(Figure 7.2), and then steal his hat and ride off laughing. His companion, Aluda,
tells him, "Thank God, that they didn't steal you, too!"

The main difference between this film and other literary accounts in which these
opposing motifs occur (i.e., the duel, the sworn brother, the romance) is that, in the
film, romance among the Khevsurs is imagined as being essentially a form of premarital courtship, in that it has as its goals marriage, the formation of families, and social

FIGURE 7.2: First contact with the bold, free Khevsur woman: Mzekala (Sopik'o Ch'iaureli) accepts a cup of water from the "city dweller" Imeda (National Archives of Georgia).

reproduction. In other literary and ethnographic accounts, local forms of romance are specifically opposed to marriage, and to a lesser extent to sexual relations. Thus, with respect to romance, *Khevsuruli Balada* is much more firmly grounded in the narrative and normative expectations of the Soviet version of Hollywood. Everything ethnographically specific about Khevsur romance is erased: Khevsureti becomes a place of romance, but not a place of quintessentially *Khevsur* romance.

Romance, Poetry, and Violence

The opposition between the two forms of positive and negative interaction— open flirtation between men and women and dueling between men—is represented by their direct juxtaposition in a feast scene that occurs when Imeda enters Shat'ili for the first time. In the feast scene we see the openness and boldness of Khevsur relations between the sexes, exemplified by a scene where Mzekala (Figure 7.3) and Aparek'a (Figure 7.4) engage in *shair-k'apioba*, a kind of extemporaneous verbal duel in traditional terms, using the accompaniment of the *panduri*, or traditional lute.

Aparek'a begins his poem with a traditional invocation, making the *panduri* "sing" a specific genre of poem, which he calls a *shair-k'apia*, that is, a poem we expect to

FIGURE 7.3: Mzekala at the feast (National Archives of Georgia).

FIGURE 7.4: Aparek'a singing *shair-k'apia* on a *panduri* (National Archives of Georgia).

be joking and flirtatious (*shairi*), but also one that is extemporaneous and dialogic (*k'apia*). He begins by praising her beauty:

khma amaighe panduro,	Oh *panduri*, raise your voice,
amomavali mzistvina,	For the rising Sun,
shair-k'apia amovt'q'o,	That I might compose a poem (*shair-k'apia*),
pirimze lamazistvina.	For the Sun-faced beautiful one.

Aparek'a throws the *panduri* to Mzekala (whose name means "Sun-woman"), who criticizes both his singing and his skill at playing the *panduri*:

vis rad ch'irdeba net'avi,	Who would want I wonder, and why,
e mag panduris zhghriali,	The clatter of that *panduri* of yours,
k'lde-ch'iukhebshi jikhvebsa,	Your roaring is frightening,
daaprtkhobs sheni ghriali.	The ibexes on the cliffs and crags.

Undeterred, Aparek'a wants to know whether she has a soft spot in her heart for him:

tvali mich'iravs shenzeda,	I have my eye on you,
rogorts miminos mts'qerzeda,	Like a hawk on a quail,
net'avi gamagebina,	I wish you would let me know
shen ra guli gakvs chemzeda.	What you feel about me.

Mzekala indicates is that she not going to flirt any longer, and in her reply she notes that she indeed likes someone—just not him:

am mk'erdshi ori gul midevs,	In this breast I have two hearts,
ertshi ts'vims ertshi daria,	In one it rains, in the other it is fair weather,
shentvisa shavq'ri ghrublebsa,	For you I have gathered clouds,
skhvas gavughimeb daria.	For another I make fair weather smile.

Aparek'a responds by upping the ante with praise (I have found the last two lines of this stanza in an ethnographic report from the turn of the century, so they are authentic):

kalav sul tvalts'in midgekhar,	Woman, you always stand before my eyes,
ghvidzilshia da dzilshia,	When I am awake or in my sleep,
daimaleba khokhobi	A quail could hide
sheni tval-ts'arbis chrdilshia.	In the shadows of your eyes and eyebrows.

Mzekala refuses the lute, so Aparek'a throws it to Torghva, the man who had been dancing with Mzekala earlier, who in turn throws it back angrily. Aparek'a continues by announcing his frustration with her obstinancy:

Net'ai ristvis gakebdi,	I wonder why I praised you,
ristvis davkharje dzalao,	Why I wasted the effort,
egeti enis p'at'ronsa,	The owner of such a tongue,
ra gagatkhovebs kalao?	What will make you marry, woman?

This serenade incites a duel between Torghva and Aparek'a, who are rivals for Mzekala's affection. The close juxtaposition of poetic duel between man and woman and actual duel between men shows us that Khevsurs must take the bad with the good: egalitarian, open relations of non-avoidance between sexes provoke equally open, egalitarian expressions of violence within a given sex, with the implication that Khevsur women look on the capacity and display of violence as a desirable trait of men; for instance, Mzekala is portrayed giggling with her friends when the swords are drawn.

Echoes of *Sts'orproba*

One might argue that Khevsur romance has been completely denatured, that the film *Khevsuruli Balada* owes more to Soviet versions of Hollywood than Khevsur ethnographic realities. But in spite of the obvious censorship that turned the salacious text of *White Collar* into a tamed asexual romance, where *sts'orproba* becomes a kind of courtship, just as some of the fake Khevsur poetry from the film is based on actual Khevsur poetic practices and even drawn from folkloric texts, so too are traces of the custom of *sts'orproba* present in the film, emerging obliquely in one peculiar scene.

In one pivotal scene after the duel described above, Mzekala wanders into Imeda's room at night, ostensibly to return his flashlight. Mzekala's boldness is matched only by the way this action reminds us of the parallel practices of *sts'orproba*, where a woman comes to a man at night. She lies down next to him and they talk, in much the same way as one might on a first night of *sts'orproba* (Figure 7.5). The substance of their conversation, too, touches closely on matters related to this otherwise conspicuously absent custom. Mzekala reflects that he probably has a lover in the city, which he denies. She tells him he is a liar, and reflects that the women of the city know nothing of love, though she has never been to the city, she would never go there, but still, she would like to see, from afar, at a glance, how the people of the city live and dress. In turn, Imeda takes an interest in whether Mzekala loves anyone in Shat'ili, perhaps Torghva, perhaps Aparek'a? She admits that there are many who love her, but whom she loves is a secret. He asks, more directly, if she has ever "spent the night

FIGURE 7.5: Mzekala and Imeda "lying down" together (National Archives of Georgia).

with Torghva." She replies that she has never spent the night with anyone. "Spending the night" can only be an oblique reference to *sts'orproba*, to "lying down and getting up," though, again, here it is imagined as happening exogamously, between people who might eventually be married to one another, a premarital union tending toward marriage. He touches her, one time too many, which angers her and so she gets up to leave; this echoes the rules of *sts'orproba* concerning who gets to touch whom where: Mzekala freely touches Imeda, but Imeda, it seems, is not allowed to reciprocate. She wonders if he is really a Khevsur, and prepares to leave; he ensures her that he is indeed a "real Khevsur." To reassure her he lies back, crossing his arms to show he will not touch her, but wonders if it was some "local custom" that brought her here: another veiled reference to *sts'orproba*. She leaves at dawn, though all they have done is talk. Thereafter, their relationship takes on the more easily recognizable dimensions of romantic flirtation; there is no more talk of "local customs" in the film. Here, then, we find one kind of erasure—"anti-marriage" becomes premarital courtship, leaving behind, as I have argued, only traces of itself in this strange scene.

NOTES

1   Comparison of different translations for all these quotations can be found at http://kartvelologi
    .tsu.ge/index.php/ge/journal/inner/14

2   Note that all images related to this film are photographs taken on the set from the National
    Archives of Georgia and not images from the actual film, for which I was unfortunately unable
    to secure rights. The images chosen closely parallel actual shots from the film.

CONCLUSION: VIRTUAL ROMANCE

———◆———

MODERNIST GENRES OF REALISM, from ethnography to novels and film, created a set of avowedly realistic representations in which Khevsur love stories became decoupled from actual Khevsur life and love, and started to circulate as often fragmentary objects (news stories, ethnographies, and so on) within Georgian media culture. These representations began to assume an autonomous but fragmentary existence as a series of texts and images that are now repeatedly circulated and cited. These images and descriptions of Khevsur desire and desirable Khevsurs disclose an unfamiliar world of romance to the Georgian public, but it is a world that is known only in cited and quoted fragments and that can only be reassembled with the glue and filler of the imagination. Each attempt at realist description has produced glimpses but also left gaps that make the lost original seem ever more distant and mysterious, and produced openings for the imagination of the reader to "fill in the gaps."

Such fragmentary images continued to circulate in the world of late socialism, and the virtual potential of these images were still able to be re-animated with the imaginations and desires of Georgians as resources for the erotic imagination. We have already seen some of these stereotypical images in the Introduction, in the discussion of beer ads. Here, as a conclusion, I briefly explore two cases—idealized images of Khevsur women as unattainable objects of desire in late-socialist popular art and decor, and post-socialist teenage forums on the Internet—in which these circulated, recycled, and stereotyped images of unattainable Khevsur desire come to be appropriated with the desires of contemporary Georgians.

FROM FILM TO IMAGE: KHEVSURS IN
LATE-SOCIALIST ART

In the film *Ballad of the Khevsurs*, the relationship between the frame narrative about socialist modernity and the frame narrative about traditional romance reproduces a long-standing image of the mountains, and Pshavi and Khevsureti in particular, as a living museum, an outcropping of the past in the present, in contrast to the modernity of the plains of Georgia. Frequently the metaphorical image of a photograph was deployed to capture this feeling. In the late nineteenth century the ethnographer N. Khizanashvili described these regions as "a photographic picture of the past, of the life of the ancestors. This picture we find only here, in Pshavi and Khevsureti" (Khizanashvili 1940: 1). However, after the resettlement of the Khevsurs, the life of the Khevsurs moved from being only figuratively a photograph of the past, to something that could really only be encountered in actual photographs from the past. Khevsur romance, like Khevsureti itself, thus could never again be encountered in reality; it was a lost world, a world experienced only in a mixture of photographic images, literary citations, and acts of the imagination—a now unchanging world that circulated like an old photograph.

In fact, *Ballad of the Khevsurs* was a watershed film in the history of Georgian socialist art. It both exhibits in its own structure a new set of artistic norms only possible after the death of Stalin and the fall of the Stalinist school of "socialist realism" in 1954, and also serves as a kind of advertisement for new forms of socialist plastic art that became possible during the so-called "thaw" of the Krushchev period, a period from the late 1950s to the early 1960s of relative openness and liberalization in many areas of Soviet life. Oddly, as a result, seemingly archaic, traditional images of Khevsurs and "primitivist" motifs from Khevsur art became strongly associated with a kind of "modernist" formal experimentation in art, producing a relationship between a modernist "frame" and a traditional "picture" of Khevsur life whereby modernist and archaic elements blend together into a unique hybrid that we can call "traditional modernism." The most dominant images portrayed in this traditional modernism are images of unattainable desire, beautiful Georgian women in traditional dress, usually Khevsurs. *Ballad of the Khevsurs* depicts this conversion of a living tradition into a still photograph *formally*, by using the visual device of still images juxtaposed with live actors to signal shifts between the embedded narrated ("diegetic") space of tradition, where Khevsur practices are still alive, and the enframing socialist present where they exist only as still images. A significant change between the original novel and the final screenplay is that the main character, Imeda, becomes an artist, and appropriately, the central narrative of the film is framed by his artistic representations of traditional Khevsur life. His artwork is not merely part of the diegetic world of the film, a set of objects or *props*, but also plays a key role as an *actor* in the formal visual language of the film.

The film was clearly intended to showcase not only socialist technological *modernity*, as I argued above, but also bold formal experiments in socialist artistic *modernism*, including both the form of the film and also the new kinds of modernist art showcased within the filmic world. In the original literary script, for example, in a scene that would have been brutally difficult to shoot as it combines live actors with animated sequences (it is replaced in the actual film by the poetic duel above), the artist Imeda imagines the real dancing Khevsurs at a feast turning into animated contours, a painted portrait, and then into still photographs:

> *The song continues, but the feast freezes and the real faces of people fade and are replaced with the sketched contours of people. They are sketched by a painter but the song continues. This song is real, alive.*
>
> *The drawn outlines slowly change and before our eyes is a painted canvas of a Khevsur feast. On the screen is already apparent that we have the creative work of a talented artist. His has his own manner of drawing, he makes good use of the art of old frescoes, at the same time the artwork is very contemporary.*
>
> *The song continues.*
>
> *The picture again fades, again the drawn outlines appear again. These contours fill in with a motionless, frozen photograph . . .*
>
> *Again the feast—a real, living feast of the Khevsurs.*
>
> (Mdivani 1964 S.2121. 28)

This juxtaposition of different kinds of images from various media, living actors, animated contours, and painted still life in this proposed scene is significant on several levels. On the one hand it works as part of the main theme of the film: the theme of real Khevsur life turning into a still image of a lost world that an elderly Imeda mourns. At the same time, this scene shows a writer eager to explore the new, purely formal possibilities not only of film, but also of other artforms, in the period of Krushchev's "thaw," in which film and other media were relieved of their duty of being purely neutral "realistic" conveyances of "life." If in Stalin's period such purely aesthetic experiments in form could earn one the label of "formalist" and an early grave, in this period a scene such as this, which explores the depiction of "life" across a variety of media forms, represents an exploration of the new possible languages of film and other media.

While this particular scene was never shot, this "formalist" foregrounding of Imeda's artwork remained a central device of the actual film: each transition in the film's main narrative portions is mediated by some artistic object or image—a drawing of two boys becomes a live image of two boys, the weapons of Imeda's dead father hang on his wall in his city apartment in the scene after his death in a duel, Aparek'a deduces that Imeda loves Mzekala from his portraits of her, and so on.

Imeda's artwork performs a framing function: the framed narrative of the traditional world of Khevsureti is framed on both ends by Imeda's art representing that lost world. Near the beginning of the film, his conversation with the doctor, who had heard of his artwork and expresses interest, leads him to show the doctor a series of pictures illustrating scenes and landscapes from Khevsur ethnographic life, including images of Mzekala, one a charcoal drawing, the other a metal bas-relief. The coda of the film, after Mzekala is killed, reprises the first panorama of Imeda's compositions, with the doctor and the artist standing in silence and again surveying these images, which now take on an elegiac quality: fragmentary images of a now-lost world, funereal images of a lover now dead. We are reminded not only that Mzekala is long dead, but that the world of the Khevsurs, too, is dead, now only accessible in still images.

The film also showcases a new form of Georgian modernist art being popularized at the same time as the film. The author of the screenplay is as specific about the kinds of media Imeda should work in, and the kind of style he uses, as he is about the need to show certain specific kinds of airliners at the Tbilisi airport. Repeatedly in the literary script, and in images from the film (below), we see metal frescoes, which are a particularly characteristic medium of the new, state-approved, Georgian "traditional modernist" style, as being a key part of Imeda's repertoire.

The author of the screenplay underlines this mixture of "tradition" and "modernity" in this art form specifically when he characterizes Imeda's bas-reliefs above ("*he makes good use of the art of old frescoes, at the same time the artwork is very contemporary*" [Mdivani 1964 S2121.28]), and even more explicitly: "*Among the works of the artist is expressed the style of traditional Old Georgian frescoes. At the same time, something original, contemporary, modern*" (Mdivani 1964 S2121.10).

Importantly, the themes explored in this new artform consisted largely of highly idealized portraits of Georgian women in traditional dress, depicted as unattainable objects of desire and reflecting a broader set of idealized representations of Georgian women under socialism as demure, standoffish, unattainable objects of desire, what is generally called the "cult of women." Among the most common kinds of Georgian women portrayed in this artform, both at the professional and souvenir levels, were representations of Khevsur women. At the end of socialism, souvenir versions of such bas-reliefs were commonplace; my own collection, for example, includes 12 pieces, of which 11 are generic, idealized portraits of "Georgian women," and 3 of these are specifically Khevsur women. All of these images have certain features in common: exotic head-gear, and elongated eyes, which are usually demurely downcast

FIGURE 8.1: From person to portrait: Imeda and Mzekala, with sketches of Mzekala in background and incomplete bas-relief on workbench (National Archives of Georgia).

and averted from the viewer, often directed at a flower or candle the woman is holding (Figures 8.2a and 8.2b).

These conventions found in popular souvenir works are based on the works of named artists, which also include frequent representations of Khevsur women with highly stylized faces, elongated eyes, and backgrounds that contain traditional Khevsur decorations. A good example is Khevsur artist Irak'li Ochiauri's "Khevsur Woman" of 1966 (Figure 8.3), which (probably not coincidentally) very strongly resembles Imeda's bas-relief image of Mzekala from the film of the previous year.

Traditionally the metal bas-relief form had been associated with religious figures (icons), but during the "thaw," a time of official atheism, this artform became secularized and especially devoted to portraying typified characters (*t'ipazhi*) from traditional ethnographic life, particularly Georgian women: a movement away from portraying "the fantastic images of Christian religion" to portraying "the ideal of the Georgian woman, her beauty" (Japaridze 1971: 20). This once-religious

FIGURE 8.2A AND 8.2B: "Traditional modernist" souvenir representations of Khevsur women.

FIGURE 8.3: Irak'li Ochiauri's *Khevsur Woman* (1966). Reproduced by permission of Lela Ochiauri.

artform was secularized and used to sacralize Georgian women as cult objects of the "cult of women."

Famous pioneers of this style such as Irak'li Ochiauri (himself a Khevsur) and Guram Gabashvili (whose style and themes are imitated in the souvenir versions and in *Ballad of the Khevsurs*) focused on the idealized, exotic, romanticized portrayal of beautiful Khevsur and Tushian women in traditional dress in natural contexts, holding flowers, surrounded by deer and birds (Nino Tseradze, personal communication; Japaridze 1971: 20, 29). The style of portrayal, in particular the elongated eyes, shared between the final bas-relief image of Mzekala in the film and these abundant representations of Khevsur beauty point not only to a common style, but also thematically to a common object of desire: the idealized portrayal of Georgia through the beauty of idealized Georgian women. And of all Georgian women, Khevsur women, the most frequent "type," become generalized objects of desire, placed on a pedestal within this now-secular pantheon.

Such ubiquitous bas-relief images of Khevsur women circulated in the world of late socialism in much the same way that decontextualized images of Khevsur or Pshavian men circulated as brand accoutrements on post-socialist Georgian beer bottles. Khevsur romance moved from a narrative of desire, to a kind of desire where the narrative underpinnings have been dispensed with and the "Khevsur woman," divorced from all ethnographic or narrative contexts, has become the object of desire—a movement from desire contextualized within full narratives to desire for characters independent of their narratives (Galbraith 2009). Khevsur romance, as a form of virtual potential, comes to center itself on fragmentary circulating images of Khevsur women as unattainable objects of desire, just as the film moves from a narrative in which the prototypical Khevsur woman, Mzekala, is a living moving character, to a still bas-relief image of the now-dead Mzekala, the unattainable lost object of desire for the male gaze.

VIRTUAL ROMANCE ON GEORGIAN TEEN FORUMS

On March 12, 2007, a certain "nanu" began a new forum discussion on teen.ge with an extremely long "copypasta" post of various authoritative sources about "ts'ats'laoba" (the spelling she uses), prefacing her post with the following:

NANU: At a time when even Europe wasn't "developed" to this level (in this area of course), things were happening in the mountains of Georgia that contemporary Americans would envy (I think I am exaggerating a little)

I have read nothing much about ts'ats'laoba but I have heard some things

Anyway I think it is an interesting topic :dirol:[2]

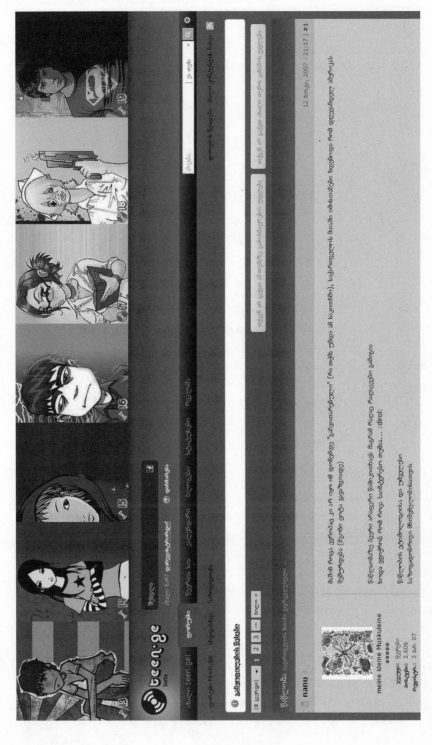

FIGURE 8.4: "nanu" opens discussion of *ts'ats'loba* on teen.ge forum.

I reproduce the ensuing discussion as best I can:

TOTOSHA: yeeaaaaaah
It's an old topic, very old
NANU: old but interesting
TIAMAT GIRL: **quote:**
ts'ats'laoba
ts'ats'loba :big grin:
NANU: **tiamat girl**
in georgian literature ts'ats'laoba is used more often
but whatever as you like
TIAMAT GIRL: **nanu**
what do i know in georgian literature i think ts'atsloba is used more :big grin:
NANU: fine as you like, but in my opinion what is more important here is that in the mountains of georgia such things were happening and at the same time very early.
today we still think of the mountains of georgia as being the most backwards (in this matter), than for example tbilisi
TEMO: yeaaaaaah and what is ts'ats'loba? :mda:
TIAMAT GIRL: sex without sex
lol :big grin:
TEMO: and whaat is that?
you've got me all confused
NANU: i don't think it was completely without sex??[1]

As this forum conversation shows, along with many other sexual topics, contemporary Georgian teen Internet forums occasionally return to the theme of Khevsur and Pshavian sexual traditions (often mixed up or treated as synonymous), so much so that some posters (such as totasha above) see the topic as being an old, worn-out theme. The relative anonymity afforded by these forums produces a public space for open dialogue about sexuality that would otherwise not be possible for Georgian teens, while the other affordances of online forums also allow different interlocutors to cite one another and to address one another, having often complex conversations in the space of a single thread (Figure 8.5). In such online discussions of *ts'ats'loba*, we find diverse streams of citation (ethnographic, literary, and so on), with their various epistemic grounds and authorities, often cut and pasted in large, unreadable blocks of text ("copypasta"), swirling and eddying together, so that different, even opposed, understandings of the custom are presented side by side in the same debate. Such

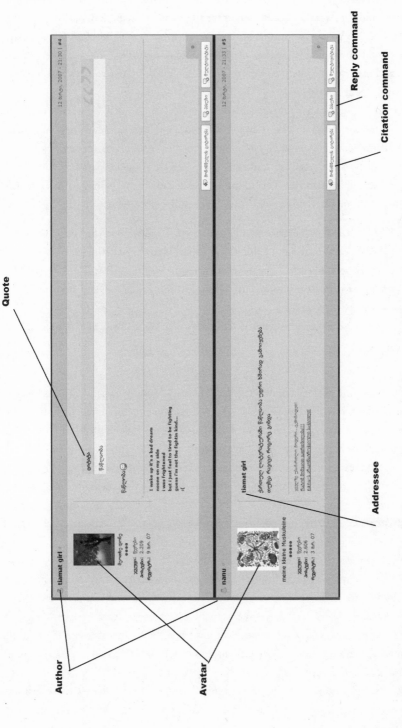

FIGURE 8.5: Exchange between "nanu" and "tiamat girl" about the proper spelling of *ts'ats'loba* (teen.ge).

forums show how these customs display a kind of virtual potentiality, a mixture of the real and fantasy: they are resources for the sexual imagination, but they are also understood to be real, so posters are continuously concerned with "what really happened" and rampant speculation based on dubious authority ("I know many Khevsurs and they say . . .") with corrections based on authoritative sources and constant demands for citational evidence ("Post links!").

In these discussions, the sexual "elsewheres" of traditional Georgian mountain regions and the "Imaginary West" become curious paradoxical doublets or even translational equivalents. For nanu, *ts'ats'loba* represents the possibility of a progressive, "European," and yet simultaneously authentically Georgian, sexuality, paradoxically among a group that inhabitants of Tbilisi, the Georgian capital city, believe to be extremely backward. A certain "Sophie Golden," in a recent blog post, echoes this perspective:

> I know a lot of Pshavians and from them I know that very very often *ts'ats'loba* ends in sex and I think that Pshavi is to this day the most "European" region, where no one pays attention to virginity. This *ts'ats'loba* is a slightly ridiculous tradition, but even so it seems kinda cool and colorful, if we consider it today.
>
> Likewise, in Javakhishvili's *White Collar* precisely this theme was used, if you remember.
>
> That was my first "erotic" book :D.[2]

Similarly, one poster in another debate, "babairo," simply considered *ts'ats'loba* the equivalent of the "European"-style teenager relationship of "boyfriend-girlfriend" (which in contemporary Georgia involves kissing in parks, albeit illegally): "If we were to translate it into contemporary language, this would be girlfriend-boyfriend minus the directly sexual act." The same commenter added later that "such displays of affection, or what contemporary teenagers do (and the police fine them for doing :smile:) had exactly this form."[3] Similarly, in the same forum "Hyperzet" facetiously offered to translate terms like *sts'oproba* and *ts'ats'loba* as being what is "called 'petting' (*p'et't'ingi*) in the classical literary language."

Because these customs are both part of the elsewhere of traditional Georgian past and yet uncannily resemble the elsewhere of the modern progressive West, the status of *ts'ats'loba* in these debates is highly variable: sometimes *ts'ats'loba* plays the role of a venerable tradition defended by conservatives and dismissed as backwardness and idiocy by progressives, while at other times it is an inversion of "correct" tradition, dismissed by traditionalists as scandalous and stupid and embraced by progressives as "European" and progressive (see also Manning 2014a).

Accordingly, some forum debates are concerned primarily with how these customs relate to the way in which the Georgian nation is poised between the elsewheres of a traditional past and a Euro-American future. Accordingly, *sts'orproba* and *ts'ats'loba* in these debates become matters of the morality of the nation, just another generic battleground for well-worn debates between positions that are really not as much about sexuality as they are about broader political divides between traditionalists and progressives. One forum participant, "»»Ş»A»L»i»A»»," wanted to know why this well-worn topic of "mountain traditions" was being resurrected once more, treating it as one more repetition of an endless forum debate about the institution of virginity, which can only lead to polarization between well-known camps: "Some say that we take nothing seriously and we have forgotten our culture.... Others post once again on 'the institution of virginity' and call out to the people that we no longer need this institution of virginity, so we can take off as much clothing as possible: 'Let's be free to have boyfriends!'"

But even in the same forum pages absolutely opposed understandings of the nature of the custom prevailed. Participants like "Rafster," accusing another forum participant, "drozera," who condemned the custom as being of questionable morality, as "understanding everything in a perverted manner and having a dirty mind ...," saw in this custom something completely chaste: "First as far as I know the man did not have the right to touch the woman, he could only stroke her hair.... Secondly this was like a pure relationship between a brother and a sister...."

On the very same page of the same forum, another participant, "sheshlili" ("crazy"), displayed a completely opposite understanding of the true nature of the custom. Having gleaned (apparently from *White Collar*, in which this is the case) that *ts'ats'loba* could happen in the nude, this person wanted to know some other things too: "So to cut a long story short what interests me [is that] I have heard that there was completely nude *ts'ats'loba* and also caressing the breasts, sex was completely forbidden, but was there caressing the sexual organs by hand and fellatio and cunnilingus or not [.] I haven't run across anything about that anywhere. And what's the deal, was there anal sex or not? There was also a widespread kind of *ts'ats'loba* called 'Aragvian *ts'ats'loba*' in this region and it even allowed fucking, but it was censured as I understand."

The virtual potential, the indeterminacies in the exact nature of "what really happened," allows *ts'ats'loba* and *sts'orproba* to play roles both as matters of concern in public political and moral debates about the nation and as fuel for private fantasy. Just as its own internal ambiguities make it an ambivalent proxy in heated political discussions between traditionalists and progressives, the indeterminacy of just what *ts'ats'loba* was—what was allowed and what was not—also opens up spaces for imagining alternative sexualities. For example, the prohibition of sex can lead to *ts'ats'loba* being interpreted as a traditional Georgian form of what Georgians now call "petting" (*pet't'ingi*, that is, "everything up to vaginal intercourse"). Or, alternatively, this prohibition notwithstanding, it is sometimes claimed that it must have routinely led to sex in actual practice. Or, if sex is taken to mean "vaginal intercourse," then *ts'ats'loba* becomes open to a series of frankly pornographic interpretations (meaning "fellatio, cunnilingus, anal sex, everything *but* vaginal intercourse"). Additionally, the absence of intercourse, and the trial of self-restraint required of both partners, frequently causes others to claim that this was in fact a form of sadism or masochism. Others in the online forums, as we have seen, occasionally see in *ts'ats'loba* nothing other than a translational form, an indigenous version, of the Euro-American boyfriend-girlfriend relationship.

Forum participants defend or embrace the tradition for different reasons. Some defend the public face of the tradition from scandalous allegations of immorality. In one of the forums under discussion here, the discussion of Khevsur traditions is largely controlled by a certain "Mtis-Yoili" (whose online pseudonym is a transcription of *mtis-q'oili* ["mountain-flower"], *q'oili* being the Khevsur dialect form of the standard Georgian *q'vavili* ["flower"]), who draws her authority both from her claims to be a Khevsur girl herself and many citations of authoritative sources, defending the honor of the tradition from unsubstantiated allegations of perversion by other posters. For example, as a native Khevsur, she upbraids other posters for relying on dubious sources like Javakhishvili, and mixing up debased Pshavian *ts'ats'loba* with respectable Khevsur *sts'orproba*. Echoing earlier sources, she sees the Khevsur tradition as having once been pure and having been degraded by Pshavian influence, causing it to be forbidden in general:

> [Pshavian] *Ts'ats'loba* and [Khevsur] "lying down" (*ts'ola-dgoma*) were at first from the beginning one and the same, then the custom began to degenerate in Pshavi into fornication, whereas a perverted form of *sts'orproba* spread into Khevsureti too a bit later.

For others, it is not so much that *ts'ats'loba* is a venerable Georgian tradition, or the equivalent of an absent, "European" kind of sexual sociability, or even an emergent kind of affection one can find teenagers expressing (and policeman fining) in any park in Georgia, but it is simply the exoticism and alterity of *ts'ats'loba* that become an object of desire, a forbidden desire one can freely express only in the anonymous space afforded by the Internet. Such posters are concerned with this tradition not as a respectable or scandalous, backward or progressive expression of national culture, but as an object of desire, an affordance for private sexual fantasy. In the same forum "amelia" wrote: "Oh I'm crazy about it, it's my dream to experience *ts'ats'loba*, but who engages in *ts'ats'loba* in Tbilisi, I seriously like it, a lot." When asked by another forum member what about the custom attracts her, she could locate it only in a purely irrational space of desire: "What do I know, it must be some sort of psychological nonsense, but to tell you the truth I haven't thought a lot about *why* it attracts me, it just

დღესდღეობით უკეთესი არ გამოგონილა ვიდრე წაწლობა 🔟

მე მინდა წაწალი
😊

FIGURE 8.6: Lomgul Orgeli's post (Tbilisis Forumi)

does." Forum participants like "amelia" treat *ts'ats'loba* exclusively as an unattainable kind of framing of private desire, filled with virtual potentiality for the private sexual imagination.

On the one hand, we have forum participants like "amelia," who only sees in it something she desires for herself. On the other hand, we have "Mtis-Yoili," who defends it as an authentically Georgian form of desire, and "nanu," who sees in it a progressive form of sexual expression, a local prefiguration of Western modernity. Lastly, we have a certain "Lomgul Orgeli," who, in a reply to "Mtis-Yoili," concluded with a striking conflation of these two modalities of desire: "In today's times, nothing better than *ts'ats'loba* has been invented :big grin: I want a *ts'ats'ali* :two people kissing:" (Figure 8.6).

I pause for a moment on the multiple voicing of this last, apparently simple, statement of desire. If uttered by a Pshavian girl of generations past, this post could be read as being perhaps no more complex than a North American girl wishing for a boyfriend: a desire for something absent, but possible. But uttered by a contemporary Georgian girl on an Internet forum today, it becomes a wish that cannot be fulfilled, an imagined virtual desire that can never become an actual consummated desire. "I want a *ts'ats'ali*," a seemingly simple statement in its original ethnographic context, becomes a declaration of a desire for something absent and also impossible: not only a specific absent sexual "other," but also an absent and impossible kind of relationship in which such an "other" can be found. The poster "amelia," for example, doesn't want a *ts'ats'ali*; she just wants to experience *ts'ats'loba* as an object of desire in itself. The problem is finding a partner willing to do it: "but who engages in *ts'ats'loba* in Tbilisi?" She doesn't want a *ts'ats'ali* so much as she needs one to realize her true desire: to engage in *ts'ats'loba*. Here the means to an end, *ts'ats'loba* as an expression of desire for a *ts'ats'ali*, becomes an end, an object of desire, in itself. *Ts'ats'loba* begins as a framing of desire for an actual other, like a frame around a picture of a loved one. Through the long chain of citationality I have described here, attention moves from the picture to the frame itself, which becomes an empty frame for impossible pictures painted by the imagination.

NOTES

1   :dirol: is a smiley face that is often translated as :cool: 8) or a smiley face wearing shades.

2   In *teen.ge*, 3 March 2007, 9:17 P.M., at teen.ge/index.php?showtopic=828 (last accessed 10 November 2013).

3   In "Ts'ats'loba—Pshauri T'raditsia," *Giq'vardet Chemnairebi!*, 11 February 2010, 10:31 A.M., at www.vasassi.com/2010/02/blog-post_11.html?showComment=1265913089667#c3591176156937520528 (last accessed 10 January 2014).

4   In *TBILISIS FORUMI*, 8 July 2011, 3:27 P.M., at forum.ge/?f=20&showtopic=34278143&st=75 (accessed 10 November 2013). The remaining citations all come from this thread.

GLOSSARY OF KEY GEORGIAN (KHEVSUR OR PSHAVIAN) TERMS

---

boseli   literally "stable"; in Khevsur usage the lower "impure, feminine" floor of the house where women and cattle sleep; in Pshavian usage it also means "hut for menstrual isolation"

dghiani   (Khevsur only) "likeable, well-known"

dobili   (1) literally "sworn sister"; (2) a kind of female demon who is the "sworn sister" of a shrine divinity (*jvari*)

dzmobili   (1) literally "sworn brother"; (2) the term that is used to refer to both "boyfriends" and "girlfriends" in a durable romantic relationship

elchi   "ambassador, envoy," someone (usually a girl) who arranges "lying down" between a boy and girl

garq'vna; garq'vniloba   "fornication, depravity," nonmarital sex

jari   literally "army"; usually it refers to a meeting of the older members of the community at any important ritual to discuss serious matters from which women or talk of women was forbidden, opposed sometimes to a parallel, less serious mixed-gender meeting of young people, the *akhalukhali*

jvari   literally "cross," in Khevsur dialect it means either a male shrine divinity or the physical shrine itself

jvart ena   "language of the crosses," the divine language spoken by the gods through human mediators

k'anoni   (Russian imperial) law

k'apia   extemporaneous, improvised verse; *shair-k'apia*, a *shairi* poem improvised on the spot, usually in a dialogic competition between two poets

khati   (Pshavian dialect) literally "icon," used in the same sense as Khevsur *jvari*

khatri   "respect"; *khatrit* "out of respect" for another person

kochriani   (1) in ordinary language, nearby groups who did not follow Khevsur rules; (2) in *jvart ena*, "Russian"

leksi-shairi   a general class of poems with the same meter (16-syllable line with end rhyme), typical of the feminine repertoire which deal with topics of everyday life, including love poetry, which can include both neutral poems on many subjects (*leksi*) or more provocative, playful insulting poems of censure (*shairi*)

leksoba   to compose a *leksi-shairi* or to recite it in a specific manner

morideba   (1) deference; reserve, inhibition; (2) avoidance; also contains notions of shyness and (feminine) modesty

nadobi   (Pshavian) (1)"sworn sister"; (2) the term that is used to refer to"girlfriends" in a durable romantic relationship

nadzmobi   (Pshavian) (1)"sworn brother"; (2) the term that is used to refer to"boy-friends" in a durable romantic relationship

namusi   honor; conscience; shame, the honor that comes from having shame

namusiani   honorable; upstanding; conscientious

panduri   three-stringed lute

paragi   decorated neck collar, usually of a woman's clothing

perobit   "by begging, entreaty": *perobit dats'ol-adgoma* is specifically opposed to lying down out of desire:"being forced to lie down with a boy or girl *without desire* out of regard for someone or other considerations" (Baliauri 1991: 189)

q'ma   literally"servant, serf, vassal," used in the sense of "man" or "male member of the shrine community (*jvari*)"

sadzmobilo, sadobilo   gifts for the *dzmobili* (in either sense) or *dobili*

sakalvazho   (poetry about) love, boys and girls; specifically forbidden from serious meetings of the *jari*

sakheli   literally"name," usually in the sense of one's masculine virtues, honor, fame

sakhel-sirtskhvili   "name and shame," i.e., honor and shame, displaying concern for which is the same as having *namusi*

samrevlo   (Khevsur) hut for menstrual isolation of women (Pshavian *boseli*)

senva, saseno   poems usually of the *shairi* class that express bitter rivalry (*senva* "bitter rivalry, poison"; *saseno*"insulting, poisonous")

shairi   poems that tend to focus on satire, insult, or censure; *shairis gakhdoma* "to become [the subject of] a *shairi*" is to lose one's good name

shesaperi   "suitable, appropriate, worthy, fitting," usually said of the suitability of potential sexual partners for each other

simghere   epic poems, with a distinctive performance style and eight-syllable meter, about dead heroes that belong mostly to the male repertoire and that can be performed in the *jari*

sirtskhvili   "shame"

sts'orperi   literally"equal-color": (1) peer, age-mate, friend; (2) casual lover *sts'orproba*   the sexual relationship between *sts'orperis*, in which one engages in *ts'ola-dgoma*

survili, suruli   "(sexual) desire"

tavdach'eriloba   masculine "self-control, reserve"

tavmoq'vareoba   "self-esteem, pride"; sense of autonomy

tav-shek'aveba   "self-restraint"

temi   a group of villages, usually occupying the same river valley

ts'ats'loba   (Pshavian) the sexual relation between Pshavian lovers (*ts'ats'alis*)

ts'ats'ali   (Pshavian) lover

ts'esi   "rule," usually in the sense of Khevsur customary laws and traditions, as opposed to Russian *k'anoni*

ts'ola-dgoma   "lying down and getting up"; the sexual practices of spending the night together in *sts'orproba*

unamuso   "lacking in *namusi*"; shameless

REFERENCES

———

Abu-Lughod, Lila. 1986. *Veiled Sentiments: Honor and Poetry in a Bedouin Society*. Berkeley: University of California Press.

Adorno, Theodor. 1991. *Notes to Literature: Volume 1*. New York: Columbia.

Ahearn, Laura. 2003. "Writing Desire in Nepali Love Letters." *Language & Communication* 23 (2): 107–22. http://dx.doi.org/10.1016/S0271-5309(02)00046-0.

Baliauri, Natela. 1991. *Sts'orproba Khevsuretshi*. Tbilisi: Tbilisi University.

Barthes, Roland. 1978. *A Lover's Discourse: Fragments*. Trans. Richard Howard. New York: Hill and Wang.

Bauman, Richard. 2004. *A World of Others' Words: Cross-cultural Perspectives on Intertextuality*. Malden, MA: Blackwell. http://dx.doi.org/10.1002/9780470773895.

Cameron, Deborah, and Don Kulick (2003). *Language and Sexuality*. Cambridge: Cambridge University Press.

Caton, Steven. 1987. "Power, Persuasion and Language: A Critique of the Segmentary Model in the Middle East." *International Journal of Middle East Studies* 19 (1): 77–102. http://dx.doi.org/10.1017/S0020743800031664.

Caton, Steven. 1990. *Peaks of Yemen I Summon: Poetry as a Cultural Practice in a North Yemeni Tribe*. Berkeley: University of California Press.

Charachidze, Georges. 1968. *Le système religieux de la Géorgie païenne : Analyse structurale d'une civilisation*. Paris: Maspero.

Ch'reladze, St. 1892. "Chveni mtis khalkhi: sabibliograpio ts'erili." *Iveria* 1:1–3.

Eckert, Penelope. 1994. "Entering the Heterosexual Marketplace: Identities of Subordination as a Developmental Imperative." *Working Papers on Learning and Identity* 2. Palo Alto: Institute for Research on Learning. https://www.stanford.edu/~eckert/PDF/subordination.pdf.

Eckert, Penelope. 1996. "Vowels and Nail Polish." In *Gender and Belief Systems*, ed. Natasha Warner et al., 183–90. Berkeley: Berkeley Women and Language Group. http://www.stanford.edu/~eckert/PDF/nailpolish.pdf

Elyachar, Julia. 2010. "Phatic Labor, Infrastructure, and the Question of Empowerment in Cairo." *American Ethnologist* 37 (3): 452–64. http://dx.doi.org/10.1111/j.1548-1425.2010.01265.x.

Evans Pritchard, E.E. 1940. *The Nuer: A Description of the Modes of Livelihood and Political Institutions of a Nilotic People.* Oxford: Oxford University Press.

Galbraith, Patrick. 2009. "Moe: Exploring Virtual Potential in Post-millenial Japan." *Electronic Journal of Contemporary Japanese Studies* 5. http://www.japanesestudies.org.uk/articles/2009/Galbraith .html

Giddens, Anthony. 1992. *The Transformation of Intimacy: Sexuality, Love and Eroticism in Modern Societies.* Stanford, CA: Stanford University Press.

Gogoch'uri, Davit. 1974. *Melekseoba Khevsuretshi.* Tbilisi: Sabch'ota Sakartvelo.

Gogolauri, Tamila. 1996. *Gana Laghi Var, Roma vmgher.* Tbilisi: Int'elekt'i.

Inoue, Miyako. 2006. *Vicarious Language: Gender and Linguistic Modernity in Japan.* Berkeley: University of California Press.

Japaridze, Gulnara. 1971. *Kartuli Tanamedrove Liton-Mkandak'ebloba.* Tbilisi: Gamomtsembloba "Khelovneba."

Javakhishvili, Ketevan. 1957. Statement about Mdivani's original script for *Tetri Saq'elo. National Archives of Georgia* S2131.1–3.

Javakhishvili, Mikheil. 1994 (1926, 1934). *Tetri Saq'elo,* in *Tkhzulebani Shvid T'omad,* 2:580. Tbilisi: Sakartvelos Matsne.

K'alandadze, Ana. 1995. "Mshobliur mits'aze uzomod sheq'varebuli." In *Natela Baliauri, Khevsuruli Kronik'ebi,* 5–14. Tbilisi: Lega.

Khizanashvili, N. 1940. *Etnograpiuli nats'erebi.* Tbilisi: SSRK mecnierebis ak'ademia.

Kulick, Don. 1998. *Travesti: Sex, Gender, and Culture among Brazilian Transgendered Prostitutes.* Chicago: University of Chicago Press.

Kulick, Don. 2003. "No." *Language & Communication* 23: 139–51.

Mak'alatia, Sergi. 1934. *Pshavi.* Tbilisi: Geograpiuli Sazogadoebis Shromebi.

Mak'alatia, Sergi. 1984 (1935). *Khevsureti.* Tbilisi: Nak'aduli.

Mak'alatia, Sergi. 1998 (1925). *Pshauri Ts'ats'loba da Khevsuruli Sts'orproba.* Tbilisi: Int'elekt'i.

Malinowski, Bronislaw. 1923. "The Problem of Meaning in Primitive Languages." In *The Meaning of Meaning,* ed. C.K. Ogden and I.A. Richards, 296–336. New York: Harcourt, Brace & World, Inc.

Malinowski, Bronislaw. 1929. *The Sexual Life of Savages in Northwestern Melanesia.* Oxford: Liveright.

Malinowski, Bronislaw. 1932. *Argonauts of the Western Pacific.* London: George Routledge & Sons.

Mamsashvili, R. [pseudonym]. 1880. "Mgzavris Shenishvnebi: mogzauroba Aragvis kheobashi (Traveller's Notes: A Journey in the Aragvi River-valley)." *Droeba* 1880, 102.1–3.

Manning, Paul. 2007. "Love Khevsur Style: The Romance of the Mountains and Mountaineer Romance in Georgian Ethnography." In *Caucasus Paradigms: Anthropologies, Histories, and the Making of a World Area,* ed. Bruce Grant and Lale Yalçın-Heckmann, 23–46. Halle Studies in the Anthropology of Eurasia. Berlin: LIT Verlag.

Manning, Paul. 2012a. *Strangers in a Strange Land: Occidentalist Publics and Orientalist Geographies in Nineteenth-Century Georgia.* Brighton: Academic Studies Press.

Manning, Paul. 2012b. *The Semiotics of Drink and Drinking.* London: Continuum Press.

Manning, Paul. 2014a. "Once Upon a Time There Was Sex in Georgia." *Slavic Review* 73 (2): 265–86. http://dx.doi.org/10.5612/slavicreview.73.2.265.

Manning, Paul. 2014b. "When Goblins Come to Town: The Ethnography of Urban Hauntings in Georgia." In *Monster Anthropology in Australasia and Beyond,* ed. Yasmine Musharbash and Geir Presterudstuen, 161–77. New York: Palgrave Macmillan.

Manning, Paul, and Ann Uplisashvili. 2007. "'Our Beer': Ethnographic Brands in Postsocialist Georgia." *American Anthropologist* 109 (4): 626–41. http://dx.doi.org/10.1525/aa.2007.109.4.626.

Mdivani, Giorgi. 1957. Letter responding to criticism of original script for *Tetri Saqʼelo*. National Archives of Georgia, S2131.4–5.

Mdivani, Giorgi. 1964. Literary Script for *Khevsuruli Balada*. National Archives of Georgia, S2121.

Mead, Margaret. 1928. *Coming of Age in Samoa: A Psychological Study of Primitive Youth for Western Civilization.* New York: William Morrow.

Ochiauri, Aleksi. 1980. *Stʼumarmaspʼindzloba Khevsuretshi.* Tbilisi: Metsniereba.

Ochiauri, Aleksi. 2005. *Kartuli Xalxuri Dgheobebis Kʼalendari: Khevsureti. Tʼomi 2.* Tbilisi: Ena da Kʼultʼura.

Ochiauri, Tinatin. 1995. From the editor. In *Natela Baliauri, Khevsuruli Kronikʼebi,* p. 4. Tbilisi: Lega.

Pascoe, C.J. 2010. "Intimacy." In *Hanging Out, Messing Around, Geeking Out,* ed. Mimi Ito et al., 117–48. Cambridge, MA: MIT Press.

Robakidze, Grigol. 2004 (1932). *Engadi.* In Grigol Robakidze, *Tkhzulebani Tkhutmetʼ Tʼomad,* 15 vols. Vol. 2: 189–224. Tbilisi: Intʼelektʼi.

Rustaveli, Shota. 1912. *The Man in the Panther's Skin.* Trans. Marjory Scott Wardorp. London: The Royal Asiatic Society of Great Britain and Ireland. Repr. 1966.

Rustaveli, Shota. 1977. *The Lord of the Panther-Skin.* Trans. R.H. Stevenson. Albany, NY: SUNY Press. UNESCO Collection of Representative Works: Series of Translations from the Literatures of the Union of Soviet Socialist Republics.

Shanidze, Akʼakʼi. 1931. *Khalkhuri Pʼoezia: Tʼomi 1, Khevsuruli.* Tbilisi: Sakhelgami.

Simmel, Georg. 1949. "The Sociology of Sociability." Trans. Everett C. Hughes. *American Journal of Sociology* 55 (3): 254–61. http://dx.doi.org/10.1086/220534.

Simmel, Georg. 1978. *The Philosophy of Money.* Ed. David Frisby. Trans. Tom Bottomore and David Frisby. London, New York: Routledge.

Tedoradze, Giorgi. 1930. *Khuti Tsʼeli Pshav-Khevsuretshi.* Tbilisi: Sil. Tavartkiladzis Gamotsema.

Tuite, Kevin. 1999. "Real and Imagined Feudalism in Highland Georgia." Presented as "Real and Imagined Feudalism in Highland Central Caucasia." American Anthropological Association conference, Chicago, Nov. 21. http://mapageweb.umontreal.ca/tuitekj/publications/Tuite-1999-feudalism.pdf

Tuite, Kevin. 2000. "'Antimarriage' in Ancient Georgian society." *Anthropological Linguistics* 42 (1): 37–60. www.mapageweb.umontreal.ca/tuitekj/publications/Tuite-antimarriage.pdf

Tuite, Kevin. 2008. "The Banner of Xaxmatʼis-Jvari: Vazha-Pshavela's Xevsureti." In *Der Dichter Važa-Pšavela: Fünf Essays,* ed. Ekaterina Gamkrelidze, 11–38. Würzburg: Königshausen & Neumann.

Tskhitishvili, Aleko. (n. d.). *Kartuli Mama-pʼapʼuri Seksi.* http://lib.ge/book.php?author=234&book=6216

INDEX

could endanger *dzmobilis*, 47
girl giving boy gifts through, 53
no *elchi* in Pshavian practices, 11
not needed for durable boyfriend-girlfriend
    relationship, 43
pairing boys and girls who were strangers, 27
as "phatic worker," 3, 5
presence or absence of, 1, 32–35
role in dissolving proposed marriage partner-
    ship, 79
sworn sisters as, 52
thankless work, 3–4
elective, Western-style "play" form of sex, xviii
elective character of romance in *Ballad of the
    Khevsurs*, 117
elective relationships, 48
"elsewhere"
    of "Georgian traditional sex," xviii, xx
    of Western sexual traditions, xviii
Elyachar, Julia, 2–3
emancipation of the serfs, xxxi, 91–92, 96
enemies, 22, 37, 49, 61, 70–71
Engadi (Robakidze), 110–11
epic or heroic "songs" (*simghere*), 69
epic "praise" poetry, 61, 71. *See also* praise poetry
erotic desire, xxvii
erotic novelistic readings of Pshavian and
    Khevsur ethnography, 113
erotic re-imagining of native romance, 110
eroticism, 107
eroticization of "romance of the mountains," 94
ethnographers' use of evidence from love
    poetry, 57
ethnographic aspects of gender, 97
ethnographic beer advertising. *See* Georgian beer
    advertising
ethnographic branding, xxi
ethnographic descriptions of *sts'orproba*,
    ts'ats'loba
    explosion (1920s and 30s), 99
ethnographic sketches, 92
ethnographies
    in Georgian newspapers, 93
    of language and sexuality, xxvii, xxxiii, 90
    of sexuality (contemporary), xix
ethnology in a living culture, xxx

exchanges of spit, 2, 42
exile from community for violating rules of
    marriage, 30, 78, 100
exogamous society, xvi, 28
exogamy, 79, 100
exotic native, 95
exoticism and alterity of *ts'ats'loba*, 136

fellatio, 135–36
female demons, 73–74
fighting, 46, 54
    brawls, 45
    dueling, 71, 117–18, 121
    following *saseno* poems, 67
"first dates," 17
flirtation (coquetry), xxiv, xxvi–xxvii, 18,
    117–18
    girls and boys could not flirt until "set up"
        by the *elchi*, 3
folk poetry, 63, 110
folklorists, 106
formal constraints of poetry, 59–60
fornication, xvi, xviii, 105, 108–9. *See also* vaginal
    intercourse
frame narrative, 117, 125
"free love," 108–9
    of the mountains, xxiv

Gabashvili, Guram, 130
Galbraith, Patrick, xix, 105
garq'vna of premarital sex, 26
garq'vnili (depraved one, pervert), 26
gender
    difference and inequality, 6
    ethnographic aspects of, 97
genres, xxvii
    of conversation, 2
    of love poetry, xxxii
    of lying down (table), 33
    relating individual erotic desire to a collective
        normative order, xxxii
    of realism and romance, 92–94
    of realistic reportage, 90
Georgian beer advertising, xiv, xxi–xxvi, 130
Georgian ethnographies, xvii, 107
Georgian feudalism, xxxi

of *dmobili* boy and *dzmobili* girl, 29–30, 78.
(*See also* marital abduction)
Khevsur customs of, xxviii–xxix, 29, 77–78
kin of one's marriage partners, 32
Russian law (*k'anoni*), 75, 77–78
separation between *sts'orproba* and, 28
sexual intercourse, 74
masculine competitions, 45
Mdivani, Giorgi, 115–16
A Meeting in the Mountains (1966), 115
menstrual isolation huts, 11, 41, 47, 96, 98
modern (the), xix
modernist genres of realism, 124
modernist novels, 110–11
modernity and tradition, 116–18, 125
morideba (modesty), 11, 60–61, 65
mountain villages as museums of traditional
life, 114
mountaineer ethnographers, 26, 101

nadobi, xv. *See also* sworn sister
nadzmobi, xv. *See also* sworn brother
"name" (*sakheli*) of an individual, 69
namusi, 22, 26, 59–61, 65, 71–72, 75. *See also*
honor
Nanuk'i's story (case study), 85–87
Natela
as figure of erotic desire for the readers, 95
a native ethnographer of the 20th century,
98–103
story of, 94–98
newspapers, xxxiii, 90–93. *See also* intelligentsia
"Night and Day" (Khevsur poem), 42, 45,
56–57
novels
and films, xvii, xxxiii, 99, 104
as sites of vicarious participation, 111
with romantic protagonists set in ethnographically realistic mountain settings, 99

oaths, 26, 49–51
obligations of hospitality and kinship, 32, 35
Ochiauri, Aleksi, xiii, xxx, 101, 106, 130
exile, 77–78

Ochiauri, Irak'li
"Khevsur Woman," 128
onanismus coniugalis, 109
"ordered anarchy," xxx
Orthodox Christianity, xxxi, 78
Orthodox Church marriage, 77

panduri, 65, 118
paragi (beaded collar), 10, 80
parallelism between linguistic and nonlinguistic
genres, xxviii
people (rural, uneducated peasants), 91, 93
perobit, 18
persuasion, 2, 5, 7
p'et't'ingi (petting), xviii, 134–35. *See also*
caresses
"phatic communion," 2
"phatic worker" or "phatic pimp," 3
photograph, 108, 125
physical intimacy, 20, 22–23
pillow talk, xxviii
platonic love (*mijnuroba*), 107
play form of eroticism and sexuality, xviii, 17–18,
28, 105. *See also* sociable sexuality
poems of denunciation, 25, 57–58
for aggressive sexual advances, 39
poetic duel, xxvi
poetic expression and sexual expression, 72
poetic genres, 69
poetry for the dead, 69
poetry of blame, censure, insult, satire, scorn
(*senva*), 60, 68–69, 77
pornographic interpretations, 105, 113, 136
potential marriage partners, xvi, 28, 78, 82
lying down with, 32
norms of avoidance or taboo, 10
potential *sts'orproba* partners, 28
overlapped with potential marriage partners,
29
praise poetry, xxxiii, 22, 60–61
replacing individual desire with desirability
in, 68–72
sociocentric perspective, 65, 69
pregnancy, 106, 109

premarital sex, 26

private sexual fantasy, 135–36

prohibition, 23, 29

promiscuity, 74

prostitute, comparison to, 26

    Khevsur word was Russian mat'ushk'a (little mother, mama), 75

Pshavela, Vazha, 99, 106, 109

    distinction between *mijnuroba* and loveless fornication, 108

Pshavi, xv, xx

    as living museum, 108, 125

Pshavian love poetry, 60–62

    articulating desire in, 62–64

    composed by both men and women, 68

    lyric, expresses the author's desire, 71

Pshavian romantic practices, 113

    the boy comes to the sleeping girl, xv, 11

    evidence from poetry, 57

    publicly known norms, 56

Pshavian sexual practices, 13, 75. See also *ts'ats'loba*

Pshavian sexual traditions, 132

Pshavians, 47

    beer, xxi

    fieldwork among, 57

    intermarriage with Khevsurs, 75

    oral tradition of poetry, 57

public, intelligentsia as, 91, 93

public performance of poetry, 68

"reading" the factual gaps in Khevsur romance, 108

real elsewheres where other ways of doing things are possible, xvii–xviii

realism understood as "civic aesthetics," 92

realist writing was critical realism, 92

realistic fiction (novels), 92

realistic genres

    in the Georgian press, 99

    of representation, 92

reported speech, 102

revolutionary challenges to question traditional order of *sts'orproba* and marriage, 77

rivalry between *dzmobilis* and future spouse of lover, 74

road vodka, 38, 40

romance

    imagined as premarital courtship, 117

    of the intelligentsia and the people, 91

"romance of the mountains," xx–xxi, 91, 94, 97, 99, 104, 110–11

romantic love

    autonomous domain pursued for intrinsic pleasure, xix

romantic realism, 94

rules for lying down, 64. See also *ts'ola-dgoma*

    Aragvian, 79–80

rules for physical comportment at first meeting, 23–25

Russian law (*k'anoni*), 81–82

    divorce under, 77–78

    marriage, 77, 78–79

    regulations on sexuality and marriage, 75

Russian Revolution, xxxi, 77

Russians, xxix

    comparison to, 26, 39, 109

    Russian-style depravity, 81

    shamelessness, 75

Rustaveli, Shota, 107–08

    "The Knight in Panther's Skin", 107–08

sadzmobilo gifts, 52–53

sakalvazho poetry, 67, 72

sakheli, xxx, 75

salekso (for the poem) gift, 60

samrevlo, 11, 96

sanctions

    against the marriage of sts'orproba partners, 30

    for transgressions, 25, 27–28

sandauri dzmobili (desired sworn brother), 48

saseno poems (poems of reproach, rivalry, or insult), 67, 69

    about women, 67

    by women, 68

satirical *shairi* poetry, 83

scandal, xx, 74, 77, 79, 107

self-control, 11–13, 26, 65

    in poetry, 64

self-esteem (*tavmoq'vareoba*), 26, 47

self-respect, 37

self-restraint, xxx, 11–13, 48, 56, 59, 71, 136

senva, 69

sex without sex, xvii
sexual "elsewheres" of traditional Georgian
    mountain regions and the "imaginary
    West, 134
sexual fantasies, 113
*The Sexual Lives of Savages in North-Western
    Melanesia* (Malinowski), xix
sexual overtones between intelligentsia male
    and peasant girl, 94–95
sexual relations, 118
sexual sociability, xviii, 28
sexual symbolism of vodka in Khevsur
    romance, 36
sexuality and identity, relations between
    culturally and historically variable, xxix
sexuality as relational and transitive, xxvii
sexuality research
    epistemological problem, 55
sexualization of gender, xxviii, xxix
shair-k'apioba, 118
shairi poetry, 67–69, 72, 77
shame, xxx, 25, 29
    namusi, 39
    sirtskhvili, xxx, 75
    verbal shaming, 25, 27
Shanidze, Ak'ak'i, xxx, 60–61, 68, 71
sharing vodka in bed, 42
shemtkhvevit, 30
shesaperi (desirability), xvi, 27, 45
    boys and girls set up together should be
    similar, 22
"signs," 15
silver
    oath of, 49
    cups, 63
    or gold, 63
silver rings, 39
    publicizing the existence of a romantic
    secret, 53
    semi-performative gift, 53
Simmel, Georg, 17–18
simple lying down
    no sense of obligation, 30
    without a mediator (*uelchod*), 31
sleeping together among others, 27–28
    a man could not force a woman easily, 26

sociability, 17
    and obligation, 30–34
sociable conversation, 17–18, 20–21
    undertaken purely for the pleasure it
    affords, 18
sociable sexuality, 21, 34, 105. *See also* play form
    of eroticism and sexuality
    only possible within certain parameters,
    34
    threatened by Aragvian rules, 81–82
social distance, xvi, 1
social realism, 92
socialism
    free love under, 108
    some peasants received education and
    became intelligentsia, 91
socialist artistic modernity, 126
socialist films about the life of the Khevsurs,
    114–22
socialist popular art
    images of Khevsur women as unattainable,
    124
socialist *rabfak* education system, 101
socialist technological modernity, 126
Soviet version of Hollywood, 118, 121
speech genre of conversation, 2, 7
spirit mediums called *kadagi* (oracle), 75
Stalin, Josef, xiii, 116
Stalinist period, 115
    cultural revolution, 108
    school of "socialist realism," 125
    sexual conservatism, 109
stealing vodka, 2, 40–41
stereotypical Khevsurs and Pshavians, xix–xxvi,
    124
    macho, gallant, romantic figures, xxii
    "mountaineer romance," xx
    tasteful and chaste restraint, xxii
sts'orperi, xvi, xviii, 22, 50, 78
    cannot be a spouse, 29–30
sts'orproba, xiv, xvi, xxix–xxx, 7, 22, 78, 99–100
    active sexual history an asset for a
    woman, 22
    advocating for more permissive practices,
    77–78
    age when boys and girls engage in, xxviii–xxix

anti-marriage, xiii, xvi, xvii, 10, 122
arranging at public events, 46
boundaries between consequential sexual
    behavior and, 25, 28
boys must never go to girls, 11
as chaste, 111
community of practice, xxviii
continuum of relationships, 34–35
couples who were not of similar attractive-
    ness, 22–23
desire to marry, 29
elective, sociable sexual desire, xvi, 25
fornication forbidden under, 108
Georgian traditional form of petting, xviii
girl is expected to resist on first night, 8
incomprehensible to the rest of Georgia, 111
instituted by God to tame desire, 6, 9–11, 73
male shrine gods and female demons, 74
must not result in marriage or childbirth,
    xvii, 25
"play form" of sexuality removed from
    real-life consequences, 105
promiscuity in, 74
relationship between equals, 18
secretive in creation and maintenance, 48
self-regulating of individual desire, xxx
ubiquitous feature of Khevsur life, 1
uses that allowed one to escape lying down
    out of entreaty or respect, 34
sts'orproba and ts'ats'loba debates, 135
Sts'orproba in Khevsureti (Baliauri)
    scandals narrated in, 100
suicide, 30, 44, 78
survili, suruli, xvii, xxx, 32, 64, 71–72. See also
    desire
sworn brothers, 35–36, 42, 106, 117
sworn-siblinghood relationship
    "forced" swearing of siblinghood, 49–50
    girls, 52
    oath in front of witnesses, 49–51
    publicly recognized obligations, 48–49, 51
    ritual, performative event, 49–50
    widened sphere of potential relations of
        sts'orproba, 52
sworn sister, 74. See also nadobi

taboos, 10, 19–20, 23
    menstrual or birthing huts as tabooed build-
        ings, 96
tavdach'eriloba, 11. See also self-control
tavmoq'vareoba, 5, 37, 47
Tedoradze, Giorgi, xxx, 43, 56–57, 101, 108–9
    on strangeness and secretiveness of Pshavian
        customs, 100
"thaw" of the Khrushchev period, 125–26, 128
"There was and there was not," xviii
They Came Down from the Mountains (1954), 115
tragic love story, 116. See also unrequited love stories
transcriptions of native poetry, 99
transgression, 25
    ways in which a lover might attempt, 27
transgression of public taboos
    intimacy achieved through, 20
ts'ats'ala, 106
ts'ats'ali, xv, xviii, 57, 99
    an insult among Khevsurs, 12
    poetry on, 98
ts'ats'loba, xxix, 75, 108–9. See also Pshavian
    sexual practices
    Georgian traditional form of petting, xviii
    girlfriend-boyfriend minus the directly
        sexual act, 134
    local prefiguration of Western
        modernity, 137
    must not result in marriage or childbirth, 25
    in the nude, 112
    online discussions of, 130–38
    salaciously and sexually framed, 111
ts'esi, 6
ts'ola-dgoma, 8, 18. See also lying down and get-
    ting up
twice-given rings, 54
Tuite, Kevin, xiii, xv, xvi, 7, 13, 25–26, 29–30, 42,
    46, 52, 61, 99, 106

unamuso, 26
unrequited love stories, 62, 64, 93
Uplisashvili, Ann, xxi

vaginal intercourse, xvi–xviii, 74, 113, 135–36. See
    also fornication

village communes (*temi*), 76

virginity, xvii, 112, 135

virtual romance on Georgian teen forums, 130–38

virtual sexuality

"play form" of sexuality removed from real-life consequences, 105

vodka, xxxii

appropriated from public currency for purposes of romance, 40

boy could drink with friends (showing he had a girlfriend), 40, 42, 51, 53

could point forward to an anticipated meeting with a lover, 39

as currency of social life, 36–37

currency and symbol of durable romantic relationships between boys and girls, 36, 38

for *dzmobili* could become vodka for the forsaken one, 41

for newborn child, 38

gifts of vodka (when visiting as sworn sibling in another village), 52

girls hid bottles of good vodka, 40

hiding it meant the relationship was secret, 41

not present in *sts'orproba*, 43

oaths, 37

performative role in declaration of love, 51

portability and durability, 37, 38

reminder of a breakup, 39–40

role in creating, maintaining, and ending relationship, 38

saving vodka measured time spent apart, 41

stolen bottles of vodka that girls save for boys, xxxii

that a girl gives to a boy, 40, 51, 53

visiting vodka, 38

wanting (*ndoba*), 10

warfare, 13

warlike nature of the Khevsurs, 60, 62

Western imports of *Playboy* magazine and pornographic videos, 113

Western modernity, 137

Western sexual life, xvi, xviii, xix

Georgians' fascination with, xvii

White Collar (Javakhishvili), 113, 115, 135

salacious text, 111, 121

Who do you know (double entendre), 20–21

women's lives (phases), 6, 28–29